Standing Under the Wrong Rainbow

G. DEON THOMPSON

abbott press

Abbott Press books may be ordered through booksellers or by contacting:

Abbott Press
1663 Liberty Drive
Bloomington, IN 47403
www.abbottpress.com
Phone: 1-866-697-5310

Because of the dynamic nature of the Internet, any web addresses or links contained in this book may have changed since publication and may no longer be valid. The views expressed in this work are solely those of the author and do not necessarily reflect the views of the publisher, and the publisher hereby disclaims any responsibility for them.

Any people depicted in stock imagery provided by Thinkstock are models, and such images are being used for illustrative purposes only.
Certain stock imagery © Thinkstock.

ISBN: 978-1-4582-1716-5 (sc)
ISBN: 978-1-4582-1718-9 (hc)
ISBN: 978-1-4582-1717-2 (e)

Library of Congress Control Number: 2014912583

Printed in the United States of America.

Abbott Press rev. date: 09/12/2014

Contents

Note: **bold,** *italics,* and <u>underlined words</u> added throughout the text for emphasis unless otherwise indicated.

Dedication

It may sound so very cliché to begin a book by giving thanks to God because the expression seems so watered down today. But I stand as witness that this book could not have been written without the support of my Father, Yahweh. Thank you!

To my wife Ana Paula; what a wonderful inspiration you have been to me. There is something so unique to an individual that walks by the faith of things not seen. When there was nothing seen in me by others you maintained a realization of who I could be. May I always dedicate my life to you as a faithful husband, lover and best friend. Thank you.

To my parents Audrey & Godfrey, what a wonderful opportunity to let the world know that you both deserve my thanks. I know that it is difficult to be 'good' parents throughout a lifetime but you have both stuck to your manuscript by being a precedent to me. You have continually asserted God first and that has been more valuable than gold to me. Thank you.

To all persons walking in the Christian faith; persevere! Continue making a difference and do not give up hope. Be a witness and let them all see peace, joy and love in your lives.

Acknowledgements

I pick up inspiration form many people, things and places in my life but specific acknowledgement should be brought to the support I have received from Bahamas Faith Ministries and very specific to Pastor Richard Pinder. I appreciate your candour and insightfulness.

I would also be remiss if I did not herald the timely and effective 'ear' of Mr. Terrance Hanna. You are an exceptional person with a genuine heart.

I also would like to acknowledge Pastor Phillip Stubbs. When I was but a child and would watch you dress for school; your care and pride to properly put on that tie, inspired something deep in me. I never forgot how I wanted to 'look' and be as smart as you are.

Introduction

Isaiah 24:15 – 'Therefore in the east give glory to the LORD; exalt the name of the LORD, the God of Israel, in the islands of the sea.'

'The unintended writer' is a fair cliché of who I am in relationship to this book. It was never my intention to write in-depth or engage the topic of marriage with such fervour. What started as a written opinion on a social network has turned into a book of my convictions.

Writing this book was a struggle from the very start because I didn't want to waste time writing something as if I were embroiled in an online debate where passions run rampant and words become bitter. I knew that such an approach would make my opinions too prejudicial. This intro alone has changed several times because I found myself writing as if I were still in a blog.

The final (and most important) impetus for writing came from the Holy Spirit. As a testimony, I have not worked consistently for about one year. In the time that I was searching for a job, I started writing poems and having extended dialogues in Facebook. That small exposure raised my interest to explore my critical writing skills. Week after week as I was searching the job market and becoming more frustrated, I would turn to writing in blogs as a tangible way to release frustration and experiment with my creative edge. I started having a deep conviction to commit my time to writing.

Some years prior, I had started writing two books simultaneously. I did achieve a substantial amount of work on each but because of the circumstance of work and school; I ended up neglecting both books. I started to feel a sense of guilt so one day I picked up one of the books and began writing again. With the amount of time I had on my hands I needed to not only justify my use of time but I was longing for that lost sense of accomplishment that comes with having job security. One comes to learn that not having a job is an easy way to lose one's sense of self-worth.

Where my passion really ignited one day was in an online blog from a Bahamian journalist who posed a question about gay rights and marriage in The Bahamas. I found myself riveted to the topic. I started commenting online where my interest peaked as persons started responding to my comments. The debate was surprising as I discovered the tenacity and defiance of the conversation. Albeit, the topic is a true hot-potato in the US but in The Bahamas, I had assumed that it would be more placated. I foolishly expected that gay rights advocates in The Bahamas would be a quiet minority who found themselves unwilling to vocalise a defence of their position. There is little doubt that many Caribbean nations are very conservative on the issue of Gay Rights and marriage. That perception fuelled my astonishment as this topic mushroomed into a full blown political and social debate in The Bahamas supported by a surprising level of gay rights enthusiast.

Well, if it was the guidance of the Holy Spirit to take me to that debate, which I honestly now believe the case to be; I conformed by putting aside the other book to focus on this topic.

The one thing I knew immediately was how large the topic of gay marriage is. It was obvious to me that the topic was far too large to capacitate words only to The Bahamas. Jurisdictions like The Bahamas which are reliant (mostly due to geography) on the socio-economic stability of the US are also aware of a harrowing socio-political and philosophical fact; when the US surrenders or changes its moral composition, the philosophical borders in many other sovereign countries (especially The Bahamas) start to experience the effects of those changes.

That proposition for me was far too threatening as a litmus test to not challenge the current changes occurring in the US on Gay

Rights. My opinions therefore are mostly pragmatic to the perspective of the American debate because it sets a higher precedent from which conclusions can be drawn. Based on my online debate, I found that the implications flowing from the conversations created a need to validate truths on subjects far beyond the rudimentary debate of gay rights and marriage. Most of the arguments were steeped in philosophical and fundamentalist belief systems which are exact polar opposites. The topics have universal and societal changing properties. The subject matter challenges the sovereignty of laws, traditional reasoning, moral standards, and biblical inerrancy whiles also opening up the debate on man's existence.

From the stand-point of a person who is facing virtual unemployment, nothing is more daunting than undertaking something which is not considered a tangible part of my professional acronym to earn a living. I simply do not consider myself a writer in the purist sense of career orientation. That thought transferred into having to sit each day and write, but the results at the end of each day did not calculate into billable hours. That can be very disconcerting. For that reason; the early stage of my commitment to writing was joined to my guilty conscience of sending out CV's or offering legal counsel to a few matters that would come to me via email.

After a while I decided to commit to the book full time. That was scary because I am certainly not a certified minister of the Bible and most of the subjects are trenchantly religious and 'seemingly' far outside my field of knowledge. I could virtually guess that there are 'experts' who will be quick to use degrees as ad hoc arguments in dismissing much of what I write as intellectual heresy.

One day I got an answer to my uncertainty about writing, which was so surreal for me that I literally began to cry. I was up early and thinking about writing. When I finally started to place thought to paper, I stopped and read the few lines typed. It seemed like utter nonsense what I had written. For me personally, the hours in that particular day was turning out to be an abject failure. Something spurred me on beyond the few words I had written. I started to research a phrase that I needed to understand within the context of the way I wrote it. I was being drawn into reading a few Biblical annotations of one of the words I wrote. When I finally traced the last used context of the word into the book of Romans; I was stopped dead in my tracks. What a revelation! I read the verse and it dawned on me that the very same words that I had written were contained in this verse. The same words I had called 'nonsense' were sitting in front of me. I had to look back and forth between what I wrote and was reading. I was stunned. This is when I felt the Holy Spirit urge me on. The message I received was to give no heed to the distractions and doubts because I can do all things through Christ Jesus who strengthens my mind, body and soul. What an assurance that was. There is no feeling greater than the inspiration of the Holy Spirit.

That was the real impetus and inspiration to carry on writing and to stand up for what I believe.

To this end, I also realise that another conversation should take place to justify my writing. I do believe that God is using my passion to bring clarity to a subject which I have been very critical about.

Growing up in The Bahamas was awesome for an adventurous spirit like myself. I have often told friends that I felt like the 'Huckleberry Finn' of The Bahamas growing up. My world has always been steeped in masculine bravado. That sense of certainty about who I was as a boy and individual melted well with the prevailing heterosexual environment found in The Bahamas. To be very honest, I grew up having a visceral dislike for anything with a homosexual overtone. The real irony to my feelings is that I became convicted as if the Holy Spirit was showing me two unique perspectives to consider.

The first perspective was deep rooted memories that I had basically suppressed. I would be the first to accept that this may be the real reason that I harnessed such hatred towards homosexuality. On two occasions during my childhood, there were attempts to sexually molest me. Thank God that the act never took place; but, the mere attempts brought me to a place of understanding and has allowed me to address this with a real perspective. The attempts were very superficial and happened through persons un-associated with my family. In one incident I was approached by a tourist when I was about 6, who acted as if he was enamoured by my accent. I was an avid swimmer and spent hours on the beach by myself in many instances. When he began to touch me on the shoulder I thought it only a friendly gesture but I realised quickly and with a sense of deep fear that his intentions were beyond plutonic as his hands started to glide too my lower extremities. By the grace of God I believe that I was delivered from that situation because just as this man had leaned into me in a 'trapping' position; my cousin road up on her bike about 25 yards away and beckoned me to her side. She had no clue what was happening but simply wanted me to leave the beach with her.

On another occasion, I was enrolled in a summer camp for boys and girls. My uncle was a counsellor at the camp so he had me sleep in the intermediate dorm where he was. I was about 8 at the time but most of the boys where about 10 to 12. I remember being on the top bonk where all the beds formed a large canvass because they were pushed together. There were at least 20 persons sleeping in close proximity. I have always been a light sleeper so fortunately any disturbance to my surrounding kept me alert. I awoke to the feeling of a hand on my lower leg. It was the most subtle touch. So subtle that I actually woke thinking it was a spider moving on me. I must have slightly startled this man because he pretended to snore at that point. I was still drowsy and I assumed it was another case of a bad sleeper so I paid no real attention and started to fall asleep again. Right away this predator started moving his hands up my leg in a slow, calculated manner. I was frozen in fear because this was a counsellor in the camp but I knew that this was an abnormal situation. As he reached my groin area; he started to grope me. With the loudest shout ever; I woke every person in that dorm including my uncle. It was funny looking back at his reaction because he thought I was having a nightmare and had failed to live up to the standard of being 'matured' like the older boys. The whole incident died without a single person really asking me why I started screaming. The predator had literally rolled over into four or five spots away from where I slept. The very sad part to this story is that I was aware of another boy who slept close to my bed; he became notorious for wetting the bed. Although he was older, he would wake every morning with socked pyjamas. In hindsight; I do believe that this boy was being molested by this predator. Years later, I found out that this man, Patrick, was very wrapped into the gay Bahamian community. This gave me the perspective on how the gay community separates itself from acts such as paedophilia, as if it is expressly different than any other sexual perversion; yet heterosexuals and homosexuals are both guilty of involvement in sexual perversion. Both groups can commit sexual crimes against children and both groups are guilty of this sin. My goal here is to give my personal perspective of the fallacies relative to homosexuality in the wider debate.

My second perspective is in understanding why I was writing this book. I started, and changed several times much of what I was writing. I felt as if I was taking on a personal vendetta which would turn into a crusade against homosexuals. I was really 'gong-ho' to lay my words into the gay community like a spear piercing the jugular. Something happened that actually put a sword through me instead. The Holy Spirit chided me one day as I was watching TV and listening to a heated debate on the matter in the US. I was so annoyed at the TV debate that I jumped out of my seat and headed towards the kitchen. I was actively speaking with myself as if going mad when the Holy Spirit showed me that it was this mad attitude that was hindering the church in reaching gays. The Holy Spirit enlightened me that one of the main objectives of the church in terms of the message of Jesus Christ is to teach the Kingdom of God on Earth as it is in Heaven. The Holy Spirit showed me that the Kingdom message was not a message of violence but of love as Jesus did teach. I was in no way walking in that message. The biggest revelation that came to me though, was that I was not simply writing to place a perspective on the whole gay rights conversation but to actually wake up and bring focus to the Christian community. I felt as if my words were to shock them and move them from such a docile position. What the Holy Spirit showed me was that the Christian community on one hand was portraying itself as haters and mad men in language;

whiles also allowing the homosexual agenda to increase through better organization because Christians have become too lazy and nonchalant in addressing the hard facts and issues.

The Bible verses in Ephesian 6:13 - 17 came to me; "*But everything exposed by the light becomes visible—and everything that is illuminated becomes a light. This is why it is said:*

> *"Wake up, sleeper,*
> *rise from the dead,*
> *and Christ will shine on you."*

Be very careful, then, how you live—not as unwise but as wise, making the most of every opportunity, because the days are evil. Therefore do not be foolish, but understand what the Lord's will is.

Parts of this book for me are more about convicting the Christian community than casting aspersions towards the behaviour of persons who label themselves as 'gay'. My perspective here is to filter into many of the arguments being put forth and to re-establish viable alternative arguments which offer true and practical solutions and begins to take back much of the ground so easily surrendered by the Christian community. Christians need to know that their silence is only an open door for chaos and untruths to ensue.

The perspective on gay marriage has certainly changed. Persons who were once against gay marriage and who 'appear' to be Christians are steadily renouncing Biblical propositions on the topic. Meanwhile, gay rights advocates have become more emboldened and their actions are at the opposite end of the spectrum; they absolutely abhor with irreverence anything remotely religious (Christian especially) and they are fighting with resilience.

What this book will confront are the key debates or issues which need realignment. Some of it will be ideological and political whiles other parts will address scholarly issues and sociological issues. However the debate is viewed, it will point out the undeniable and clear divisions seen between persons who have defined, shared beliefs in 'a God of standards' and persons who maintain a diminished view of a deity which can range from atheistic to Deistic.

Because there seems to be two distinct sides to the discussion, the focus will remain on defining those objectives. The detractors on opposing sides will be classed in general (but not exclusive) as the protagonist who are Humanist or the LGBT community and persons such as myself, will be called the antagonist (Christian or conservative).

To also be fair and transparent to the argument, my personal abridged view embraces the concept of one God (the Trinity) who is Omnipotent and has transferred an infallible testimony called The Bible to man. That will be the antecedent for the majority of premises from my perspective, throughout.

It is anticipated that many will say that the views presented are one-sided and prejudicial. I accept that as long as I am fair and truthful to the word of God. That is more important to me so that the integrity of my opinions would be capable of withstanding the barrage of criticism and scrutiny. For the most part, it is impractical to believe that one can make a 'stand' on an issue and not come into stark opposition. Indeed; milk and lemon juice do not naturally mix.

At one point in the online conversations, it was asked of me by a protagonist to stop quoting scriptural references, which he considered 'archaic' and impractical. That request was considered simply because the person was willing to have a very public, engaging conversation. That consideration was important at the very least, to keep the conversation on the border of the gay advocates philosophical comfort zone which was to him, a perceived logical rationality. That objective was not achieved in this book. It's important to stress from the beginning that I believe in the Word of GOD and the truth that is derived from it. We know that the Word tells us that 'faith comes by hearing, and hearing by the word of God'. Christianity can ill-afford to water down its doctrine when presenting or arguing the veracity of truth and risk becoming another camp-fire dogma of 'Kumbaya'. I am presenting this book from a Christian perspective heralding belief in a 'living' GOD of standards against a Humanistic creed, with a general view of self-actualization and inner revelations of metaphysical absolutes.

At the end of this book, it is my hope that what is written will give greater resolve to those who have either lost faith, lost perspective or believe that the issue does not affect them, so that they may rethink their stand. I do further hope that the reasoning will be a testimony of sorts to convict a re-assessment of thought among those who have supported principles that are now being depreciated and called into question. It is not my intention that my words cause further division between the two belief systems but that the truth of what I say will be consumed as a 'pot of love'. There is much truth in a pot cooked with love.

Unfortunately and as conceded; many of the topics are far more complex than what has been presented here. Although it may appear as if there is an extensive written dialogue; the breadth of facts and opinion have been extremely abbreviated so that the conversation could take place in a much smaller window.

What has been noted and determined is that much of the existing debate is far too emotional and the facts are seldom properly researched. For this reason, a somewhat laborious effort has been made to objectivity present salient facts from both sides and expand on those specific facts while still being concise and not adding too much 'fat' to the issue. The conclusions are drawn from those facts using the same logical methodology that is contained and addressed in each topical tier.

My writing style 'may' or may not be consistent but my readers may also come to notice that I sometimes switch between different Biblical translations of verses. I am pretty much in agreement with most Bible translations such as the King James, New King James and the New International Version; but sometimes I do also use the Living Bible or Amplified because they tend to offer very common language.

Before venturing further; here are final issue disclaimers.

All too often this conversation has experienced the vitriolic response to Christianity and conservatives by Humanist who say that they are nothing more than barbaric extremist exalting hate-mongering and homophobia. Besides the fact that I perceive most of that language as only escapism to conjure public sympathy and the fact that there will be a direct answer to the question of prejudice (within the writing); it is believed that there is stark importance to say upfront that this is not a campaign of 'gay-bashing'. It is an attempt to state a well-reasoned belief system from a logically considered rationale.

As a Christian, I make or imply no hierarchy over my fellow man. I believe that all of mankind has sinned and fallen short of the Glory of GOD. This is a theme that I will express throughout my discourse. What that means to me, is that I live by the standard that man has a sin nature. I do imply that the only difference between me and a Humanist or gay is that my belief system tells me that sin is wrong and that I have chosen to embrace the Grace of God and live according to the command in Romans 6: 12 – 18 which concludes in Romans 6:23 by saying:

For the wages of sin is death, but the gift of God is eternal life in Christ Jesus our Lord.

Chapter 1

What Rights Are We Talking About?

I can recall laying on my bedroom floor years ago listening intently to the vinyl recording of the 'I Have a Dream' speech by Martin Luther King. That speech built a sense of pride in my soul as I held onto each word he uttered. My understanding back then was more attached to the eloquent way he spoke and the image he painted of children playing together in peaceful harmony.

Years later and I find myself cringing each time that I listen to a debate on gay rights and someone attaches the walk of African Americans who fought for naturally ascribed 'life' rights, to the agenda of gay rights activist.

Automatically that agenda became a topic of discussion for this book. To me; the extended debate on Gay Rights and the synergy to Civil Rights (of African Americans) has become a defence mechanism (this term will be repeated several times throughout this writing in acknowledgement of other similar actions) of sorts for gay rights advocates who use it as a certified precedent. In my personal opinion; this mechanism (similar to the 'race card') has drawn sympathy and support from many in the African American community.

The entire question of rights is brought to the debate table to understand whether blacks are entitled to constitutional rights based on naturally ascribed rights; or whether their fight was based on an expression of <u>assumed</u> rights simply from a desire or misdirected belief that they should participate in life endeavours similar to an elite (white) race of people. I also needed to qualify whether gay rights are mirrored to the rights of African Americans and why.

Natural Rights

Let me say first that, I believe the foundation of all human rights was established by God in Genesis and throughout the Bible. I believe these rights to be natural to man's existence. Here are just some of the rights God gave to man.

i.   Genesis 1: 26 – God gave man the right to have **dominion** over all things on Earth (fish, birds, cattle, bugs). The word dominion in Hebrew, primarily translate as 'radah', which means to either rigorously rule or dominate. God's intention therefore, was to issue charge of the world to man. He gave man the right to be masters (**equally**) over his earthly surroundings. This means that man has dominion rights to property and land; rights to food and housing.

ii. Genesis 1:28 – God gave man the right to walk in His blessing. God's blessing is never to be taken for granted.

    ➤ His blessing gives us the right to walk in the wealth of His liberty and happiness without extortion and cruel suppression according to Proverbs 10:22.

    ➤ His blessings gives us a right of reprieve against injustice; a right to mercy; a right to peace; etc. (Matthew 5:12)

iii. Genesis 1:28 – God gave man the right to have a family.

iv. Genesis 9:6 – God gave man the right to be free from attack and murder because he states that man is made in His own image and therefore a punishment exist for those who would spill the blood of man.

Man's 'God-given' right to have 'dominion' was a right which did not discriminate. It did not speak of specific ethnic types or races. It spoke of mankind. What I have not found in the Bible are specific rights which are only proportional to homosexuals. That is not shocking because neither have I found rights specific to Blacks or Whites or Asians, etc. What I did find was that rights were attributable to 'man' universally which meant that everyone is entitled.

Where the problem comes in, is interpreting homosexuals into a 'new' or different class of humanity as if they are a race unto themselves who deserve a special consideration of rights entitlement.

WHAT ARE RIGHTS?

What are the rights entitled and where do they come from? I would say that I have already answered that question but let's take this further. If we consider the question of 'what is a 'right' within the context of gay rights and civil rights of African Americans; we would have to place that question at the doorstep of the US constitution which was formed as a result of independence. The formulation of those rights had to be based on a tangible quality which was able to be standardized.

Here is what the Declaration of Independence conveys in its' very first line as justification of why the 'act' of independence must take place and where the precedent authority for the rights sought in the act, come from; '*When in the course of human Events, it becomes necessary for one People to dissolve the Political Bands which have connected them with another, and to assume among the Powers of the Earth, the separate and equal Station to which **the Laws of Nature and of Nature's God <u>entitle them</u>**, a decent Respect to the Opinions of Mankind requires that they should declare the causes which impel them to the Separation.*'[1] From that

---

[1] United States Declaration of Independence (1776); Constitutional documents United States Congress; Wikisource. http://en.wikisource.org/wiki/United_States_Declaration_of_Independence

stand point it would appear clear to me that the act of independence was based on natural entitlements that were ascribed from God.

Let's examine the rights further as they relate to African Americans and the LGBT community.

Throughout the development of the ancient world and world religions, there are numerous instances of qualifying rights which various societies naturally attributed to citizens. The 'right to be free' is a theme that can be found preserved in history as far back as the story of Moses[2] and throughout Roman[3] society where persons who were kept as slaves could work and buy their freedom.

'Human Rights[4]' as a collective theory, although encapsulated in the Bill of Rights in the US, really came into force due to concerns about possible atrocities being committed during World War 2.

In a modern context and germane to this debate; when persons refer to or speak of 'rights', they are referencing either to civil rights or civil liberties. In the US, those rights evolved from privileges enshrined in the Bill of Rights which initially protected freedom of religion, the right to keep and bear arms, freedom of speech, the freedom of assembly and the freedom to petition.

Significant to the rights of African Americans in the US is the fact that they could not exercise rights ascribed from the constitution because circa 1870, slavery remained legal in many States. It was a time when Black people were seeking the <u>entitlement</u> offered through the words[5] of **Thomas Jefferson**, which although quite true, fell short of delivering

---

[2]   King James Bible, Exodus 6:2-7

[3]   Keith Bradley, Slavery and Society at Rome (Cambridge University Press, 1994), pp. 2–3.

[4]   The common definition or defined as 'inalienable fundamental rights to which a person is inherently entitled simply because she or he is a human being'. Human rights reference handbook (3rd ed. rev. ed.)

[5]   Thomas Jefferson was an American Founding Father, the principal author of the Declaration of Independence and the third President of the United States United States Declaration of Independence, 2nd sentence; Constitutional documents United States Congress http://en.wikipedia.org/wiki/All_men_are_created_equal#cite_note-7

the truth of his decree. He said in the Declaration of Independence that *"We hold these truths to be self-evident, that **all men are created equal**, that they are **endowed by their Creator** with certain unalienable Rights that among these are Life, Liberty, and the Pursuit of Happiness."*

CIVIL RIGHTS and THE AFRICAN AMERICAN

The path to civil rights for African Americans is a deep quagmire of historical facts which could be considered from the crossing of slave ships from African states such as Ghana, Sierra Leone, and Nigeria into the New World of the Americas and the Caribbean; then all the way to the riots in Birmingham, Alabama.

The illegality given to the act of slavery did not truly begin to dissipate until the Thirteenth Amendment to the United States Constitution outlawed slavery and involuntary servitude. The Amendment abolished Slavery but most Blacks still had to struggle against an engrained culture of prejudice. So whiles the intention was for African Americans to enjoy rights under the liberty afforded in the Constitution; their struggle continued as a literal fight for the right to be acknowledged as equal citizens and ultimately equal human beings.

The African American Civil Rights movement started to really take shape over 80 years later when blacks began to organise non-violent protest as a form of civil resistance. Two of the early protest of note would have been the Montgomery Bus Boycott which began in 1955 and the March on Washington 1963.

Specific to this conversation, the rights[6] which African Americans fought for were:

- The right to vote – From the 14th Amendment in 1868 to the 15th Amendment in 1870, blacks in the US had the constitutional

---

[6] It is important to note that many black leaders in The Bahamas fought for and went through the struggle to liberate blacks in The Bahamas. Events such as the

right to vote. Unfortunately, white supremacist, mainly in the Southern states, mounted arguments that convinced the US Supreme Court that the Civil Rights Act of 1875 was unconstitutional. By 1883[7] the Supreme Court was acting to strike out the gains started under Abraham Lincoln's 'Reconstruction' and disallowing or disenfranchised blacks in the right to vote.

- The fight against segregation – Southern white supremacist had a racist cultural joke which started from a performer who would paint his face black to assimilate a negative stereotype of black people who they called "dandified coons". This character became known as Jim Crow. In 1881, the state of Tennessee started a rolling snowball among Southern states by passing a state law unambiguously[8] called Jim Crows law to segregate blacks from whites. The case of Plessy vs. Ferguson in 1896, which is a Supreme Court ruling, made it legal to segregate on the bases of race (whites and blacks) in public facilities.

- The Fight against racial violence – The 'race wars' or riots of the Civil Rights era can be defined from roughly 1955 to 1971. This is truly a misnomer of sorts because racial violence *in the US* can be categorised from the beginning of slavery around

---

Burma Road Riot of 1942 and Black Tuesday in 1965 were but a few instances of the valiant struggle of black history in The Bahamas. The issue of Gay Rights has much more of a foundational argument in the US so the trek into US history is unintentional towards marginalizing the historical significance of the Black Movement in The Bahamas. The African American Movement is being put forth as a wider platform to show the dichotomy between the two movements.

[7] Civil Rights Cases (1883); Supreme Court, 8-1 decision of the Court was delivered by Justice Joseph P. Bradley, with John Marshall Harlan of Kentucky alone in dissent. The Court decided that the Civil Rights Act of 1875 was unconstitutional. Information Please®, ©2005 Pearson Education, Inc.

Read more: Civil Rights Cases (1883) http://www.infoplease.com/us/supreme-court/cases/ar06.html#ixzz2kTYib6N9

[8] Historical and legal pundits use the term 'Disambiguation' which Websters 7th New Collegiate Dictionary defines as capable of being understood in two or more possible senses; combined with (dis) which means reversing, the word then connotes a specific and unambiguous term.

the 1700's to modern cases today. From the mid 1800's all the way to the 1960's blacks were subjugated to a legal system which allowed for 'trial by mob'. Many Blacks [9]suffered the indignation of extrajudicial trials by ravenous mobs which resulted in lynching. At the height of its strength[10] in the 1920 it is estimated that there was between 3 to 6 million registered members of the Klu Klux Klan. This organization carried out 'witch-hunts' against blacks; one such atrocity being called the 'Mississippi Burning' Case.

- The Fight against economic repression and exploitation – Many blacks were discriminated against in ways which kept them economically marginalized. The struggle to achieve equal employment, housing opportunities under the 'Fair Housing Act 1968, and educational equality were major platforms of the Civil Rights movement. These rights had unprecedented growth during the movement where blacks saw rights being increased against unconstitutional actions[11].

GAY RIGHTS AND THE STRUGGLE

The context of '**Gay Rights**' is also based on a history of struggle.

In terms of establishing major criteria on the need for 'gay rights', one can start with the insanity of the Nazi regime. History will show that along with the other heinous acts committed by the Nazis, some

---

[9] The Tuskegee Institute has recorded 3,446 blacks as being lynched in Southern states

[10] Wikipedia via McVeigh, Rory. "Structural Incentives for Conservative Mobilization: Power Devaluation and the Rise of the Ku Klux Klan, 1915–1925". Social Forces, Vol. 77, No. 4 (June 1999), p. 1463.

[11] Wikipedia - George Wallace, the Governor of Alabama, in a symbolic attempt to keep his inaugural promise of "segregation now, segregation tomorrow, segregation forever" and stop the desegregation of schools, stood at the door of the auditorium to try to block the entry of two black students. "George Wallace: Settin' the Woods on Fire: Wallace Quotes". The American Experience. Public Broadcasting Service. 2000

5,000 to 15,000[12] gays were incarcerated in concentration camps. Throughout the German society, it was confirmed that some 50,000 persons were also placed into the prison system after being sentenced for homosexuality. Of the 5 to 15,000 in 'death camps', perhaps 60% did not survive.

The Gay Rights movement and struggle in the US can be measured from the period of 1924 to modern day. Subjectively this is an anomalous statement in view of the fact that there is no struggle against 'slavery' in the history of gays; burnings on crosses; or even records of the National Guard called out to prevent the enrolment of gay children into the education system[13]. The history of gay's looking to achieve some level of recognition or equality is much more analogous to a 'pressure' group or lobbyist like Green Peace, who espouses a belief system and petition government to abide. This is not to say that the LGBT has not suffered legal struggles and many grievances.

In 1924 The Society for Human Rights in Chicago[14] was formed as the first organization representing 'gay rights' in the United States. The organization published a newsletter which covered topics of interest for gay men. It was not until 1962 that any major 'rights' were achieved by gay activist; Illinois[15] made it legal for two consenting adults to have homosexual relationships in the privacy of their own home.

On June 27, 1969 The Stonewall riots took place in Greenwich NY, which resulted as a form of 'Gay Power' stand against police that raided a bar frequented by gay men, lesbians, bisexuals, and transgendered people. The raid turned into a riot when the patrons of the bar refused

---

[12] Persecution of Homosexuals, United States Holocaust Memorial Museum; 100 Raoul Wallenberg Place, SW Washington, DC 20024-2126 http://www.ushmm.org/learn/students/learning-materials-and-resources/homosexuals-victims-of-the-nazi-era/persecution-of-homosexuals

[13] Brown v. Board at Fifty: "With an Even Hand"; Library of Congress; http://www.loc.gov/exhibits/brown/brown-aftermath.html

[14] "Timeline: Milestones in the American Gay Rights Movement". PBS. WGBH Educational Foundation.

[15] The American Gay Rights Movement: A Timeline; http://www.infoplease.com/ipa/A0761909.html

to adhere to police procedure [16] and revolted. The revolt was seen as a significant stand by the gay movement to fight for their 'right of assembly'.

By 1980 and as far as rights are concerned, the Gay Rights Movement received another boast when the Democratic Party, in support of the gay movement, included a statement in its party mandate, which read as: "All groups must be protected from discrimination based on race, color, religion, national origin, language, age, sex or sexual orientation."

By the year 2000 and beyond, the gay rights movement starts to see significant growth in a political and legal context.

i.   2000 – State of Vermont recognizes civil unions as having legal force.

ii. 2003 – The essence of gay rights is confirmed in the case of Lawrence v. Texas where the Supreme Court ruled that sodomy laws violated the autonomy of self which embraces the liberty to have self-expression/belief/thought and intimate conduct.

iii. In the same year the Massachusetts Supreme Judicial Court decided it unconstitutional to restrict the civil union of gay and lesbian couples. By the 17 May the state made same sex marriage legal.

iv. From 2004 to March 26 2013, most issues remain focused on gay marriage. In May of 2012, President Obama backs the notion of same-sex marriage and by March 26 of 2013, the Supreme Court of the United States convenes for legal discussions about the constitutional validity of same-sex marriages.

Within the context of this debate, what are the rights that the LGBT community is fighting for? After completing a concerted

---

[16] Standard procedure was to line up the patrons, check their identification, and have female police officers take customers dressed as women to the bathroom to verify their sex, upon which any men dressed as women would be arrested. – Wikipedia, Stonewall Riots. Wikimedia Commons has media related to Stonewall Inn (New York).

search to determine with certainty what rights are being denied to the LGBT[17]; I found at the ACLU web-page a full and concise layout of what appeared to be generally agreed rights which the LGBT is fighting for. To quote the ACLU[18], their mission is; *'the creation of a society in which lesbian, gay, bisexual and transgender (LGBT) people enjoy the constitutional rights of equality, privacy and personal autonomy, and freedom of expression and association.'*

The 'Rights' are:

- Discrimination – The Fourteenth Amendment of the constitution adopts an equal protection clause which requires every state in the Union to provide equal protection to all citizens under the law. The LGBT asserts that there is wide discrimination against their community and the ACLU has taken on a mission to protect the LGBT against discrimination of any determined form. According to the ACLU, *'no LGBT person should experience discrimination in employment, housing, or in businesses and public places, or the suppression of their free expression or privacy rights'.*
- Parenting – Whiles the issue of parenting is somewhat mute considering that thousands of gay men and women are parents the salient issue extends itself to adoption by gay couples and the rights thereof. Currently in the US, full joint adoption by same-sex couples is fully allowed in 21 states. State to state adoption laws are very diverse and can have a duplicitous meaning when left to interpretation from one judge to the next. (Note the 'best interest of the child'- what studies have been done?)
- Relationships and Marriage – The issue of gay marriage is such a 'volcanic' topic that it carries serious political consequences

---

[17] Perhaps I was out of my element but I found scarce information that was placed forward in an organized manner that gave a full few of the areas of constitutional or legal dogma that depraved the rights of the gay community.

[18] American Civil Liberties Union, website of the American Civil Liberties Union and the ACLU Foundation. http://www.aclu.org/lgbt-rights

in the US. The political divide on the issue is very contentious. At the heart of the debate is The Defense of Marriage Act (DOMA). Section 3 of DOMA *'codifies the non-recognition of same-sex marriages for all federal purposes, including insurance benefits for government employees, Social Security survivors' benefits, immigration, and the filing of joint tax returns[19].'* The US Supreme Court on June 26, 2013, after hearing arguments pertinent to '**UNITED STATES v. WINDSOR[20]**', decided that **S**ection 3 is unconstitutional. Whiles the ruling certainly redefines the approach to DOMA, the language of the Law has yet to be overturned such that it still officially recognises marriage as 'between' a man and woman.

- Youth and School – The LGBT and their representation by the ACLU has determined that the rights of young people who are of the LGBT influence must be protected in their rights to properly integrate into the public school system. Specific to the rights in contention is the right to freedom of expression such that LGBT children would attend school dances with dates and the freedom to cross-dress. *The First Amendment (Amendment I) to the United States Constitution prohibits <u>abridging the freedom of speech.</u>*

D. Fundamental differences between Gay Civil Rights and African American Civil Rights

After laying out the precedent on fundamental rights fought for by African Americans and the LGBT movement, I had to sit back and think about the premise of the two movements being inextricably linked under the same cause.

---

[19] 104th Congress Public Law 199][From the U.S. Government Printing Office] http://www.gpo.gov/fdsys/pkg/PLAW-104publ199/html/PLAW-104publ199.htm

[20] UNITED STATES v. WINDSOR, EXECUTOR OF THE ESTATE OF SPYER, ET AL.; SUPREME COURT OF THE UNITED STATES http://freemarry.3cdn.net/4dbd426fcdde01533f_92m6i6slj.pdf

I will list my objections below more clearly but I demur immediately primarily based on my first instincts and rationale on the premise. Although I acknowledge that my thinking on the subject is majorly subjective and personal; I needed to make a stand 'here' enough to say that the core comparisons between the two movements are remote and vague with only a brief similarity in the area of personal attacks and atrocities (but all races and people suffer personal attacks).

As a race of people, blacks in the US and around the world have endured a third class existence for hundreds (if not thousands) of years. To compare the rights and fight of the LGBT community with the God given right of all humans to live free from the tyranny of slavery, is ridiculous and reeks of mindless frivolity. The direct comparison with the African American movement dilutes the repression, psychological carnage and criminality that slavery and segregation impressed on blacks[21] based on racial heritage. Imagine; Jews were systematically targeted and 'mandated' for extermination in the millions. Their fight against the atrocities committed is a result based on the repression of 'Jewish Rights'. Most current organizations which defend the history and plight of the Jewish nation defend against anti-Semitism; which is essentially a fight against prejudice towards a 'race' of people. The criminality committed during WW11 was tried at Nuremberg which established a criminal standard by which all humanity must live. That standard protects gays, blacks, Jewish people and whites. It is an international legal standard against 'aggression and Crimes Against Humanity'. For this reason, my premise is set that there is a difference between the rights of all humans to live free from slavery and the criminality committed by whomever against groups or individuals.

Therefore; the primary differences between gay rights and civil rights of African Americans are:

1. The right to vote; the fight against segregation; the fight against racial violence; the fight against economic repression and

---

[21] People of any 'race', should not be subjected to slavery.

exploitation are completely different issues contextually to what the LGBT is fighting for. **There is a difference between fighting for rights which are enshrined in the constitution but legally denied and rights which are protected under the constitution but are being expanded on an activist bases.** For instance; there is no difference between a black man or white man walking in a store and being denied service compared to a gay person walking in a store and being denied. Constitutionally, both scenarios lend themselves to illegality and a breach of civil law of which recourse is to prosecute the offender pursuant to established law. There is absolutely no need to open a new interpretation to codify the law where The Fourteenth Amendment already adopts an equal protection clause. That clause protects, Caucasians, African Americans, Asians, Latinos etc. and disallows discrimination based on race and citizenship. It states, '*No person could be denied "equal protection of the laws."* It is obvious that the imperative 'No person' refers to all human beings including gays and does not seclude a class of people. To expand these rights to a class of people, who are activist with an agenda, would be wrong. If this 'Pandora's Box' is opened, every specialist, separatist, unique group, agency or people would apply for 'qualified rights' under the same veil.

2. **Whiles Constitutional, Natural Rights and Civil Liberties seem to coexist, there is a difference between those established rights and an 'issue' which develops from a right.** When African Americans demonstrated for certain 'rights', they were exercising their God-given 'natural rights' and constitutional right to declare 'equality' and to insist that those established rights were being institutionally infringed upon. Blacks were literally, systematically, and legally being denied civil rights which were already recognized and attributed to them. I have already illustrated this through the U.S. Declaration of Independence states;

*"We hold these truths to be self-evident, that **all men are created equal**, that they are **endowed by their Creator** with certain unalienable Rights….."*

We are all aware that the role of government is to protect the constitutional rights of citizens. Rights which are enshrined in the constitution, transfer to citizens certain freedoms which flow from the establishment of those rights. That means that all citizens have a right to certain freedoms or liberties within the context and boundaries of those rights. The problem is to decipher whether establish rights have sufficiency such that gays are protected under the law to exercise their freedoms. Every gay person is a citizen under the constitution. Are rights attributed to them? Yes!

Is gay marriage a right or an issue and if it is an issue, should it be enshrined as a right? Under the Constitution the Legislation has the power to make laws. It is widely argued that law must be constitutionally sound and meet the criteria's of what the 'Framers' intended. Is DOMA an unconstitutional and unjust law by protecting marriage between a man and woman or is the LGBT community being unfairly denied this right? Did the Framers intend for marriage to extend itself to **anyone or anything**?

The real fact is that the Founding Fathers/Framers did not define marriage in a way that would conclude this subject. What can be said, is that many decisions by the Legislation have been interpreted based on the values that the forefathers espoused or intended. I would venture to say that the Framers may never have imagined that 'Gay Marriage' would be an issue or right to debate. Here are excerpts from pundits, just to scratch the surface of the beliefs which these influential men who helped to shape the Constitution, adhered to:

i. George Washington said[22]; "*Of all the dispositions and habits which lead to political prosperity, **Religion and morality are***

---

22 George Washington was the first President of the United States, the commander-in-chief of the Continental Army during the American Revolutionary War, and one of the Founding Fathers of the United States Rediscovering George

> *indispensable supports. In vain would that any man claim the tribute of patriotism, who should labor to subvert these great pillars of human happiness."*

ii. Samuel Adams said[23]; "While the People are virtuous they cannot be subdued; but when once they lose their Virtue they will be ready to surrender their Liberties to the first external or internal Invader."

iii. James Madison said[24]; "*The belief in a God All Powerful, wise, and good, is essential to the moral order of the World and to the happiness of man.*" He also said, "*We have staked our future upon the capacity of each and all of us to govern ourselves, to sustain ourselves, according to the* **Ten Commandments** *of God.*"

iv. Thomas Jefferson said[25]; "The Christian religion is the best religion that has ever been given to man"

v. Benjamin Franklin said[26]; "*I believe in one God, the Creator of the Universe. That He governs it by His Providence. That He ought to be worshipped.*"

Here are five very significant individual who were framers of the Constitution. I cannot see the logic in deriving, from what is obviously

Washington; PBS online. http://www.pbs.org/georgewashington/classroom/religious_liberty2.html

[23] Samuel Adams, American statesman, political philosopher, Founding Fathers of the United States Samuel Adams Heritage Society; http://www.samuel-adams-heritage.com/quotes/morality.html

[24] James Madison. the father of the U.S. Constitution. He was also the fourth President of the United States. He was the primary author of the Bill of Rights, One Nation Under God America's Christian Heritage http://www.leaderu.com/orgs/cdf/onug/madison.html

[25] Thomas Jefferson; The Religion of Thomas Jefferson By David Barton, Founder and President of Wallbuilders and Ecclesia College Regent; http://www.ecollege.edu/about-us/veritas-aeterna/383-religion-of-jefferson

[26] Benjamin Franklin was one of the Founding Fathers of the United States, **Letter from Benjamin Franklin to Ezra Stiles** Benjamin Franklin *March 9, 1790;* http://www.beliefnet.com/resourcelib/docs/44/Letter_from_Benjamin_Franklin_to_Ezra_Stiles_1.html

their core values, an interpretation that 'Rights' should be extended to a philosophic group or issue which was never intended to be protected.

GAY RIGHTS; THE ISSUE vs RACE RIGHTS

Gay marriage is an issue under Civil Liberties and not a right. It is an issue that is debatable within the context of whether gay individuals are being systematically withheld from rights or discriminated against and contravening constitutional rights. By systematically, I refer to the intentional and nationalized behaviour by a legislative body to exclude gays from specific rights which are enshrined or <u>intended</u> the same. If it is not a natural or constitutional right, it is not automatically ascribed. Holding to my point; protagonist cannot then say that they are being denied a right. What they are fighting for is an issue!

A few issues which have been debated as bills, regulated and some turned into laws (but were not constitutionally or naturally ascribed), are:

- Abortion was an issue about a woman's right to regulate her own body. It is an issue which became a law or legal right.

  A movement is established to reverse the abortion right which is called 'The Right to Life Movement' concerned with the **right** of all foetuses to live. It is an issue which has a strong legal argument that a foetus is a human being and has the same rights as humans under the constitution.

- The issue of a national health-care system or Obama-care. The Affordable Care Act attempts to reform the insurance industry and the health care industry '*in order to cut healthcare costs and to provide affordable health insurance to all Americans*'. The issue is now a law.
- There was a time where speeding was not regulated in the US. It is now regulated with speed limits and there are now defined speed limit laws.

- Immigration and citizenship are issues being debated as to whether certain immigrants, who essentially meet a 'longevity' criterion, will have an automatic right to citizenship outside of the process of application. This is still an issue.
- The issue of legalizing marijuana is currently being debated and being considered under Federal law. It is an issue but not a right that is being denied.

Civil liberties which are protected under the constitution.

- Freedom of speech
- The right to privacy
- The right to be free from unreasonable searches of your home
- The right to a fair court trial
- The right to marry
- The right to vote

The **right to marry** which is a protected right (man to a woman) then becomes an issue debatable on the level of intention where same sex couples are concerned. Where the law clearly offers rights as between marriage of a man and woman, the LGBT community is asserting that the law was '**intended**' to cover them as a group also. If it were intended; then a systematic and prejudicial legal landscape has been incorrectly formed against gays. Again; what was the intention of the framers of the law?

The complexity of the subject can be taken from the words of **Thomas Jefferson; he said,**

> *"Special provision has been made by one of the amendments to the Constitution, which expressly declares, that 'Congress shall make no law respecting an establishment of religion, or prohibiting the free exercise thereof, or abridging the freedom of speech or of the press:' thereby guarding in the same sentence, and under the same words, the freedom of religion, of speech, and of*

> *the press: insomuch, that whatever violated either, throws down*
> *the sanctuary which covers the others, and that libels, falsehood,*
> *and defamation, equally with heresy and **false religion, are***
> ***withheld from the cognizance of federal tribunals.***"

Many will argue that the purist interpretation of these words separates any establishment of religion or religious standard. That could not be any furthest from the truth. Such ad hoc interpretations normally neglect to see the pragmatic consideration of why the constitution was written and who wrote it. It was not written arbitrarily on an existential plain. It was written based on established **ecclesiastical law** and philosophical conclusions which were relied on to establish a foundation. The consideration that was given came at the conclusion that the belief injected into the constitution was justified and righteously concerned to govern a country. The most glaring omittance by the established 'learned' clergy on constitutional matters is the non-acceptance that it was written primarily from a legal ecclesiastical perspective. If it were not so, murder (thou shall not), adultery (thou shall not), theft (thou shall not) etc., would not be infractions under the law.

If the company Honda writes a manual on the use of a Honda car; can one interpret, or delineate the intentions of Honda by amalgamating a Ford concept into the intentions of Honda? Clearly the Framers were men of Christian faith and values and used their knowledge of proven values to give a manual or guideline for how society should be regulated. They allowed for 'pluralism within borders'. This meant that rights were given but had definitions or 'stakes' as to where the stake extended. It makes absolutely no sense and is illogical to conclude that a person would hold Christian values as an axiom of truth but have the intention to indorse the gay lifestyle.

Common knowledge is that some founders such as Washington, Jefferson and Franklin had slaves. This is contrary to Christian values. Those Framers abolished the issue of slavery for the moral right of freedom. That means that even though they were slave owners; they did not justify their wrong behaviour.

The issue of gay marriage extends beyond the rights that the Framers intended to allow or protect in the constitution or through legislation. The issue removes the boundaries that the Framers established and those boundaries were intended as moral absolutes (standard, a post/ceiling/cap). If the post to the boundary is removed, who then will have the moral positioning to re-establish a post? Can a person simply move a land boundary post and encroach on another's land merely as a 'thought of right'? No! There are persons waiting in the wing to move that post even further. How could the LGBT community ever justify to a polygamist or a gay polygamist any position which does not support multiple mates in a 'loving' relationship? Which standard would be argued against it? Where would the LGBT acquire the moral 'fortitude' to justify being against polygamy or necrophilia and bestiality (the last two are speculated to still be practiced as burial rights and cultural rights in some cultures)[27].

3. **Civil Rights for African-Americans was and is about discrimination against a race of people and not a SEXUAL ORIENTATION.** The real argument for the LGBT community is establishing and confirming whether 'gays' are in general socially predisposed or are genetic inheritors. If so; do those facts attribute a natural and constitutional right to them separate and apart from defined rights already ascribed to 'all men'.

If the conclusion to the aforementioned statement is to the affirmative, then the same criteria would confirm rights to the LGBT community (The argument of genetic predisposition is taken into account more extensively below).

The real challenge to the African American community is whether they are prepared to accept such a watered down version of their genetic heritage

---

[27] PLEASE NOTE THAT THE INFORMATION CONTAINED IN THIS REFERENCED LINK IS OFFENSIVE TO MANY. Kunisada|Utagawa Kunisada]]'s series, "Eight Canine Heroes of the House of Satomi", 1837 http:// en.wikipedia.org/wiki/Zoophilia

such that any group of persons who ascribe to a behavioural proclivity can attach their dispositions to the same historical and fundamental fight for rights against racism that all Africans have fought for.

Allowing the 'Civil Rights' of African Americans to be analogous to 'Gay Rights' is tantamount to land dispossession where blacks are relegating the achievements of their struggle to be pirated away by a parasitic ideology which does not have the same moral scope under the theme of discrimination as blacks do to claim the accompanying rights under racism.

Blacks must have accountability to what their struggles established in the past, such that their struggles in the future are given continued credence.

In the history of the world; I can account for no historical event which has been laudable that did not have the moral force fundamental to being observed in successive generations. What this means is that Hitler is not lauded throughout history but instead it was the liberation forces that are lauded. Nobody fundamentally recalls or celebrates into history the people who were against the liberation of blacks; they remember Lincoln. History will recall with great acclaim the work and struggle of Nelson Mandela but those who stood against him will be placed in the annals of shame.

Causes which do not have moral force do not withstand the test of time. African Americans must understand the clear demarcation between the rights that they have fought for throughout their entire history and the precipitous rights being attached to their struggle by the gay rights movement.

Having the conviction to separate fact from fiction is becoming a task in every society considering the wave of populous sentiment. Facts on the civil rights attributable to African Americans have a pedigree of unchallengeable girth but mixing those facts with popular sentiment waters down the heroic actions of hundreds of black leaders and disrespects God given rights.

African American Christians must begin to move away from the loud blaring music and the spellbinding dance of popular sentiment to regain the honour of standing for time tested truths and facts.

CHAPTER 2

The Dimensions of Marriage

Breaching the barriers of marriage

The topic of gay marriage will always be a very difficult subject to discuss. There are deep emotions involved and zealously held beliefs from opposing sides of the topic. For many people, simply quoting the Bible to them will cause immediate resistance because of their own belief system. Because I do trust in the power of the word of God and I do think (as I will attempt to demonstrate later) that it is rational and logical; I will try to create enough balance that gives my reasoning from a combination of secular and Biblical perspectives. The dialogue has to be extensive enough on all angles in the chance that 'protagonist' may see the rationality of truths presented.

Marriage is a very big institution when considering how many people are under legal contracts. It has great dimensions to understand. Although much of the debate about gay marriage is still centric to the Christian church it also has pronounced traction in the legal realm where the contentious issue is specific to the Constitutional debate of 'rights', and the protection of freedoms as well as the issues surrounding tax incentives.

The most difficult part to the debate is to understand the apprehension and aversion to granting marriage to gays? We have already tackled the concept of what is or is not a right. When the phrase 'right to marriage' is so boldly placed forward it leaves another question wide open; what is marriage?

Marriage Defined

1. Dictionary definition - I looked up the word marriage in the 2002 Oxford Student's Dictionary. Oxford defined marriage as, the state in which a man and a woman are formally united as husband and wife. I went online to find a modern definition and was somewhat surprised to find that the definition was very much the same except that it did include the words 'typically as recognized by law'.

2. Bible definition - In the Bible, it is quite clear that all references to marriage is secured through a man and woman or husband and wife. It would be safe to assume that the Bible translates the relationship and the meaning of marriage as a 'union' of man and woman or reconciling so as to coexist in harmony[28].

Here are Bible references which specifically define marriage:

- Genesis 2: 22 – 24 – 'Then the LORD God made a woman from the rib he had taken out of the man, and he brought her to the man. The man said, "This is now bone of my bones and flesh of my flesh; she shall be called 'woman,' for she was taken out of man." For this reason a man will leave his father and mother and be **united to his wife, and they will become one flesh**.

- Mark 10: 6 - 9 - "But at the beginning of creation God *'made them male and female.'* 'For this reason a man will leave his father and mother and be **united to his wife, and the two will become one flesh**.' So they are no longer two, but one. Therefore what God has joined together, let man not separate."

- Matthew 19: 4 – 6 - "Haven't you read," he replied, "that at the beginning the Creator 'made them male and female,' and said, 'For this reason a man will leave his father and mother and be united to his wife, and the two will become one flesh'? So they

---

[28] 1Corinthians 7: 1 -16

are no longer two, but one. Therefore **what God has joined together, let man not separate**."

There are a plethora of other verses which give clear evidence that the Bible references the definition of marriage as between a man and woman. Perhaps the most powerful text is taken from 1 Corinthians 7: 1 -16 which gives a stringent guideline and context of marriage. It reads with a governed authority for the parameters of the relationship, man and woman, as if a priest is issuing a verbatim context of vows. This chapter is an indomitable instruction on the proper character and maintenance of the marriage relationship between a man and woman.

3. The US Federal government definition – The US Government has defined marriage under the Defence of Marriage Act (DOMA) pertaining to the terms: 'marriage' and 'spouse'. In determining the meaning of any Act of Congress, or of any ruling, regulation, or interpretation of the various administrative bureaus and agencies of the United States, the word 'marriage' means only a legal union between one man and one woman as husband and wife, and the word 'spouse' refers only to a person of the opposite sex who is a husband or a wife.'

4. The LGBT community definition – This may be surprising to read, but I had a problem finding an official definition from any organization associated with LGBT which defined the word 'marriage'. It appeared to me that there was no philosophical cohesiveness on the definition. The only relative phrase that I found was that of 'same-sex or marriage equality'. On the site Wikipedia, the definition of 'same-sex' marriage was marriage between two persons of the same biological sex and/or gender identity. Legal recognition of same-sex marriage is sometimes referred to as marriage equality.

A. New Paradigms

There are a few significant reasons for placing a face on the definition of marriage. With the level of debate currently it makes sense to understand not only the differences in definition but the similarities also. That allows a visual reference of understanding which can account for extreme changes in the average accepted definition.

I made an attempt to define 'rights' and the context of how those rights are attributed. That being the case, one has to understand what marriage is to then amalgamate the meaning or purpose of marriage with attributable rights.

The whole framework of rights accredited to marriage must be contextualized based on the meaning and purpose of marriage. The definitions listed above take on new girth and significance when placed into different paradigms such as **cultural, legislative, social and religious significance**. That significance is important because any debate about legitimising gay marriage must determine whether gay marriage is contextually within the ascribed definitions or whether the meaning delineates from the general definition thus creating a new paradigm.

1. **Cultural significance** – Cultural Anthropology is very concerned with the relationships of people in a historical, modern and future context. Where families are concerned, Anthropologist have traditionally focused on the relationship based on **consanguine**, which is relationships by blood or **affinal** which is relationships by law (marriage). Marriage has a wide berth of cultural norms within the milieus of acceptance and meaning. Different cultures accept various standards for marriage but it is largely and principally viewed as an institution between a man and woman where there is legal recognition of an intimate interpersonal relationship. In many Arab States the culturally accepted phenomena of **consanguine marriage** is prevalent. Such marriages are permissible under the *shariah* and first cousins are allowed to marry. Under Australian

law there is also an allowance of first cousin marriages. In the US such marriages were legal up to 2010[29].

Although consanguineous marriage is largely frowned upon due to a profound risk of developing a range of genetic disorders[30] there is a key reason why it was widely accepted throughout Europe[31] and Asia in the first instance; it gave legitimacy to the original intention of protecting family dynasties through the process of selective 'breeding' among certain families.

Under consanguine marriage all attributable legal tender similar to affinal relationships are assigned so that the relationship is officially recognized.

The key intention or purpose of consanguine marriage is procreation.

Anthropology[32] has traditionalized through **affinal relationships** that marriage achievies four core objectives as a definition:

- *Marriage regulates sexual behaviour* – *which is essentially a way to places prescribed barriers on how individuals manage the process of child birth and rearing.*
- *Marriage fulfills economic needs* – *by giving stability to individuals who live via ascribed marital status where finances are combined.*

---

29 The United States has the only bans on cousin marriage in the Western world. Associated Press. "Md. lawmaker: Ban first-cousin marriages as unsafe." February 18, 2010.

30 **Scientists: Incest Doomed European Royal Dynasty**
    Published April 16, 2009. http://www.foxnews.com/story/0,2933,515982,00. html#ixzz2U3DQktVI

31 The kings of the Spanish Habsburg dynasty (1516–1700) frequently married close relatives. Alvarez G, Ceballos FC, Quinteiro C (2009) The Role of Inbreeding in the Extinction of a European Royal Dynasty.

32 Bonvillain, Nancy. 2010. ''Cultural Anthropology'', 2nd edition. Boston: Pearson Education, Inc. http://wikieducator.org/Cultural_Anthropology/ Social_Institutions/Marriage

- ***Marriage perpetuates kinship groups*** – *not only through the culture of consanguine but also as a general means of securing inheritance, financial stability and social status.*
- ***Marriage provides institution for the care and enculturation of children*** – *marriage gives children legal, genetic and financial heritage, as well as inculcates a 'sense of person'.*

Changes in culture can't be underestimated. Keeping in mind that there may be subtle changes to the dynamics of culture in various societies every day; let's try and maintain the potential impact of that change as it relates to the cultural identity of marriage.

What we have shown above is that the secular culturally accepted norm of marriage is focused on shared qualities such as economics, sex, family security and children.

If we were to be honest; a surface evaluation would show that gay marriage can achieve 3 out of 4 of the objectives and the last objective is artificially achieved through adoption or surrogacy.

That means that gay marriage can be justified from a cultural standpoint of anthropology; or can it?

Place this thought into perspective; there is an immediate reason why social scientist and even the US government chose to define marriage with the context of a 'shaped' definition. It was necessary to have not only a standard but to set up protective borders. The unequivocal nature of defining an affinal marriage as between a man and woman is a concerted effort to establish certainty and control over a definition which can lead to confusion and create a circus environment. Here is proof of this assertion.

- In 2007, Liu Ye of China[33] decided it would be better to marry himself than be single. The best part is that he married a foam-board cut-out of himself dressed in a lovely red dress. Ye admits to being 'narcissistic', but said of his nuptials, "There are

---

[33] Chinese man married himself; Via: www.shortnews.com) http://culturetown.org/chinese-man-married-himself/

26

many reasons for marrying myself, but mainly to express my dissatisfaction with reality."

- Bestiality is in Vogue. Here are a few very strange stories from around the world.

In 2006, a Hindu[34] woman in India claimed she had fallen in love with a snake and then married the snake in accordance with Hindu marriage rituals. What was amazing is that it was reported that over 2,000 people showed up and participated in a celebratory procession, on the notion that the ceremony would 'bring good luck'. The apparent 'groom' which was the snake, did not have live representation but was presented as a brass-likeness of itself.

In the same story line there was a bizarre continuance of animal marriage which spoke of situations in Sudan. Persons there are aware to be careful who or what they are 'caught being intimate' with. The law of marriage there overlapped into the ridiculous. **In 2006, the law of marriage was applied to a goat. 'Charles Tombe was caught having relations with the goat and was forced to marry** it, and pay a dowry to its owner, as a form of public embarrassment'.

Even in Israel we find that the oddity in law is possible. A British lady who had apparently become enamoured with a dolphin through a '15-year courtship', decided to marry the mammal. She made statement to the extent that the animal was "the love of my life." It is reported that the marriage was 'sealed' with a kiss and the dolphin given a herring.

- Inanimate love legitimized. In 2000 a man by the name of Davecat decided that he wanted to marry his sex 'blow up doll'. He is quoted as saying, "She provides me with a lot of things that I can't get out of an organic partner, like... quiet". The man and his partner were the focus of The Learning Chanel show, 'My Strange Addiction.'

---

[34] 15 of the World's Weirdest Marriages, 'I Now Pronounce You... What?!' By Kathy Landin, The FW; http://thefw.com/weirdest-marriages-of-the-world-photos-videos/

- Marriage game fantasy. It is reported that a Japanese man who went by the name Sal9000 married a character from a virtual dating game. The character's name was 'Nene Anegasaki from the Nintendo DS video game "Love Plus,". The marriage ceremony was accounted as a legal union even-though the bride was an 'imaginary object'. The man's wife is a resident of Nintendo DSi LL/XL. Invited guest to the marriage witnessed a virtual kiss between the man and his wife.
- Finally; in Korea a man determined that he was in love with a pillow which had a picture of a woman attached. The pillow which is called a 'dakimakura' had a picture of a character from a Japanese anime. He married the pillow with the consent and blessing of a local priest. The ceremony was purported to have been carried throughout the local media there.

As bizarre and as unfortunate it is to show such extreme stories, it becomes prudent and necessary that these extreme angles are reported to drive home the very serious point; which is, that many people have philosophical beliefs on what their rights should be in relations to marriage. The stories above actually constitute legitimate, all be it strange, marriages.

I believe then that it is safe to posit that every change in society can have effects that can be minuscule or very evident. Some change will deteriorate held standards and be detrimental whiles some will be purely positive. We can entertain a conversation that defines a vast array of strange cultural events which have varying degrees of change and effects but once again, the primary focus is to stay on marriage.

The one thing that stands out the greatest when evaluating the legitimacy of gay marriage as a cultural norm or the enigma of change is the lack of data, which can form a comparative conclusion.

For instance; in a recent article[35] about prostitution a very interesting fact emerged. In countries like Germany and Sweden which had moved

---

[35] The Monkey Cage, Legalized Prostitution Increases Human Trafficking by Erik Voeten on June 13, 2013 http://themonkeycage.org/2013/06/13/

to liberalize the sex industry, the initial objective was to protect women by placing them under the 'guise' of the law and to regulate the industry for tax purposes. I won't speculate on the level of study which took place before such legal change was enacted but clearly this cultural change is having far ranging effects on the cultural development of those countries and not in a positive way.

Another report printed much earlier in The Examiner[36] outlined concerns from a police chief that showed drastic statistics based on a period from the changing of laws and the time of the report. It showed that sex trafficking had increased into Germany by 70%. Quite scary was the stat that 70% of child related trafficking was with children under the age of 14. Because the country allowed prostitution the traffickers were able to better disguise their activities such that many Eastern Europeans and African women were being abducted and forced into work in Germany. Women have become more of a commodity and most of the assumed 'positives' of legalizing are being viewed as negatives.

Therefore, the question remains; what would be the cultural impact in a 10 or 20 year period of legalizing gay marriage? Many critics are quick to speak of the unfairness of not allowing same-sex couples the rights attached to heterosexual couples. What's more interesting to me is how the voice of dissenters to prostitution laws (as a tangible example because we have proven statistics) have been muffled. These persons who would have stood up in opposition to say that it's unfair to live in a society which agrees to change laws such as prostitution; are now negatively impacted, having to live with broad exposure of the law and its' results on their families. Young children and specifically young girls are seeing the cultural influence and exposure to a law, which lends itself to accepting women as a commodity. It's very possible that young boys will grow up comprehending that women are actual business tools for sex. In another

---

legalized-prostitution-increases-human-trafficking/

[36] German's legalized prostitution brought more exploitation than emancipation to women   Youngbee Dale May 26, 2010, The Examiner. http://www.examiner.com/article/german-s-legalized-prostitution-brought-more-exploitation-than-emancipation-to-women

10 years to come; imagine what those children will contribute culturally to their society based on their view of cultural norms.

2. __Legislative significance__ – Legal marriage is nothing less than a contract which attributes various rights and benefits to the subscribers therein. The significance to the subscribers is that those legal rights attached to marriage are protected by governments and legislative bodies who also have an invested and constitutional duty to protect the welfare of its citizens. On average, marriage is the largest single investment that individuals make. That investment normally entails offspring, property ownership, legal rights of survivorship, spousal benefits, and other marital amenities.

In the US, the United States Supreme Court stated in *Maynard v. Hill*:

> Marriage, as creating the most important relation in life, as having more to do with **the morals and civilization of a people** than any other institution, has always been subject to the control of the legislature. That body prescribes the age at which the parties may contract to marry, the procedure or form essential to constitute marriage, the duties and obligations it creates, its effects upon the property rights of both... and the acts which may constitute grounds for its dissolution.
>
> The recent challenge to DOMA has resulted in about 14 states[37] (at the instance of this writing) supporting the right to marry by gay couples.
>
> Many other states have written in 'mini' DOMA laws that do not recognize the entitlements supported by the other states. The status of DOMA is still intact. That

---

[37] The 14 states where gay marriage is legal, in one ma By Sean Sulliva; The Fix; The Washington Post http://www.washingtonpost.com/blogs/the-fix/wp/2013/10/22/the-14-states-where-gay-marriage-is-legal-in-one-map/

means that the language of the Federal Government still recognizes and defines marriage as a union/relationship/ legal joining of a man with a woman.

This is obviously subject to change[38] based on the numerous challenges before the Supreme Court of the US, which has a full slate of constitutional arguments to consider.

Principle to the debate of gay marriage is the case of *United States v. Windsor[39],* which is being litigated on the constitutionality of banning gay marriage. The acceptance of redefining marriage in the US has far ranging Federal affects such as tax incentives for first time 'gay-couple' home owners, inheritance tax issues and rights under divorce laws. The LGBT community clearly asserts that attaining those rights under legislative amendments are primarily important in the effort to redefine marriage.

For the short term, the key significance of marriage in a legal sense is the protection of the estate, survivors and liabilities which flow from the union of marriage. Into the future, gay marriage will raise significant legal dilemmas towards understanding the purpose of marriage.

Here are a few of those instances which are legal challenges to heterosexuals but the instances will exponentially increase as well as the variances under Homosexual scenarios:

a. If a gay[40] couple uses a surrogate who wants to remain anonymous, and the baby develops a life threatening disease

---

[38] Section 3 of DOMA has now been declared unconstitutional as of June 26, 2013. The New York Times; Between the Lines of the Defense of Marriage Act Opinion; By JOHN SCHWARTZ.

[39] United States v. Windsor, http://en.wikipedia.org/wiki/United_States_v._Windsor.

[40] U.S. News on NBC (online) Kevin Murphy, Reuters, http://usnews.nbcnews. com/_news/2014/01/23/22421999-kansas-sperm-donor-to-appeal-ruling-that-he-

or has a life development that requires blood donated from the surrogate; would the parents of the child have any legal right to violate the anonymous discretion of the surrogate?

b. Conversely, if a gay couple pays to have a surrogate and the child inherits a genetic disease from the surrogate; who bears the risk and the outcome?

c. If same sex marriage is ever deemed illegal what would the fallout be to those families if it is also determined under the 'best interest' policy that adopted children are subject to unnatural psychological indoctrination which is abusive?

d. The 'best interest of the child' concept usually holds the blood mother instantly responsible for the health welfare of the child. Does surrogacy change that dynamic pursuant to a contract and are two 'fathers' then deemed naturally in the best interest of the health and welfare of that adopted child?

e. What happens in a same sex relationship if one partner wants to revert to a heterosexual relationship; can one partner object to exposing the child to a heterosexual lifestyle?

f. How will the law regulate surrogacy to stop the exploitation of selling babies as chattel (slavery)? There is a real threat that selective genetics and birthing mothers can change surrogacy into a high stakes auction selling game; are consumer and commercial laws relevant?

g. Where society has been reluctant to remove children from the care of a mother in divorce; what will be the new criteria for a custody battle where the reason for the divorce is irreconcilable differences between two men? And; what rights would a woman have in a lesbian relationship where the 'birthing' partner is the only blood relative?

The legal discrepancies can go on and on. This area of law is in flux and will no doubt develop into legal quagmires if it has not already.

---

must-pay-child-support?lite

I'm sure that sceptics will immediately suggest that there may be exaggerations in my legal analysis but most amazingly, I found this legal story almost whiles I typed. It[41] is a very interesting case (cited below) found in the news which concerns a same sex couple, a male surrogate and divorce.

Many Legislative bodies have heard debate that centres' around the ambit of fairness[42]. From a legislative position, it is a very spurious line of reasoning to use towards establishing gay marriage because the standard for fairness can be too subjective. Measuring whether justice is seen to be done in an equities manner to determine an inadequacy of law is a proposition that must correlate to strict amalgamated and 'tested' legal standards. Consider whether it is fair to stop a 'heterosexual pride' parade. Apparently the subjective standard of fairness would say that it is fair to do so. Here is a quote from a proponent of limiting such a parade; "The celebration of heterosexual pride is **inappropriate because it belittles the just cause** of the LGBT community," the statement added. "Unlike homosexuals, heterosexuals are not discriminated against simply for being heterosexuals[43]." The very fact that the statement attempts to block the rights of heterosexuals to stage a parade is an oxymoron in fairness. What is the criterion for understanding the legitimacy of entitlements being increased?

Any legislative argument for fairness (similar to the one listed) **where <u>the love of two individuals</u> is used as the criterion for fairness** in entitlements, is perhaps the most dangerous premise in legislature logic. It assumes a standard that has no legal force to withstand scrutiny.

---

[41] Kansas judge hears arguments in case of sperm donor sued for child support By Jim Doblin and Matthew DeLuca, NBC News http://usnews.nbcnews.com/_news/2013/10/25/21150280-kansas-judge-hears-arguments-in-case-of-sperm-donor-sued-for-child-support?lite

[42] Diane J. Savino: The case for same-sex marriage; TED http://www.ted.com/talks/diane_j_savino_the_case_for_same_sex_marriage.html

[43] ROB HALFORD Says Brazil's 'Heterosexual Pride Day' Proposal Is 'Childish' Read http://www.blabbermouth.net/news/rob-halford-says-brazil-s-heterosexual-pride-day-proposal-is-childish/

For instance, if we affirm that two persons love each other and are entitled to various legal protections and advantages; how could we not use that very same standard to justify entitlements were 'love' is claimed between heterosexual polygamist; or homosexual polygamist.

Love is an abstract concept which can be claimed in virtually any relationship. If it is the impetus for legal entitlements through the concept of fairness; there are no levels of certainty to establish the voracity of the claim.

Legislative bodies which are acting ad hoc in creating these legal precedents are driving agendas which are pushing the borders of normative legal and moral positions to abnormality such that legal force and cogency is threatened. The significance to have legislative bodies adhere to correct interpretation and application of the law is absolutely essential.

Issues which have 'moral scope' should be determined by a standard of Ecclesiastical law which is tried and tested and codified in the constitution; and legal standards should not be so easily established by the 'fairness' movement.

3.   **Social significance** – Much of what I state here is woven into the cultural significance. There is only a thin line of reasoning which separates the two.

In a pluralistic society such as the US, it is becoming more distinguishable what effects the whole gay rights and gay marriage debate is having on that society. Between 1996 and 2012, a period of approximately 16 years; there has been a drastic change in persons who now believe that 'same-sex' marriages should be legalized and who have accepted a realignment of the terminology which advocates marriage as a partnership between a man and a woman. The social definition of marriage in the US is evolving.

A Gallop Poll taken in March of 1996 showed that only 27% of persons polled supported same-sex marriages. By May of 2012, that number in a Gallop Poll was now recorded at 50%. The effects of this statistical increase are being seen throughout all levels of the American society. From the President to famous athletes; from movie stars to celebrities; there is a concerted, determined effort to have same-sex marriage accepted and any persons opposed are seen as socially 'incorrect'.

This is a fundamental change in the 'moral theory' of the American society. The significance of the change is that philosophically, humankind has started to redefine homosexual behaviour. It is no-longer universally seen as an abnormality of behaviour but as an alternative normal life style. Even more significantly, is the fact that the premise being used to justify homosexuality has a **'relativity to other behaviours'**; those abnormal behaviours, such as polygamy or incest, can adopt and pattern the same argument for the same intended social success.

For persons who are quick to dismiss this statement, more thought should be given to the fact that when considering the core arguments by the gay community; their normal justification for acceptance is that they are being discriminated against. That is a fundamental argument used.

Discrimination is one of those constitutional words that has a double edge effect. It is so far ranging that it protects the rights of all in one instance whiles allowing others to be protected as a way of legitimizing perverse agendas. Many sexually perverse groups such as nudist, sex offenders, persons in bestiality are using the veil of protection behind this legal and constitutional right, in an effort to mount very legitimate challenges. Note this posting on the 'Family Research Centre[44]' website; **"Some homosexual activists defend the historic connection between homosexuality and pedophilia**: Such activists consider the defense of "boy-lovers" to be a legitimate gay rights issue." At the very heart of that statement is an argument based on the same principles I have implied. For instance; if a homosexual man asserts that he is 'born' gay (without supporting empirical evidence) and it is accepted, there is no

---

[44] Homosexuality and Child Sexual Abuse 2013 Family Research Council; http://www.frc.org/?i=IS02E3

way of justifying **the discrimination** of not accepting the very same argument from a paedophile. It will be argued that my comparison between paedophiles and homosexuals is unfair because children are being unfairly exploited as sexual minorities. There is much truth in that statement; but the no-standard mandate is allowing children to express themselves as sexually liberated individuals. In many communities the age of children[45] actively involved in sex is drastically dropping. Far worse is the fact that many children are allowed to voice strong opinions on their sexuality at an age where their knowledge of sex should raise the red flag of alarm and declaring[46] a sexual proclivity should be an unknown dynamic in their lives.

I ask; what are the true effects on society pertaining to gay marriage? To beat the drum again; there is no data to prove one way or the other what the true effects would be so it leaves me in an open field of unqualified assumptions but perhaps in a very pragmatic way.

Looking back at the anthropology of marriage and understanding the affinal position; one has to wonder how gay marriage plays out in the grand scheme of things.

We are all basically optimist it seems, about the nature of man to find the best common denominator of 'upright' behaviour; but unfortunately, history proves that thought incorrect. The stats that were aforementioned in regards to prostitution have shown the digression of behaviour based on legalizing. In Colorado (US) I was watching a program where every law officer that was interviewed, spoke of the proliferation of illegal activity due to the ambiguity of law in that state in relations to marijuana.

Let me take a statistical guess that homosexual behaviour will proliferate. The increase will not happen because more homosexuals are being born (as perhaps the LGBT would like to assert), but because

---

[45] **Children are having sex at younger ages,** Wainwright Jeffers, WALB News; http://www.walb.com/story/10972974/children-are-having-sex-at-younger-ages

[46] Black Media Scoop; http://www.blackmediascoop.com/r-kellys-teen-daughter-comes-out-as-transgender/

exposure to a **social trend** will cater to attitudes and behaviours being shaped towards vast acceptance.

Is it unfair to speculate that society may become more 'socially sterile' into the future where procreation is concerned and population explosion will go into a decline? Since gay male couples (and female) are unable to procreate; the need of a surrogate to produce an off-spring as well as adoption, will continue to become the choice way to have families in this community. Lesbian women will also continue to proliferate birthing methods. That introduces vast social dynamics where family lines, population ecology etc. and some of the concerns introduced under 'legislative significance', will lag behind in proper analysis. Without these issues being seriously addressed the role of surrogacy as a potential black-market business can have devastating consequential effects on the 'moral' compass of communities.

The **social significance** of sterility along with the business of child birth can produce an uncontrolled black market effect as couples become more desperate because market dynamics may produce high prices or even poor scientific techniques in a rush to capitalize on a new consumer market. The combinations are all nebulous but where money is involved, unregulated debauchery will ensue and is realistic.

I mentioned in the introduction of this book, that I started my interest in gay marriage from an online conversation. In that blog, I needed to address an insinuation by a specific protagonist, where he stated that a gay couple would be superior parents in comparison to single mothers (he was specific to mothers).

He posted an article[47] to me which was used as a backdrop to qualify his contention.

I must admit that I was somewhat perplexed as to why this article was chosen in lieu of the proposition he was putting forth. He had

---

[47] Capitalism and Inequality, What the Right and the Left Get Wrong By Jerry Z. Muller; Foreign Affairs, published by Council on Foreign Relations. http://www.foreignaffairs.com/articles/138844/jerry-z-muller/capitalism-and-inequality?page=2

made the point that, **'it would be better for a child to be adapted into a 'loving' and well-adjusted gay relationship where there would be more financial stability as opposed to a child raised by a single mother who would obviously be (paraphrased) "living in poverty and a sexually irresponsible lifestyle"**. He inferred that it would not be in the best interest of the child to be with the single mother in his scenario.

The reason that I decided to highlight that personal debate, is because this is another fallacy that often finds its way into the deemed prerogative of gay rights advocates.

Technically, I agree that a child raised by a single person, who acts irresponsible and is financially challenged, retards the proper upbringing of a child. What I am unprepared to do is to substitute one bad situation for another. Child adaption by gays is a new phenomenon. My somewhat simplistic research has indicated that there is insufficient data of a statistical variance and significance to make scientific prognostications. This means that neither I nor any protagonist to the gay cause can make assertions or conclusions because there are no verifiable facts on the outcome of gay adoption.

It is easy to guess that there were fundamental reasons to assume that a two parent home is fundamentally better than a single parent home. Imagine this; as a social experiment gone bad (to simply characterize the explosion of single parent homes), the statistical analysis of data[48] produced from single parenting is across the board dismal. It has shown that many social ills in today's society are directly and indirectly attributable to single parenting.

I can immediately hear the retort which is; gay homes would rear children under a couple scenario. That is a legitimate argument, but here is the problem. Over 70 years ago when there were far less single

[48] The Father Factor National Fatherhood Initiative, Howard, K. S., Burke Lefever, J. E., Borkowski, J.G., & Whitman, T. L. (2006). Fathers' influence in the lives of children with adolescent mothers. Journal of Family Psychology, 20, 468- 476. -: http://www.fatherhood.org/media/consequences-of-father-absence-statistics

parent homes and people took their marriage as an 'unbreakable' commitment; all of those statistical anomalies above were virtually non-concerns. It was only after society started moving towards the social experiments of liberalization that we started to recognize radical changes in communities. As a 'type' of social experiment, the more society accepted and did not frown upon single parenting and the proliferation of the 'free sex revolution'; society ventured blindly into a social experiment that changed the landscape of social society in the most profound negative ways.

What I conclude from that (even though I will repeat parts of this below) is that the social experiment of gay couples without any data or analysis on how it will affect future generations; can potentially bring communities to a halt.

Unfortunately the voracity of what I have said is progressively underscored by the fact that gay couples are currently adopting children.

Gay parenting is one of the most perverse and unintelligent social experiments ever if properly conceptualized within a purpose for marriage and parenting.

Here is an immutable fact; children can only be born to a woman. In the very article sent to me, it was posited that the most practical social equation for capitalism is the financial dynamism of families. I don't think it would be a leap to see that children, who are completely philosophized and socialized by gay parents, would contribute to a declining birth rate. It would have the exact impact that children from heterosexual relationships have. That is; there would be reverse socialization were those children would see loving relationships within the context of same sex orientation. Whiles my assertion is only theorized, I would challenge anyone to rationalize or produce data which can be feasibly relied on to challenge this hypotheses. What I am insisting here is that apples don't fall far from the tree; so it would make no sense to find a social juxtaposition, where more apples become oranges.

It is true that an identifiable percentage of children have grown up under heterosexual parents and still go into the gay lifestyle. It is also true that the percentage of children who maintain their heterosexual identity from socialization under heterosexual parents is substantially higher. Factoring in the influence of socialization under parents whether gay or non-gay is a significant contributing element. There is no understatement by psychologist of the innate affects parents have on early and latent cognitive and social skills of children. Psychologists from Freud to Maslow have written extensively on childhood development and how parents significantly influence children.

The question then becomes; if parenting shapes early development, what would be the end results on children brought up to view the most nurturing relationship in their life as being a same sex union? Why would a child brought up by same sex parents, not have a much higher proclivity to adapt the same sexual orientation. We know that children who watched their parents smoke, have a higher probability of smoking. It follows that children who grow up under domestic violence also have a higher inclination towards violence of some nature. As a matter of fact; it is estimated by UNICEF[49] that, "the single best predictor of children becoming either perpetrators or victims of domestic violence later in life is whether or not they grow up in a home where there is domestic violence". Very stunningly it is estimated that 1 in 5 to 1 in 3 of teenagers who were subject to viewing domestic violence also experienced or became violent during teen dating[50].

If the equation of kids becoming more like their parents holds as true; how would gay marriage maintain the status quo of procreation? The point here is; gay parenting as a social experiment will inevitably fail within the affinal purpose of marriage considering that the primary function is procreation. Even evolutionist recognizes the importance of procreation as an essential part of man's evolutionary drive to perfection.

---

[49] Behind Closed Doors The Impact of Domestic Violence on Children; UNICEF Child Protection Section Programme Division 3 United Nations Plaza http://www.unicef.org/protection/files/BehindClosedDoors.pdf

[50] Sexual Assault Survivor Services (SASS) Facts about domestic violence. (1996)] via Wikepedia; http://en.wikipedia.org/wiki/Effects_of_domestic_violence_on_children#cite_note-SASS-7

Man cannot strive generationally without the sensory stimulation of opposite sex pheromones which encourage the process towards birth. The professor in the article mentioned above, theorized all of this more succinctly. He said:

> *"The role of the family in shaping [an] individuals' ability and inclination to make use of the means of cultivation that capitalism offers is hard to overstate."* **He goes on to state that median family homes are not simply a place for collection and depletion of necessities as well as procreation for offspring; but the equally important life events of socialization, 'civilized' adaptations, and education, all occur which further shape 'habits' which in turn also influences 'their subsequent fates as people and as market actors'.** *He eloquently states the belief that in the "language of contemporary economics, the family is a workshop in which human capital is produced."*

My conclusion on the **social significance** of gay marriage or marriage is that, the definition of a family must go beyond a value of simply raising a child. There has to be something more tangible to establish a hierarchy of standards in raising children. We know that in today's world, anyone can lay claim on parenting; as legend has it, even wolves achieved the feat in the story of Romulus and Remus.

What is the preeminent parenting situation for the best interest of the child? I could not support any situation which promotes single mothers/fathers as a panacea for the model family. **Whiles many single parents can be commended in the circumstance and do an extraordinary job, there is ample statistical data which shows that single parent homes have had a degenerative effect on society as a whole.** On the other hand, there is no data which I can rely on (other than my own conjecture) which remotely suggest that gay couples are better positioned to raise children through marriage. I have posited a reasoned approach on the essential flaws of gay relationships where two key purposes of marriage (procreation and heritage) are unachievable. Combine those facts with the possibility of psychological abnormality along with confusion, and it becomes another risky social experiment.

Having said that; **it has always been logically accepted that a heterosexual marriage is the model family unit**. Families actualize the very concept of mankind by setting an example of structure, such that generational existence is cultivated. Throughout the whole animal kingdom, animals mate and parent children with the clear expectation that children would replicate the behaviour and secure lineage. Biological reproduction remains essential and assuming anything less is a major faux pas. Whiles there can be maladaptive behaviour by gay adults and heterosexual adults which would not be conducive to child rearing; it is still indisputable that a stable heterosexual family unit is the model dynamic of child rearing.

4. **Spiritual/Religious** – I won't go very far into this area as would be expected because this will come up for full consideration under another section, so I will stay on the periphery.

Of all the major Christian denominations in the US (American Baptist, Anglican, Assemblies of God, Catholic, Southern Baptist, Evangelical Presbyterian Church and Orthodox Presbyterian Church, United Methodist Church and Seventh Day Adventist), there has been no significantly visible statement of support or change of definition; but smaller church organizations such as The Metropolitan Community Church, Protestant Episcopal Church in the United States of America[51] and The United Church of Christ have supported and redefined the issue.

In terms of the non-Christian religions, there has not been any aggressive support from major movements such as Islam, Hindu and Judaism.

---

[51] The Huffington Post, Yasmine Hafiz; Rev. Cameron Partridge Will Be First Openly Transgender Priest To Preach at Washington National Cathedral; http://www.huffingtonpost.com/2014/06/06/transgender-priest-national-cathedral-pride_n_5459762.html

Even though major religions have not changed their stance on gay marriage, it is obvious statistically that parishioners are quietly harbouring favourable views. It means that individuals are philosophically being impacted by the LGBT community. Whether churches will be made to adhere to any strict legal policy is beyond speculative but if the LGBT community would like to also have marriage recognized in a religious context in the very near future; they may need to establish a registered religious movement or attend one of the smaller denominations that do support.

The true significance of this debate from a religious perspective is the moral challenge Christians and other religions will have in accepting a law/s, which promotes and legitimize the gay life style including gay marriage. For the Christian believer there can't be anything more burdensome. Humanist, LGBT, and general non-believers will assail the heresy of the church towards their agenda as hatemongering and religious irrationality but by the standards that Christianity has set; there is a theological rational why Christians argue against the homosexual agenda becoming law. It is a **rationality that will be shown further on.**

The most conspicuous affront to the Christian belief is the Bible being dismissed as simply a text on ancient history with many of the stories having a fable quality. Christianity would not exist if the Bible lost its' validity.

For this reason, Christians hold to the Biblical verses which say:

- "His eyes observe the nations; do not let the rebellious exalt themselves."(Psalms 66:7) The Bible accordingly gives insight to God's involvement as He looks in on each individual nation and warns the rebellious ones.
- "Righteousness exalts a nation, but sin condemns any people." (Proverbs 14:34)

The LGBT will argue vehemently that Civil marriages under licence of the state have nothing to do with the ecumenical service performed by churches. As I will assert below, I do believe that marriage has an attachment to God but the LGBT assertion is spurious in another way.

Principally, what many advocates of the gay community have emphasized is that they are being discriminated against. One has to ask; if a church stopped Blacks from being married, would that decision be subject to scrutiny by the legislation? I would be bold to say that real pressure would fall upon the church to change that policy. So if the LGBT is already using the principle or precedent of civil rights being violated similar to the African American movement; how could we not see a natural inclination or progression to put pressure on the church to conform. Indeed it is already the case. Many churches are vilified as 'racist (which is nonsensical) or homophobic for not allowing gay marriages.

What the LGBT community is not aware of and what many church communities have failed to represent properly is that the church has a mandate to allow every person, be they black, white, yellow, homosexual or bank robber, into the church. The church is to receive all with open arms. What that does not mean is that a person who believes in smoking marijuana can assert his belief that the church is discriminating by not allowing him to smoke in the church. It does not mean that drunks can drink in the church and it certainly does not mean that the church should allow gay marriages to occur. In the story of Jesus entering the temple; we are shown the exact precedent by which the church is to operate. Matthew 21: 12 -13 says'; '*Then Jesus went into the temple of God and drove out all those who bought and sold in the temple, and overturned the tables of the money changers and the seats of those who sold doves. And He said to them, "It is written, 'My house shall be called a house of prayer, 'but **you have made it a 'den of thieves**.'"* Imagine; should the church turn itself into a den of abomination in line with how the Bible references homosexuality.

Continuously throughout the Bible, there is demonstration that God dealt with the **unrighteousness of a nation**. According to Psalm 66:7, God is always looking at individual nations and He warns the rebellious ones*; "His eyes observe the nations; **do not let the rebellious exalt themselves**."*

In the Bible, governments which were impartial to the law established by God and subjected its' citizens to corruptible law, found themselves under the wrath of God. A story which Humanist will dismiss as frivolity and the LGBT will use as an example of why the Bible is worthless as a reference (theorizing that it 'promotes' hatred); the story of Sodom and Gomorrah. That government and nation of people was burned from the Earth because the culture (government) embraced bestiality, homosexuality, paedophilia and incest.

"Woe to those who call evil good and good evil, that put darkness for light, and light for darkness; that put bitter for sweet, and sweet for bitter!..." (Isaiah 5:20)

Scoffers of the law are mindfully warned that the judgement of God is just. There is revelation that God's wrath will come against unrighteousness and ungodliness.

For the Christian, the Bible offers no compromise. What the LGBT and Humanist community assume are inconsequential decisions are blasphemous in the Bible. In fact, many Christians should see the agenda that is assailed by Humanist and LGBT as revelations of the road to the Apocalypse predicted in the Bible.

Conclusively, the purpose of marriage has traditionally come down to 'procreation' and the protection of the consequences which flow from marriage and procreation; gay marriage threatens to change the scope and purpose of an age old institution. Redefining it will open up catechistic questions on conformity, acceptance and theological relativity. Jurisprudence will find new legal loopholes to ponder and debate. Social institutions will acclimate, bend or break under the strain of re-socialization.

I could not refuse to highlight a recent interview which was conducted in the magazine, The Huffington Post Live with host Josh Zepps[52]. I can't speak to the political persuasion or philosophical leanings

---

[52] Huffington Post, Entertainment 8 May 2013 http://www.huffingtonpost. com/2013/04/18/jeremy-irons-gay-marriage-interview-out-of-context_n_3110957.html

of Jerome Irons but I can state that his interview raised the ire of the liberal community when he chose to question the logic of 'gay marriage'. In the article, Mr. Irons speaks rather candidly about issues to which he feels the discussion of gay marriage opens the proverbial 'Pandora's Box'. In the interview, he evokes an answer to a very provocative dilemma. Here is what he said;

> *"Could a father not marry his son? It's not incest between men [because] incest [law] is there to protect us from inbreeding, but men don't breed," Irons said in the original interview with The Huffington Post.*

Mr. Irons then goes further. He starts by saying that men are incapable of birthing; therefore, incest is not relevant in this instant between an adoptive male parent and adopted son who decide to marry due to the very fact that there is no "breeding". He cynically states that no person would have reason to be against such possibilities because no "birth" would ever result from it in relations to incest. His final and most poignant point being an allusion that a male parent may in fact marry his adoptive son as a means of tax evasion as such an arrangement would avoid death taxes under intestate or inheritance laws.

The interviewer then notes that the comments got a little stranger (in his opinion) from Mr. Irons. *"I don't have a strong feeling either way. Living with another animal, whether it be a husband or a dog, is great. It's lovely to have someone to love."*

The writer goes on to quote Jeremy Irons in such manner which implies that Mr. Irons maintained throughout the interview a strong fascination with the possibilities of same-sex marriages "opening the doors" for this potential tax evasion loop-hole. Mr. Irons then finally says, *"It seems to me that now they're fighting for the name. I worry that it means somehow we debase, or we change, what marriage is. I just worry about that."*

On a later interview on Real Talk, which also views on the BBC; he clarifies his position on the subject by stating that he thinks the real purpose of marriage is **procreation.**

What this interview establishes primarily is that if sensible questions can be raised by a man such as Jeremy Irons, who the writer describes as 'a rock-ribbed Libertarian'; then, how much more should the conservative caucus present common-sense and tangible questions towards the logic of gay marriage.

Whiles the secular world is prepared to use terminology (in a reversal of prejudice) such as 'homophobia to create a veil of legitimacy against so-called 'racist'; it becomes more obvious that the agenda to legitimise gay marriage is based on principles of emotionality that have no grounds to stand on because the arguments are created with no cohesive footing and in unproven experiments.

Gay marriage in fact does create a new paradigm outside of traditional definitions. When rights were ascribed to African Americans those rights did not create new paradigms. African Americans were simply 'brought into the fold' of God given rights and constitutional rights that were natural to them.

Gay marriage creates new dynamics in the definition of families. Some families will have transgender males living with a woman who may or may not be transgender. Other families may start with adoptive kids growing up to accept two male fathers where one dad has a midlife crises and wants to embrace his 'feminine' side more; so he decides to become a she. Mind you; this is no different than any other dysfunctional heterosexual family were kids can be traumatized by an emotional divorce; sexual misconduct etc. But from a Christian perspective; it does change the natural course of abnormal normality. It makes it abnormal abnormality. It's akin to an example of a sober drunk telling a child not to drink as opposed to a drunk drunkard relaying the same message. One situation obviously exacerbates the problem more.

Heterosexual marriage can be very dysfunctional. I am not lost on that fact. I am simply not allocating wrong for wrong. I'm not prospering a solution which is in fact a problem.

Chapter 3

The Born Identity

"Sexual love ... is intended only for a man and woman in marriage, where children can come about naturally," said Prominent U.S. Cardinal Timothy Dolan[53]

There is a sexual identity crises in the world. There are persons who assert that they are born homosexual; bisexual; born with a predilection for the transgender lifestyle; born with a propensity towards sex with children; born predisposed to sex with animals. Many other examples of man's predilections can be cited but which statement is true?

The Genetic Fallacy

It would be easy to assume that the LGBT community would reject Cardinal Dolan's statement as scientific heresy on the bases that it does not account for the one element that they believe tips the scale of the debate to their interest. A majority of gays hold to the conjecture that being gay is not a learned response but a genetic disposition. It is the one argument that they believe (perhaps correctly so), would change the complexity of the debate.

---

[53] Cardinal Timothy Dolan: gay people only 'entitled to friendship' Global Post; Samantha Stainburn; http://www.globalpost.com/dispatch/news/regions/americas/united-states/130331/cardinal-timothy-dolan-gay-people-only-entitled-

Here is the theory in a nutshell.

If homosexuality is a genetic predisposition, it would mean that gays are genetically born with the single determination of being gay. From conception to birth, every gay person would have an inalienable predilection for same sex relationships. Any genetic inclination would also mean that religious groups (specifically Christianity) holding to the theory that GOD create 'man & woman' for love exclusive in monogamous relationships, and with the purpose to procreate; they would be supporting a very false premise. Any person holding to the theory of exclusive heterosexual relationships would indeed be perpetuating hate and prejudice. Exclusivity of man to a woman would be a bold lie!

As far as I have researched and found; the theory of genetic disposition gained traction in the early 1990's when a self-proclaimed homosexual scientist by the name of Simon LeVay produced a study to show that neurons known as INAH 3 in the region of the hypothalamus 'were reduced in size in homosexual men'. This was significant because such an irregularity of neurons in the hypothalamus where it is said sexual behaviour is regulated, would give credence to a biological persuasion on behaviour.

The study was followed by a group of geneticist from the highly acclaimed National Cancer Institute lead by Dr. Dean Hamer. They produced results using genetic markers from 76 pairs of homosexual male siblings. The report was sighted to show that there was a genetic link between each sibling such that a conclusion from those premises could only be that there was a hereditary genetic link in families of gays. This report can be found in the July 19, 1993 edition of 'Science' magazine.

The story was presaged in significant journals such as TIME, USA TODAY, and NEWSWEEK as if it were the 'piece de resistance' of genetic studies.

That sentiment started to change by the mid to late 90's. The results of Dr. Hamer were unable to be duplicated by any other study to authenticate it. Scientific American printed an article that mentioned the doubts in the scientific community over the genetics of homosexuality. It said in essence that LeVay's findings, "have yet to be fully replicated by another researcher" and that the report by the geneticist lead by Hamer, had "been charged with research improprieties ". This was an indictment of sorts. By 1999, another group of noted scientist, namely George Rice and George Ebers indicated in their published results that, they were unable to duplicate the results of the Hamer Group, and that the results "do not support an X-linked gene underlying male homosexuality".

Subsequent to this, the study of gay genes is now focused on a new theory. It postulates that environmental factors which are social, physical, and cultural dynamics can influence the genetic biological organism and the organism may influence its own development. Sergey Gavrilets a researcher at the National Institute for Mathematical Biological Synthesis says that the link to genetics and gays is not "genes, it's not genetics. It's not DNA. It's not pieces of DNA. It's **epigenetics**".

The less complex version of what he said is that homosexuals may (not proven) have had a sensitivity to hormonal imbalances in the womb or they may have an abnormality in their body where testosterone is concerned.

'If' this study is correct, it then indicates that homosexuals can receive treatment for a disorder the same way that a schizophrenic can be treated for a chemical imbalance.

There is acknowledgment on the facts that this conversation can be far more comprehensive in all facets of the debate but no matter where the debate goes or how long the discourse; the end result of all accepted scientific studies to date, is that there is no 'gay gene' or the research is inconclusive. This means that some gays will still argue the possibility.

Contemplate this; there are men who consider themselves completely heterosexual but have had a homosexual experience. How would these men be classified? If homosexuality is genetic, how would a person switch from one persuasion to another? Can a black or white person switch from being black genetically? If not, how would a gay person ever 'become straight' (considering we have seen this happen many times)?

We are aware that sexual reassignment is possible as a transgender operation but the genetic make-up of the person never changes. Besides the fact that hormones taken by a transgender man/woman may in fact make them infertile, the transgender woman still has the facilities as a born woman (with womb) to carry a child and the transgender male may still get a woman pregnant because the 'bio-life material', sperm, is never converted. All that a male converted surgically to a female can produce is sperm.

In what is still one of the most bizarre and inane stories I have read; a woman undergoes reassignment surgery to become a man, to live with a female lover. The couple wanted to have children so the transgender male (instead of the natural female partner) decided to stop taking testosterone and underwent artificial insemination. Mr. Beastie (the transsexual) has now had three children for his wife. The point is that genetics do not change but the will of an individual certainly does.

If being gay is not a learned behaviour, the LGBT community has an uphill task in explaining how genetics could evolve to influence the changing persuasion of persons who either switch from being gay to straight, straight to gay or maintain a split personality of being bisexual. There is even a movement afoot to qualify persons as "non-binary[54]" gender (gender not along the lines of man or woman).

On the argument that being gay is genetic; I unequivocal assert that this is a fallacy and that being gay is a learned behaviour which is an indictment on all of society which has poorly addressed and understood how to have proper parenting, spiritual knowledge and environmental controls to allow for better social adjustment in children.

---

[54] The Non-Binary vs. Genderqueer Quandary; October 18, 2011 by marilynroxie via http://genderqueerid.com/post/11617933299/the-non-binary-vs-genderqueer-quandary

Chapter 4

The Practical Truth about Truth

If Billy Graham accepted an invitation to serve as president of the Atheist Alliance of America in agreement with the proposition of a 'god-less' existence; would that be a shocking revelation to Americans? Would such an act be debated among Christian apologist to voice concern about the implications of heresy in the church or would the church surrender to this position?

I would not be surprised to find anyone aghast at the implications of such hyperbole in my opening query. My challenge to the reader is to consider the implications of ascribed authority which is at the beginning of many speculative truths. What that means to me is that any proposition can be conclusive and be rationalized as the truth, if the premise to which it relies on is perceived as an authoritative fact. What exactly is practical truth today?

The Spoken Truth; The Learned Truth or The Observed Truth. Which one is true?

"Education without values, as useful as it is, seems rather to make man a more clever devil." - C.S. Lewis

At first glance one may ask why the implied questions on the rationality of truth are relevant to a topic on gay rights and marriage, but they are in fact very essential elements in the conversation. Any debate that involves two opposing theories will inevitably absorb every angle to prove each position. Each theory will argue a rationale from knowledge it assumes is the truth. The debate on gay marriage and gay rights is no different.

This conversation can normally be defined by two distinct sides; protagonist in support of the gay agenda and antagonist against. Many groups and organization[55] that are classified as anti-gay are also generally considered conservative with a Christian perspective. On the other hand, most groups, organizations and persons in support of the gay agenda are a bit more eclectic as a group where there are found broader appeals to various philosophies. For the most part, it would be safe to classify many supporters of the gay agenda as liberal Humanist.

Whiles I have offered humanist as the protagonist; I did not give an immediate reason why. Humanism as a philosophy can be accounted for from the 13 and 14[56] century. Although it is considered that Francesco Petrarch[57] is the father of Humanism due to his deep conviction towards self-expression and learning; it is the modern evolution of the movement towards deification of self that draws this distinction as the protagonist in this conversation. As Humanist figures such as Brunetto, and Shakespeare pushed the barrios of scholastic secularism modern thinkers have adapted a self-expression that seem avowed to embrace the self-fulfilment of enlightenment of thought, achievement and existence. Key values in the modern Humanist[58] is the self-ascribed 'non-religious' or agnostic attitude which allows a host of other personal values to closely and comfortably associate; those would include, atheist, freethinkers, Secularists, and sceptics. The common denominators between the groups being the rejection of any notion of a 'one true

---

[55] Family Research Council; http://www.frc.org/

[56] Humanism – a history of the noble but forgotten Credo of our species Encyclopedia Britannica, Robert Grudin http://humanism.ws/featured/a-history-of-humanism-robert-grudin/

[57] Petrarch. peter@petersadlon.com; http://petrarch.petersadlon.com/petrarch.html

[58] Professor AC Grayling; British Humanist Association; https://humanism.org.uk/

God' and the notion that human values are the universal impetus for all quality of life.

SECULAR HUMANISM

Modern Humanism[59] or more precisely **Secular Humanism** is by no means as organized as it once was and does have dissenting fractions but the general association with a humanistic way of thought has proliferated and can be heard in every corner of society. It is an attitude that gives no reticence towards long held Christian beliefs and acts as if believing in anything remotely Christian is usurping the dynamics of intellectual rationality and superiority. Not surprisingly, their level of liberal secularism seems attractive to the LGBT community because it embraces a 'self- made' and evolving moral structure that indorses freedom of expression and no moral absolutes. For this reason; my opinion has placed a face to this movement to streamline the conversation.

Putting a face to both sides of the argument is important as an analysis of the fundamental assertions being made. As was observed, many of the protagonist in support of gay marriage and rights spoke with such hubris, in my conversations, that any uninformed person would easily accept their position. That confidence and indifference is an expected response between advocates to a debate but what was quite leery was the way in which every Christian, or more precise, Biblical position was being systematically dismissed, as patently insignificant and irrelevant. Following with what I said previously, the conversation felt as if Humanist asserted a scholarly and 'enlightened' superiority. That became important because it opened up the debate on **which**

---

[59] *On Conceptions of Humanism, Freethought, Atheism, Rationalism, Skepticism, etc.* By Norm R. Allen Jr. Institute for Science and Human Values http://instituteforscienceandhumanvalues.com/articles/norm%20allen/conceptions-freethought.htm

philosophy came from knowledge that could be relied on as the truth.

Both philosophies embrace moral standards (which will also be addressed) but differ on where and how those standards are obtained. There has to be empirical pragmatism to differentiate between both.

The question then becomes; is Christianity or Humanism adequate as a reference to or for social standards (moral absolutes)? Further; is Christianity antiquated as a philosophy of knowledge and is Humanism the new modern way to practical knowledge? The questions certainly do not stop here; knowledge has to be traced back to the very existence of man. One can't have this conversation in the shadows of the most complex, important and stellar question of them all; how does man exist? That question is very pertinent to the origins of truth. If one can understand the origination of truth the answer reverberates to the essence of which philosophy provides a tangible truth enough to be believed?

To begin to answer those questions (primarily to the origination of existence) a complex degree of subject matter had to be explored. Indeed, one can't legitimize an answer without understanding **what knowledge is** and **how it is attained; what truth is** and **how is it derived**; and also, **how is truth validated**.

1. **What is knowledge and how is it used by Humanism and Christianity?** Rudimentarily said; knowledge is the applied result of understanding reasoning through *experience, intuition* or *education*[60].

Knowledge that is explicit is the practical observance and application of physically learned <u>experiences</u> which then gives credence to reasoned conclusions. The word physical can be that which is seen, heard, touched or tasted to validate the experience.

---

[60] Answer derived from reading of the given material; http://en.wikipedia.org/wiki/Epistemology

Knowledge that is implicit comes from a cognitive suggestion of some irrationality that is then rationalized. Cognitive is more perceptive based and hypothesized to reach an educated conclusion.

Christianity and Modern Humanism[61] use both forms of knowledge gathering to formulate the conclusions which are fundamental to their belief system. The branch of philosophy concerned with understanding how knowledge is assembled, applied, disseminated and gives latitude to knowledge is **Epistemology[62]**.

In this limited window the depth of this philosophy can't be regurgitated considering the protracted amount of information found on Epistemology. That level of understudy would turn this area of science into a full thesis. But; the importance of understanding epistemology to validate the two philosophies can't be understated so the most condensed approach in my words has been selected to make a reasoned attempt of producing a level of understanding.

Epistemology is the fundamental base of categorizing philosophies into knowledge defined systems. There are many knowledge based philosophies but the primary methods to define or attain knowledge in Humanism and Christianity reflects through; Empiricism, Rationalism, and Fideism.

I. In a general context, **Humanism** as a philosophy has more of a costumed fit with the practicalities of Empiricism and Rationalism. *Secular Humanism* and *Scientific Humanism* mirrors much of the ideological jargon set forth in the two competing theories on knowledge.

---

[61] Corliss Lamont, March 28, 1902 – April 26, 1995), was a socialist philosopher and leading proponent of Modern Humanism as opposed to Secular, Religious and Christian humanism. He defined it as "a naturalistic philosophy that rejects all supernaturalism and relies primarily upon reason and science, democracy and human compassion." American Humanist Association, What is Humanism by Fred Edwards

[62] http://en.wikipedia.org/wiki/Epistemology

Empiricism promotes the innate qualities and physical perceptions such as sight, touch, sound, taste to man's sensitivity towards self-actualization. It is more of a secular philosophy which does not embrace any idea of predetermination of purpose and meaning in a theistic way but **indorses man's ability to reason his own determination** based on science. **Rationalism** uses reasoning as the principal basis upon which man derives knowledge. Its chief methodology is asserting intellectual capability towards understanding man's entire existence.

Empiricism espouses inductive axioms which are hypothesized based on sensory observations through scientific methods, whereas; **rationalism espouses deductive axioms** using the conscience to extrapolate meaning from 'logical' thinking.

To contextualize the two propositions in Humanistic understanding the following examples are offered:

> ➢ The palaeontologists are prepared to conclude **after observation**, *"Although we only know Nyasasaurus from fossil fragments, the anatomy of its upper arm bone and hips have features that are unique to dinosaurs, making us confident that we're dealing with an animal very close to dinosaur origin..."*[63]**Empiricism**
>
> ➢ Without language we would have no reason, without reason no religion, and without these three essential aspects of our nature, neither mind nor bond of society.[64] **Rationalism**

Modern Humanism brings more clarity to its practicality as a science or philosophy by **embracing both knowledge based**

---

[63] The Independent online, Monday 10 June 2013; quoting Paul Barrett, from the Natural History Museum.

[64] Johann Georg Hamann (August 27 1730 – June 21 1788) was a German philosopher of the Counter-Enlightenment, Sämtliche Werken, ed. Josef Nadler (1949-1957), vol. III, p. 231

disciplines; 'relying primarily upon reason and science'. That unity of thought means that any question of truth will imply both induction and deduction which are seen as reciprocally reliant on each other.

II. **Christianity** is essentially a philosophy or doctrine which shares minuscule straits from Empiricism, (such as the role experience may play in shaping knowledge) and with Rationalism, (emphasising deductive reasoning in a secular scientific vain) in verifying knowledge; Christianity can be seen as <u>using</u> but not fully ascribed to the relative knowledge propositions defined in the branch of **Fideism**[65]. It holds that the relationship between faith and reason is analogous to mixing oil and water; the two simply do not mix. Fideism further maintains that faith is essential, and that faith 'may be held without evidence or reason, or even in conflict with evidence and reason'.[66] Although Christianity is analogous to Fideism, it is heavily reliant on its own rationality of ***logical faith*** as an explanation for its existence and **knowledge**.

Christianity authenticates its knowledge base through belief in the exegetical statements from the Biblical book of Hebrews chapter 11, beginning with verse 1 through verses 39 and 40:

> ➢ *¹Now faith is the substance of things hoped for, the evidence of things not seen. For by it the elders obtained a good testimony. By faith we understand that the worlds were framed by the word of God, so that the things which are seen were not made of things which are visible.³⁹ And these all, having obtained a good report through faith, received not the promise:⁴⁰ God having provided some better thing for us, that they without us should not be made perfect.* **Fideism**

---

65 http://en.wikipedia.org/wiki/Fideism
66 Wikipedia, Faith and rationality

Further affirmation of that 'Faith' and the building of faith is reflected in the Bible verse; 'So then **faith *comes* by hearing, and hearing by the word** of God[67]'.

Primarily, Christianity has an attachment to Fideism through the use of faith as a practical discipline in having knowledge.

Let's examine how those knowledge bases are authenticated as applications of truth.

2.   **What truth is** and **how is it derived**

The American philosopher Richard Kirkham has argued that the only definition of knowledge that could ever be immune to all counterexamples is the infallibilist one. He said; "*To qualify as an item of knowledge, goes the theory, a belief must not only be true and justified, the justification of the belief must necessitate its truth. In other words, the justification for the belief must be infallible*"[68].

I consider this an interesting place to qualify the practicalities which provide the base for knowledge; truths.

Truth is from my perspective a word that can only be looked at objectively because one man's truth is another mans' lie. What is probably more important in understanding truth is having a central coherent formula which can be relied upon in verifying the veracity of that truth. Both Humanism and Christianity adhere to certain truths. The challenge for both is moving beyond authentication of knowledge to verification of the truth of that knowledge. One common thread between Christianity and Humanism is the fact that both do rely on logical syllogisms to authenticate knowledge as the truth.

Logic[69] from the Latin, 'logica' is the science used to verify abstract reasoning which conclude various truths. Logic is a fundamental part

---

[67] Romans 10:17

[68] Richard Ladd Kirkham (born 18 June 1955). American philosopher. Author of 'Theories of Truth' (MIT Press, 1992) http://en.wikipedia.org/wiki/Richard_Kirkham

[69] The Free Dictionary; http://www.thefreedictionary.com/logic

of the Humanist equation which commonly uses the abstraction of deductive and inductive reasoning. It is also vitally important to the Christian foundation which asserts that it's belief system is based on 'The Truth '; this, a declaration of logical reasoning which takes us back to the American philosopher Richard Kirkham who prospered the **theory on infallibility.**

I. Secular Humanism and truth – Establishing truth for the humanist[70] is consistent with reasoning through either Rationalism or Empiricism. Each discipline uses what I would refer to as truth axioms which can be either deductive or inductive.

> ➤ An empiricism deductive axiom in logic is a scientific method deploying syllogistic presuppositions much like quantitative reasoning. Each presupposition is a premise which asserts an individual truth and is relied upon to conclude a fact which could only be derived from the truth of the previous assertions. The syllogistic variance is normally from a generalized context to a specific context. It is considered a very disciplined or strict line of reasoning.

Example of deduction:

If something does not exist in space-time, then it cannot have a shape or form.

God does not exist in space-time 2nd premise of truth

Things without any shape or form cannot be either male or female. 3rd premise

---

[70] http://en.wikipedia.org/wiki/Humanism

Therefore: God cannot be either male or female. Conclusion

The conclusion derived at is one of a number of conclusions that could be made. We could have concluded that 'a male is not God'; or 'a female is not God'. Whatever conclusion is reached has to act as the 'sum total' of truths contained in the premises.

> ➤ Whatever answer cannot be derived from the ridged nature of deductive reasoning; the Humanist can then use the syllogistic form of reasoning in inductive reasoning to compensate.

Inductive reasoning is very akin to the epistemology of Rationalism. Where deduction has more emphasis on the scientific method of observation, induction focuses on the thought or cerebral reasoning. Rationalism[71] constructs a logical premise that asserts that reality is innately a 'logical structure' which can be disseminated by reason. Inductive syllogisms are the exact opposite in nature to deductive ones. The axioms used are more 'open-ended and exploratory[72]' as opposed to the narrow and more specific deductive axioms; whiles the conclusion tends to be a generalized assumption

Example of Induction:

Moses raised his rod over the Red Sea.

The Red Sea parted on a Monday when Moses raised his rod.

Therefore: Every-time that Moses raises his rod the Red Sea will part.

---

[71] http://en.wikipedia.org/wiki/Rationalism

[72] Deductive Reasoning Versus Inductive Reasoning, Ashley Crossman; About. com Sociology http://sociology.about.com/od/Research/a/Deductive-Reasoning-Versus-Inductive-Reasoning.htm

The way that the truth is derived from both branches of epistemology is that Empiricism utilizes deductive reasoning to 'test' through the scientific method certain hypothesis; whiles Rationalism is more 'exploratory' towards inducing a logical rationale.

For the Humanist, these are adequate avenues of truth analysis that allow their propositions to stay compatible with their philosophy. There is obviously much more to the complexity of truth propositions used by Humanist in terms of evidence but those will be addressed through Christianity since much of the methodolatry is cohesively used by both theories. Stating the full method for Humanism, even if used sparingly, would be like constructing another book.

The reader is fully able to have their own comparative analysis based on the structure presented here.

II. Christianity and truth – I hesitate somewhat to precede here because this answer requires a definition of God. That will be answered completely throughout specific chapters of this book but I will streamline an answer here within the context of Christian truth.

Christianity as a religion takes its' truth from the very existence of God as 'the Creator'. It can be said that this is a line of deductive and inductive reasoning. It sets out that if God created the universe and if God created everything; then God must be the creator of man. That is deductive in terms of its' syllogistic style. It also follows that if there is a sun, moon, and Earth life sustaining system and there is an animal and plant on Earth life sustaining system; there must be someone maintaining the sustenance of the system. That is inductive as a hypothesis of reasoning.

What Christianity does (as well as any other 'god' head religion) is that it boldly proclaims that all truth that exist comes from the master purveyor of that truth, who is in fact God. It then embraces the context of Richard Kirkham by stating that the God of Christianity is **infallible**. This is also a logical presupposition which can be seen as inductive because it implies that any 'god' that can create everything has to have the constitution of infallibility or omniscience or omnipotence.

Whiles Humanism utilizes the relativity of deduction and induction as verifiers of its reasoning they also both methodizes knowledge gathering through **testimony, authority** (expert opinion) but differ vastly on **revelation**.

> ➢ **Testimony** – There has not been a recorded time in historical development that testimony was not used as a form of knowledge verification. In English law it is used as direct evidence/ original evidence and sworn statements of witnesses. Christianity observes and holds that the Bible is the inerrant Word (2 Timothy 3:16)[73] and the living testimony of God to man according to Isaiah 59: 21 which says; *"As for me, this is my covenant with them," says the LORD. "My Spirit, who is on you, and my words that I have put in your mouth will not depart from your mouth, or from the mouths of your children, or from the mouths of their descendants from this time on and forever," says the LORD.*

Epistemology[74] uses intrinsic questioning to give credence to the testimony of a subject by asking; does the subject believe that which is said; is the belief justified; is it rational; is it warranted; is it sufficiently supported by evidence and is the subject entitled to believe.

---

[73] 16 All Scripture is God-breathed and is useful for teaching, rebuking, correcting and training in righteousness, New International Version (NIV)

[74] http://en.wikipedia.org/wiki/Epistemology

> ➢ **Authority** (expert opinion) – The transference of knowledge has been dispensed through the 'authority[75]' concept for thousands of years. Any child that attends school is within a system of cognitive learning from an authority; that direct authority is normally the teacher. The word itself has various definitions but within this context it is generally associated with a person who knows more than other individuals on a given subject area. Aristotle, Plato and Socrates were all considered leading authorities on philosophy; physics and politics. Much of what they thought and wrote on is still followed today as sound reasoning on those given subject areas.

Christianity holds that the authority of the Bible is directly from God as inspired in man. Romans 13: 1 says; " *Let every soul be subject to the governing authorities. For there is no authority except from God, and the authorities that exist are appointed by God.*"

What Christianity must maintain through that conclusion is that the truth of any knowledge which it adheres to, is truth derived from the knowledge and authority of God.

> ➢ **Revelation** – The Oxford dictionary[76] defines revelation in two ways; a surprising and previously unknown fact that has been disclosed to others and the divine or supernatural disclosure to humans of something relating to human existence.

Of all epistemic propositions there is none more contentious than revelation on the issue of reliability. That proves to be so because revelation (especially within the context of Christianity) has to rely on a predication derived from an existential plain beyond human

---

[75] http://en.wikipedia.org/wiki/Authority
[76] Copyright 2013 Oxford University Press.

comprehension; God! That places this premise in direct contention to the Empiricism and Rationalism of Humanism.

The epistemology of revelation is fused into many religions and cultures. The Waashat Religion developed amoung Wanapam Indians, was led by the spiritualist Indian Smohalla.[77] Smohalla was one of many Indian spiritualists that claimed to lead, based on revelation given to them.

It is believed in the Muslim religion that the Prophet Muhammad received the first oration for the Quran whiles he was 'in solitude in the cave on Mount Hira' from 'the Angel of Revelation, Gabriel'[78].

From Grigori Rasputin to Michel de Nostredame; from Thomas S. Monson to Madame Helena Petrova Blavatsky; self-proclaimed psychics, prophets and mystics have all written into history claiming to have access to revelations which speak to the human persuasion.

What authenticates revelation?

- Confirmation - Common sense dictates that any prophetic revelation can only make a claim 'as such' if it is actualized as existing from that revelation. In the most simplistic explanation, if x predicts as a revelation that the lost city of Atlantis will appear in 50 years, and in 50 years, y (of full credibility) is at the lost city of Atlantis as a witness and in observance of that revelation; it is reasonable to assert that the revelation is confirmed.

- Probability of occurrence – The voracity of a claim which implies revelation can be tested in an equation of probability. If an astronomer claims a revelation, saying that a 30 foot meteor will hit the Earth within five years; on the probability that it would happen, is it sufficient as a revelation? Every occurrence has a degree of probability but the greater the implausibility of

---

[77] Andrew H. Fisher. "American Indian Heritage Month: Commemoration vs. Exploitation; Native American religion, Wikipedia.

[78] Muhammad's Biography (part 3 of 12): The First Revelations IslamReligion.com. 2006-2013

occurrence as a mathematical anomaly; the greater credence to a claim of revelation.

- Inimitability – whether the revelation is exceptionally unique must be taken into account. If in June of 1876, at the Battle of the Little Bighorn[79], General Custer had claimed a revelation that he was headed into an ambush by Crazy Horse and tribes from the Lakota, Northern Cheyenne, and Arapaho, and then halt his progress; would that change of mind be considered unique enough to be clarified as a revelation? Hypothetically, factors contributing to General Custer's revelation could be as simple as seeing 'smoke rings' in the distant sky or a cluster of birds flying from trees. Certainly human beings can relate to having intuitive feelings which change the scope of their actions. Premonitions are many times simply called 'mother's wit' or innate intelligence. Both premonitions and intuition are variables which can occur for reasons outside of a divine revelation. The uniqueness has to be beyond the vagaries of chance and attributable to a purposeful divine transference of information to a human vessel.

III. How do both philosophies verify their positions to then justify existence?

I have shown to a small extent that Christianity and Humanism both use logic in various ways. They both implore forms of deductive and inductive reasoning.

Where the two philosophies drastically depart ways is on the rigid application of the logical equation to which Humanist adhere; it does not allow for unanswerable variables to be accounted for such as pre-existence. On the other hand; Christianity accepts many conclusions of the strict logical equations used in the scientific method such as verifying the various elements like oxygen etc.; but its belief system in 'faith' allows

---

[79] Kershaw, Robert (2005). Red Sabbath: The Battle of Little Bighorn. Ian Allan Publishing. pp. vi–5

it to go beyond the certainty threshold and rationalize man's existence from an unanswerable variable. This is where the Humanistic approach if using inductive reasoning, could potentially use a syllogistic hypothesis to reason the existence of a 'creator dynamic' but it rationalizes another 'unproven' dynamic that it prefers to hold as the truth. This is the proverbial 'line drawn in the sand' between both philosophies.

Christianity begins its' rationale from a written testimony which gives a reasoned account for the existence of man; this is seen through the book of Genesis. For the Humanist, this Christian position is a problem because neither method of analysis which they use can produce the certainty they seek in a superlative mathematical logical formula or a hypothesis which has a rational they accept.

The Christian question of existence implies an irrational scientific anomaly (God's existence). To account for an answer which suffices questions of existence, the Humanist configures 'scientific' rationalities (such as evolution and The Big Bang Theory) with complex deductive syllogisms which they adjust inductively to accommodate reasoning about irrational anomalies.

For the Humanist, any theory on the existence of man based on Darwinism and the evolutionary construct is attributed to deductive scientific proof on the same level of equations. Holding the two theories, Darwinism and Evolution, as logical truths, (in my opinion) contradicts the strict deductive logical syllogisms that Humanism embraces. As theories, Darwinism and Evolution cannot come to 100% conclusive ends. The reasoning is inductive at the very least.

Let's make the following consideration; Evolution and Darwinism assert facts which are not only unproven but the conclusions tend to be improvised as inductive reasoning.

Case in point; in 1912 Charles Darwin used scientific reasoning based on the evolution model to present the 'missing link' in the evolutionary chain of man. The archaeological find was called *Eoanthropus dawsoni or* Piltdown Man[80]. It was seen as the key link between man's transition from ape to Homo sapiens. Deductively, the verification of this truth was based on bones which were literally reanimated and reasoned to be a new species. It was not until 1953 (43 years later) that fraud was attributed to the find; yet Darwin was unaffected and his theories are still given credence as logical truths.

The complete failure of this theory is not limited to Piltdown Man. There is a copious amount of 'supposedly' Neanderthal finds which have either been determined as fraud, out-rightly disproven, or hovering in a proverbial wasteland of un-provable notions. Discoveries[81] of Homo Erectus which included Java Man, and Peking Man, were all considered major evolutionary finds by various anthropologist but have failed to meet the level of scrutiny to be classified as the true missing link[82] and remain as only inductive conclusions.

Humanism remains unperturbed by such findings within its secular and scholastic fraternity. This for me is one of the fundamental flaws of the Humanistic construct. It becomes so stuck in a 'belief' system that even where there is vast controversy it seems that the protagonist are incapable of accepting any other explanation.

Let's now consider the perspective of Christianity; how does Christianity use theistic logic to account for the truth in direct comparison to Humanism?

---

[80] Piltdown Man: Britain's Greatest Hoax; Kate Bartlett; BBC History. http://www.bbc.co.uk/history/ancient/archaeology/piltdown_man_01.shtml

[81] Fossil Humans: The Evidence, James L. Hall; Centre for Creation Studies, Liberty University.

[82] Shocking new theory: Humans hunted, ate Neanderthals; Science; Larry O'Hanlon; Discovery News, NBC online. http://science.nbcnews.com/_news/2013/05/21/18399982-shocking-new-theory-humans-hunted-ate-neanderthals?lite&ocid=msnhp&pos=7

Where the Humanist line of reasoning fails due to rigidity in the logical construct; the Christian theory actually succeeds because it does not place limitations on questions which go beyond the realm of reasoned probability. The Humanist does not believe in God so accounting for man's existence is derived from a logically theorised argument ('the big bang') that wants to rely on deductive reasoning but finds results which are more inductive.

Christianity counters the 'existence' argument by accounting for man based on a creative GOD. Very simply put; the Christian uses God as the foundation of its logical syllogism. It reasons that God exist and all of creation flows from that existence. Where Darwinism and Evolution can't inherently account for or agree with all life having a purpose and a plan; Christianity embraces these as the inevitable predestination of man.

The logic of Christianity actually has the same dimensional problem as Humanism. It has to account for 'the mystery' of existence. Where Humanism accounts for existence coming about from 'nothingness' and an intelligence evolving from 'nothing matter'; the Christian concept relies on a **faith model** that places a logical syllogism together which concludes a 'master design from a master designer'. This equation is what I will call a 'causal nexus'. It is used in other theistic arguments such as Ontology, Teleology, and Cosmology which subscribe to the belief that the universe and life itself is the result of a grand master or God.

This is admittedly, a very complex and long-winded area to cover. Trying to tie together the myriad of philosophical thought in this area in a concise manner is virtually impossible but there is enough common ground on the logical structure to have a succinct conclusion.

It would be true to say that the range of theistic theories all rationalize GOD in the logical syllogism of 'Creationism or Scientific Creationism'.

Consider the degree of complexity between understanding a created world compared with the combination of 'the big bang' theory and evolution.

How does a Humanist or atheist or 'belief dynamic' verify the truth of those theories? The theories are so very complex that for the most part one would get the impression that anything placed before the media as fact would simply be accepted. From Geophysicist to Quantum physicist, persons contributing to verifying evolution are the who's who of scientific thought.

Can deductive reasoning be used to determine the truth of a theory that says that the earth is 4.5billion[83] years old (the universe 13 billion) when so many of the variables are not conclusive or not provable? I will admit that I am sceptical. Besides the vast amounts of atheist scientist who would swear by the figures; how many independent organizations would have the capability to verify calculations in molecular or nanotechnology? How many persons will question or can question the veracity of Astrophysicist's accounts? That may be another debate all together but the salient point is that many proclamations of truth are verified by 'agenda' based theorist who are essentially too close to the situation to give an opinion that can't be ascribed as unbiased. Herein I refer to the Darwin Piltdown Man; as faulty as much of his work is, most scientist who have an invested amount of time into the school of evolution can ill-afford to deconstruct this theory starting with the unacceptable result of being alienated from their fraternity.

Where is the degree of scepticism which is thrown so readily at Christianity? With the scarcity of proof which is the 'hallmark' of the Humanist proposition; one would think that there would be a middle ground created which entertains the possibility of a 'god-figurehead'.

Let me step outside the box for a second. Considering that Darwin had a failed 'proof positive' test; would it not cause the scientist to open up a plethora of questions flowing from this 'father' or **authority** in the

---

[83] How Old Is The Earth? by FRASER CAIN; Universe Today. http://www.universetoday.com/75805/how-old-is-the-earth/#ixzz2kYm2asFB http://www.universetoday.com/75805/

area of evolutionary thought? I would think that such a quagmire would boost more questions as opposed to the host of acceptance in theories that stretch the boundaries of reason.

For instance, a forensic look at the evolutionary tree, where Neanderthals became Homo-Sapiens; there should be a considerable amount of evidence where the very nature of procreation would have 'birthed' millions ('perhaps' billions) of prehistoric men over the vast period of time that evolutionist build their theory on. There should simply be a plethora of evidence scattered over the earthly plain which would be easily found and verifiable. In other words; there should be physical DNA and fossils everywhere as evidence of the earlier existence of Neanderthals or whatever they say existed. If we simply look at recorded history from say, 1300 A.D. to 2013 A.D., the Earth has a record of 7 billion[84] persons existing. That is only a range of 700 years; imagine how many persons should have existed and left a DNA (or bone) imprint over say 1 million years? Scientists are quick to render anthropological evidence of dinosaurs (which are mostly accepted by all schools of study) but any modelling of Neanderthals or Denisovans are from small fragments such as a tooth or a toe bone.

Has anyone stopped to ask how absurd this is considering the way species are today? For instance; even if Blue Wales or Siberian Tigers or Polar Bears go extinct, how much DNA and fossil evidence would still subsist as proof of their existence in 5000 years or even 10,000 years?

Better yet; we have been told by evolutionary scientist that dinosaurs lived about 65 million years ago[85]. By some scientific standards found, it is affirmed that on average carbon 14[86] (which is used for dating organic

---

[84] Worldometers; http://www.worldometers.info/world-population/

[85] BBC/ABC online news. http://www.abc.net.au/dinosaurs/chronology/65/default.htm

[86] Carbon-14 By Lynn Poole; Whittlesey House, 1961. http://www.chem.uwec.edu/Chem115_F00/nelsolar/chem.htm

matter) can only produce about 10 half-lives which would mean that it can only date as far back as 50 -60,000 years[87].

How could carbon dating formulate such exact composites of time when it is restricted to a 50 -60 thousand range of measurement? I would be sceptical of the formula added to compensate.

Even where Uranium 235 or 238 is used to measure the age of the Earth; there is now vast discrepancies found[88].

If ever there were grounds for a conspiracy theory, it would exist when recognizing that evolutionary scientist have calculated (supposedly) that the Earth is 4.5 billion years old. They are adamant about those figures, yet, when asked to simply calculate how old bones are, there is extreme prevarication on a clear answer. Whiles two different methods are used to calculate the age of the earth and age of fossils, it still makes no sense that a stable variance on decomposition can't be widely agreed on. The major problem for the evolutionist is accounting for timelines where the existence of 'pre-man' should correspond with dinosaurs. Most evolutionary genetic studies (if you trust the results), suggest that a primitive relative of 'modern' man emerged from other mammal gene-pools about 85 million years ago[89]. Where is the missing gene pool that should be found along with dinosaurs?

How about this find reported in the Smithsonian;[90] and the implications it has on timelines as well as carbon14 dating? In this article, it looks at results found by Mary Schweitzer's a palaeontologist at North Carolina State University. She was having problems examining bone fragments from the '68 million' year Tyrannosaurus Rex found

---

[87] Doesn't Carbon-14 Dating Disprove the Bible?
by Mike Riddle; The New Answers Book. http://www.answersingenesis.org/articles/nab/does-c14-disprove-the-bible

[88] It's Official: Radioactive Isotope Dating Is Fallible; Brian Thomas, M.S.; Institute Creation Research http://www.icr.org/article/its-official-radioactive-isotope-dating/

[89] the GeoWhen database. by Martin Smith http://en.wikipedia.org/wiki/Human_evolution

[90] Dinosaur Shocker, Helen Fields Smithsonian magazine http://www.smithsonianmag.com/science-nature/dinosaur.html

in Montana. She turned to the molecular biologist Gayle Callis who through her team of scientist, found that there was blood in the bones of the T-Rex. I can't imagine what shock waves that sent through the lab but it is actually more shocking that the find (which was verified through a process of reverse probabilities to eliminate the possibility that it was in fact blood) has not been widely published. Since evolutionist/biologist have already established as indefeasible the timeline in which soft tissue can survive in fossils, this find turned their theories on its back. There is no way that they can account for it. It can't even be considered an anomaly because it would give way to possibilities which they have denied vehemently.

Here is another scenario that I played out in my mind. About 13 billion[91] years ago was the 'Big Bang' and then the earth formed around 4.54 billion[92] years ago. Then 3.5 billion years ago[93] a simple cell was formed called Prokaryotes; 800 million years later the phenomenon of photosynthesis occurred and by 2 billion the world finally saw the first complex cell organism called Eukaryotes. After billions of years of evolving and adapting, where fish, plants, anthropods, insects, amphibians and reptiles came into existence; the first man appears as Homo Habilis. This happened at about 2.3 million years ago[94]. There can be only one conclusion drawn here; Man evolved through a gene pool which included birds and amphibians.

That being the truth; how is it that we can't identify genes that would link us to those species? Even more perplexing is the fact that the word evolution cannot escape its own infinity, because it should never

---

[91] **Gustav A. Tammann,** Astronomer, University of Base http://www.spacetelescope.org/science/age_size/

[92] How Old Is The Earth? FRASER CAIN Read more: http://www.universetoday.com/75805/how-old-is-the-earth/#ixzz2kYuMuC5d

[93] Boyce Rensberger; Life Itself, Exploring The Realm of the Living Cell. http://etap.org/demo/biology1/instruction3tutor.html

[94] the GeoWhen database. by Martin Smith. http://en.wikipedia.org/wiki/Human_evolution

stop. How is it possible that there is absolutely no proof of anything evolving today? If 'today man' appeared 200,000 years ago with the full cranial capacity that we have now, why is it that there are no drawings (empirical data) or anything that shows that man recognized somewhere in the evolutionary process, a change in himself or another sister specie? There are over 7 billion persons on the Earth currently. If at this very moment we started to evolve (all at once -spontaneously); one million years from now would there be no evidence that we existed or would the evidence be a few fragments of bone found here and there? Would 'future' mankind look at the primal paintings of say, 'Matisse' and comment on how undeveloped our brain was?

Here is another confounding question; if man is a derivative, as such, of other species why did we not continue to evolve to a perfect state? The mere fact that we had amphibians in our heritage would mean that we should have moved to the ideal state of being; the ability to breathe under water or the ability to fly as our ancestors (birds) do.

There is yet another perplexing question that is not answered.

When did all of the species on earth form a coalition or co-operative and decide that all of creation (including plants and micro-organisms) would all stop evolving at the same time?

How is it possible that within the evolutionary equation, there has been no evolution of any species according to evolutionist from about 200,000 years ago?

Every question I have posed is relative.

In **creationism**, the logic is simply that GOD created the universe and all things thereafter. It obviously takes a leap of faith to believe in any god who creates or the Christian GOD that created; but for those persons who dismiss the laurels of faith, they have not made more intimate considerations.

The faith which is exhibited by Humanist who loyally subscribe to the story of evolution, is a deeply embedded faith. Humanist are not recognizing that it takes far greater faith to believe that an anomaly of physics which has never happened again, and produced an astronomical event; displays spectacular faith. The 'one time' event of the 'big bang' produced an astrologically perfect universe; what are the chances of that? Is there a physicist that can reproduce that quadratic equation or any theory of relativity which would aptly equate the probability of every part of man's existence being perfectly formed? Think about it; the sun is perfectly placed; the moon is perfectly placed; the planets are perfectly placed; there is water on Earth so man is perfectly placed; there is food so man is perfectly placed. What is the probability that the combination of these events would occur and produce such a perfect result and all coming as a result of a perfect anomaly called the Big Bang?

Finally; perhaps the most overlooked fact about the story of creation and the book of Genesis is the timeline where we place the writing of the book itself. If at the time of Moses the biblical timeline would have been about 1275B.C. (most scholars tend to agree), one would have to know that there was no real written history or geometry or physics established. This would mean that inspiration for the elements of this book had to be inspired directly by GOD because man had a very primitive knowledge of the universe. But if you read Genesis, you would come to realize that rather complex subject matters such as the beginning of the universe and the dynamics of Pangaea[95], were being described in a simple way but covered all the complexities. How would the author know these things or even hypothesize such things when we all "agree" on more modern discoveries such as Galileo who discovered the existence of other planets between 1564 AD and 1642 AD.

On a noted 'Blog Site', television producer David L. Wolper attempted to reconcile the creationist timeline with the evolutionist timeline. What he was able to achieve is a remarkably simple illustration of a comparative analysis of what Moses wrote and what evolutionists believe. I am not in agreement with the time analysis but it is a great hypothesis to demonstrate that the Evolutionist consideration fits into a 'neglected' biblical dialogue. Mr. Wolper's experiment gives a digestible

---

[95] Genesis 1: 9 - 10

example of how the story in Genesis is not void of scientific theory such that it has no worth towards scientific consideration. Of special note is the simplicity of Genesis compared with the complexity of evolution; but the relativity of events and knowledge attributed to what Moses wrote were knowledge 'events' that was yet undiscovered. Here is a small example of what he wrote.

God's Creation account VS Evolution[96].

Genesis: (Second day) -- *4.5 billion to 3.75 billion years ago* "God said, 'Let there be firmament in the midst of the waters and let it separate the waters from the waters.'"

Science:
Water-rich asteroids and protoplanets collided with prehistoric earth, bringing water. Later, gaseous emissions from volcanoes added additional water. This occurred approximately 4.4 billion years ago. Over the next several billion years, as the earth cooled, water vapor began to escape and condense in the earth's early atmosphere. Clouds formed and enormous amounts of water fell on the earth. The waters were separated, water on earth and water in the atmosphere. So day two fits with science and is in the correct order.

My conclusion will not justify the full extent of what this conversation can be. What I have written is but a small percentage of justifiable reasoning in the Creationism dialogue (and the Evolutionist dialogue for that matter). I am first to acknowledge the taint of bias; after all, this is written from my perspective of what Christianity brings to the equation. But what I would like the Humanist and docile Christian

---

96 Genesis And Science: More Aligned Than You Think? http://www.huffingtonpost. com/david-l-wolper/genesis-and-science_b_500201.html

believer to recognize here is that the level of tangible questions raised is perhaps very comparable to the questions that would be raised in understanding truth in Christianity. As a matter of fact; the variables that I have presented are seemingly far easier to comprehend from a faith position than trying to calculate a scientific formula that can't be answered or reasoned within the logic of that equation. It is very simple for me to reason that everything must have had a grand design which came from the mind of a supreme designer. It makes more sense for me to believe in a great creator, GOD, who created me (even if I don't and can't know of His genesis) than to believe in an existence that started by an anomaly from nothing! My reasoning of existence and truth stops at the door of something I admit I am limited to understand beyond. The Bible tells us that we are limited to go beyond the knowledge of God as read in the book of Isaiah 55: 8 – 9 (TLB for emphasis) which says'; '*This plan of mine is not what you would work out, neither are my thoughts the same as yours! For just as the heavens are higher than the earth, so are my ways higher than yours, and my thoughts than yours.*' This will seem self-defeating to the Humanist that I would accept a limitation but it is the practicality of reasoned logic that the creator of everything would have knowledge beyond my own. What Humanist assert is a scholastic arrogance which assumes that they are demi-gods or capable of all knowledge. That attitude is a mirror of exactly what happened in the story of satan, Eve and Adam in 'the garden'.

The derisiveness of the arguments which Humanist place forth is so reflective of the context from Romans 1: 18 -25 that I find myself using these versus throughout my writing and in full context below. There cannot be a better way to state how callous and arrogant humankind has become in their thinking. The verses were written by Paul to the Romans who had become an elite society. Paul was in an environment where Roman scribes, aristocrats, and leaders all felt as if they had transcended into a time of great knowledge. We are aware that the leader of Rome Caesar[97] had declared himself 'god-incarnate'. In fact it

---

[97] Julius Caesar; Joshua J. Mark. http://www.ancient.eu.com/Julius_Caesar/

was the Caesar Nero[98] that commissioned the death of Paul and Peter. It is easy to understand why Paul issued the prophetic words which he did.

Romans 1: 18 – 25 (TLB for emphasis)

But God shows his anger from heaven against all sinful, evil men who push away the truth from them. For the truth about God is known to them instinctively; God has put this knowledge in their hearts. Since earliest times men have seen the earth and sky and all God made, and have known of his existence and great eternal power. So they will have no excuse when they stand before God at Judgment Day.

Yes, they knew about him all right, but they wouldn't admit it or worship him or even thank him for all his daily care. And after a while they began to think up silly ideas of what God was like and what he wanted them to do. ***The result was that their foolish minds became dark and confused. Claiming themselves to be wise without God, they became utter fools instead.*** *And then, instead of worshiping the glorious, ever-living God, they took wood and stone and made idols for themselves, carving them to look like mere birds and animals and snakes and puny men.*

So God let them go ahead into every sort of sex sin, and do whatever they wanted to—yes, vile and sinful things with each other's bodies. Instead of believing what they knew was the truth about God, ***they deliberately chose to believe lies.*** *So they prayed to the things God made, but wouldn't obey the blessed God who made these things.*

---

[98] Romans In Revelation; Michael E. Day http://bibleprophecyfulfilled.com/art9romans.html

The philosophical relativity of faith in Christianity is further reflected and enforced in the belief of the 'One True GOD' theory. The theory sets up a logical syllogism in the book of John 14: 6 *'I am the way and the truth and the life. No one comes to the Father except through me.'*

The theory presents a logical imperative by declaring that the belief system is founded upon God who is the Truth and faith in that truth is enforced by the 'hearing of the logic' or hearing of the Word. Every implication that follows from that faith supposition or logical equation is therefore considered truth.

The expression that 'nothing from nothing leaves nothing' is a true and rational syllogism. The truth proposition that everything is derived from the substance of the original substance, who is God the intelligent creator, is a truth proposition that holds a higher value of believability than nothing existing where something is randomly created and then evolves a sensory perception to prosper in or usher in, the existence of all truth.

I posit that when people use the phrase intelligent design it speaks of a truth variable that is very in line with what the Bible teaches. Truth espoused from the testimony of God has a greater relevance and credibility because it is accountable to the question of existence where Humanist dogma is still wrestling with a notion that is either evolving or being reshaped to please their very own notions.

The practical truth about truth is that it simply needs to make sense. There is absolutely no biological organism known to man that does not have a thread of existence which takes it back to an original source. That simple reasoning trumps the rather complicated dialogue that must take place to explain existence from no source. How does one tell a child that his existence is not from the pairing of female and male chromosomes during copulation but from an astrophysics anomaly of space and matter fusing in the perfect anomaly of biological existence? Basically, that is the argument of evolution and creationism in a nutshell.

Christians must learn to question such abstractions to bring back the practical and simple truth of creation.

CHAPTER 5

The Moral Dilemma

"America needs to know that many faith leaders and theologians from diverse religious traditions strongly believe that all people have a God-given right to lead lives which fully express love, mutuality and commitment—including the right to marry[99],"

This is a very profound statement but it is also a serious moral dilemma.

Christian Morals vs. Humanistic Morals

Before I address the quote above, let me point out that the lines may appear slightly blurred in approaching a topic on 'Morals' considering that an exhausted attempt was made to establish what a truth is. Just to make sure that there are no misunderstandings about the two topics; I would like to point out that both are completely different. Truth is established primarily on the foundation of acceptable presuppositions and provable facts whereas morals can be viewed as a rationalization of appropriate behaviour or actions in association with a given scenario or fact[100].

---

[99] Reverend Debra W. Haffner, director of the Religious Institute, promoting the Open Letter to Religious Leaders on Marriage Equality
[100] http://www.merriam-webster.com/dictionary/moral

The aforementioned statement by Rev. Haffner has all the instincts of an ethical if not rational argument to support the contention that everyone has a right to marry. A closer look at the statement and one may notice that she has qualified it with a religious imperative; she uses 'God' as the qualifier of rights that all people have.

According to her blog, Reverend Haffner is a self-described 'sexologist, (religious) minister, and the executive director of the Religious Institute. On the 26th June 2013, a day in which The Supreme Court of the US struck down the Defense of Marriage Act (DOMA), Reverend Haffner is also quoted as saying that, "As religious leaders, we affirm that persons of all sexual orientations should have the right to civil marriage and its benefits. As our traditions affirm, where there is **love, the sacred** is in our midst." Once again, Reverend Haffner alluded to a deistic standard by refereeing to "the sacred" being in our midst.

Like many other persons that support the gay agenda, the reverend reverts to a qualifier or standard which is her justification for why the law should be supported. Easily digestible is the fact that the LGBT and Humanist both support the gay agenda on constitutional, political and financial reasons; but to now imagine that they also assert a moral entitlement is quite ominous and almost reprehensible.

Certainly Christians don't have a franchise right over morals but it is their usual contention that Humanist and the LGBT community are pushing agendas that are void of morals.

1. What are morals; why do they matter and who's standard should be adhered to?

Using the Merriam-Webster online dictionary; it revealed three definitions all of which fit into the ethos of this discussion.

a) Morals are described as or relating to principles of right and wrong in behaviour; or expressing or teaching a concept of right behaviour; or conforming to a standard of right behaviour.

The question of why morals matter is a very relevant consideration.

b) It's disconcerting to be on the side of wrong behaviour – Let's be honest; nobody relishes the thought of being wrong. To accept wrong would mean that, a specific behaviour can't be justified. It follows that in the courts of justice, no action of justifiable merit can be condemned; only punitive actions are justifiably condemned before the courts.

c) Standards – Having a socially recognized standard does two things:

   i. It legitimizes an action/movement/concept by establishing an acceptable sphere or environment in which to operate.
   ii. It justifies that action etc., to the extent that it becomes practical and comfortable to live within that standard.

Whose standard of morals should be adhered to?

d) An illustration of world political systems properly delineates the parameters of the question. The barrier that separates North and South Korea is sometimes referred to as the Armistice Line[101]. This 'demarcation' line is so precisely observed that even the slightest encroachment would render an international incident of potential war. Both countries survey the border to ensure that the '**post**' or line is not moved, to the extent that an unfair advantage is gained.

Posts are the physical equivalent to morals. They indicate a standard by which proper measurement can be taken to adjudicate a dispute where wrong and right must be determined.

---

[101] Established in the Korean Armistice Agreement (KAA), Article I, paragraphs 1–11 http://en.wikipedia.org/wiki/Military_Demarcation_Line

i. Humanist and the LBGT ascribe to various standards[102] of morals.

> There is the 'Golden Rule'[103] morality which essentially states that "One should **treat others as one would like others to treat oneself**". This is a universal syllogism which has broad appeal even to Christians. It is prominent in fields of religion (Christianity[104] & Hinduism[105]) as well as sociology and philosophy but is very embraced by Humanism[106].

> There is the Humanist Manifesto 3 which embraces somewhat of an evolutionary insight to standards. It stresses that **man learns ethics (morals) from 'needs and interest' which come from experience.** This is far removed from the Golden Rule theory in that it allows for a far ranging ethical standard where interest and experience can have almost infinite tangibles.

ii. Christianity has a bit more complexity and conformity in the standard that it adheres to. The complexity starts with the apical structure of this belief system which places God at the helm.

---

[102] There are perhaps more standards which can be spoken of such as 'Secular Humanist Declaration' but they have all been found to have the same common straits which are 'religious scepticism' and a value system free of divine intervention or inspiration.

[103] Antony Flew, ed. (1979). "golden rule". A Dictionary of Philosophy. London: Pan Books in association with The MacMillan Press. p. 134.

[104] Jesus of Nazareth is quoted: "Therefore all things whatsoever would that men should do to you, do ye even so to them". Matthew 7:12 King James Bible

[105] "One should never do that to another which one regards as injurious to one's own self. This, in brief, is the rule of dharma. Other behavior is due to selfish desires" as quoted from —Brihaspati, Mahabharata (Anusasana Parva, Section CXIII, Verse 8) via Wikipedia

[106] International Humanist and Ethical Union (IHEU) creed from thinkhumanism. com

➢ For the Christian, the beginning of any morality is in the beginning of existence. The very first verse[107] in Genesis starts a moral clause which says, 'In the beginning God created the heavens and the earth.' For the Christian there is no imputed knowledge beyond God who starts the 'beginning'.

➢ Christianity acknowledges God as 'The Creator', so by verse 26 of Genesis 1, when God intimates that He will create man and does so in verse 27. *"So God created man in His image; in the image of God He created him; male and female he created them"*; it becomes implied that **any form of morality standard would have flowed from the Creator to the created**.

➢ Christianity then accepts without equivocation that God has established a written standard and authority through His testimony (the Bible) to man and through man.

1. All through the Bible there is a communicated relationship between God and man where a precedent of moral standards is established. It starts from Genesis and is captured in the most intimate way in verses 8 through 19 of chapter 3. God walks through the pleasantness of the garden during the 'cool' part of the day. He calls out to Adam to speak with him. God then proceeds to rebuke Adam (verse 17) in the ensuring conversation for disobeying Gods standard which was commanded. Adam disobeyed a direct standard set by God and was penalized for contravening that standard. Christianity understands and recognizes that the

---

[107] New King James Bible

Bible is Gods testimony of His communicated standard to man.

2. From a scene which has played out famously in cinematic folklore; Moses is witness to the writing of the Ten Commandments by God (Exodus 31:18) "And when He had made an end of speaking with him on Mount Sinai, He gave Moses two tablets of the Testimony, tablets of stone, written with the finger of God."

Throughout the Old Testament mankind is bond to live by the Ten Commandment laws as a standard and the Mosaic Laws (which God also gave to Moses as confirmed in Deuteronomy 4:13-14 and 2 Kings 21: 8)

3. Christianity accepts the exegetical importance of the laws handed down to the 'children of Israel'. God's commandments and the Mosaic laws were incontrovertible and as such, the <u>consequence</u> of the Israelites <u>disobeying</u> God (**the standard**) is witnessed in Numbers 32:10-13; "And the LORD'S anger was kindled the same time, and he swore, saying, Surely none of the men that came up out of Egypt, from twenty years old and upward, shall see the land which I swore unto Abraham, unto Isaac, and unto Jacob; because they have not wholly followed me: Save Caleb the son of Jephunneh the Kenezite, and Joshua the son of Nun: for they have wholly followed the LORD. And the LORD'S anger was kindled against Israel, and he made them wander in the wilderness forty

years, until all the generation, that had done evil in the sight of the LORD, was consumed".

> The foundation of this apical formation is established in the New Testament through the words of Jesus Christ. He says in Matthew 5: 17, *"Do not think that I came to destroy the Law or the Prophets. I did not come to destroy but **to fulfil**."* For the Christian, this is a fulfilment of the logical syllogism found in John 14:6 where Jesus issues an affirmation; 'Jesus *saith unto him,"* I am the way, the truth, and the life: no man cometh unto the Father, but by me."*

In answer to the question of '**who's standard should be adhered to**'; one should look at the rationality of both standards.

Taken at its purist form, the moral ethos of the Humanist has no moral absolute. It has no moral absolute because its rationality of a standard is based on man himself. It is a type of syllogistic oxymoron to ask a fallible man to set an unfallible standard for himself. In the story of the 'Scorpian and the Crocodile', when the scorpion is asked by the crocodile, 'why did you sting me?'; the scorpion replied, *'Sorry, I just couldn't help it, I am a Scorpion!'* The meaning is quite evident. It was foolish of the crocodile to assume that the scorpion could act outside of its' nature. If the Golden Rule and the Humanist Manifesto 3 were symbiotically paired the fusion would still result in a human demigod that has all power of reason to self-regulate.

For the Christian, only He who creates can produce a manual that produces a standard that the created can follow.

The interesting dilemma is the juxtaposition this causes across all plains of theories which sometimes clash or disagree. Based on the 'no moral absolute' structure of the two Humanist rules there will always be an eventuality where two fundamental landscapes should harmonize. For example; if a gay person rationalizes that 'his' inclination towards the same sex is consequential to his genetic makeup; would it be immoral by the 'Golden rule' to preclude the behaviour of the paedophile who believes that his experience is the exact same 'birth naturalization' which verifies his behaviour? If the answer is no, as an affirmation of excluding the moral right of a paedophile, then the gay person has acted in a hypocritical way because he has denied moral rights where the standard is clearly set as an amalgamation of fundamental parts of both theories which are; '**do unto others**' and '**needs and interest**' based on experience.

If the gay person then ascends the 'moral throne' by clarifying that the paedophile has no moral cogency to their argument; it means that the moral post has been subversively moved to a new standard since the paedophile is denied the same moral framework.

How can this point be verified?

> There is ample statistical information which shows that there are homosexuals who have been molested from a young age. The molestation could have been of a homosexual or heterosexual nature but it does not negate the fact that the act itself is classified as a deviant predilection and wrong. When properly diagnosed a plethora of behavioural problems are identified[108]. According to the World Health Organization[109] one of the diagnosed problems can be 'inappropriate sexualized behaviour', which admittedly can have a wide classified range. The question is; if a young boy is continuously sexually molested by a homosexual paedophile and

---

[108] 'Understanding Child Sexual Abuse; Education, Prevention and Recovery' American Psychological Association; http://www.apa.org/pubs/info/brochures/sex-abuse.aspx?item=2

[109] GUIDELINES FOR MEDICO-LEGAL CARE FOR VICTIMS OF SEXUAL VIOLENCE; Authors: WHO Department of Gender, Women and Health; WHO Department of Violence and Injury Prevention and Disability http://www.who.int/violence_injury_prevention/resources/publications/en/guidelines_chap7.pdf

grows up with a maladaptive fixation to molest boys, why would that maladaptive 'inappropriate sexual behaviour' model be any different than another child under the same scenario of molestation but growing up with a predilection for only adult homosexual relationships? How could the standard be different when the variables of exposure are the same?

The very pragmatic adherence of Humanism to dismiss any paradigm which espouses a moral absolute, surrenders it to failure because it cannot justify placing a post of permanence where temporal change is a constant. In other words, the need to establish situational ethics as it becomes relevant or evolves, creates a moral dilemma and a philosophical misnomer.

Christianity on the other hand starts with a premise that a God of infallibility has set standards for man who is fallible. Whether one believes in God or not, the premise is more logical and **more moral**. Simple example; it is not practical to believe that a child can set their own moral standards without some level of guidance from a (god) parent.

Case in point; Cynthia Harper of the University of Pennsylvania and Sara S. McLanahan of Princeton University cited in "Father Absence and Youth Incarceration." *Journal of Research on Adolescence* 14 (September 2004) that young males who grow up with only one parent (mother) are so lacking the guidance to formulate proper living skills, that even with one parent they are "twice as likely to end up in jail as those who come from traditional two-parent families."

In 1998, the US Department of Justice under Laurie Robinson the Assistant Attorney General, produced a 'white paper'[110] that stated;

---

[110] U.S. Department of Justice, Office of Justice Programs, National Institute of Justice; Executive Office for Weed and Seed; What Can the Federal Government Do To Decrease Crime and Revitalize?. Economic Shifts That Will Impact Crime Control and Community Revitalization

'85% of all children that exhibit behavioural disorders come from fatherless homes and 63% of youth suicides are from fatherless homes'.

Christianity embraces the moral absolute and believes in the concept that we are all abnormal within the normality of life. Romans 3: 23 states; *"for all have sinned and fall short of the glory of God"*.

The caveat for the Christian is in the importance of understanding the imperfection of who man is in relation to the standard that God has set. The Christian understands the imperfection of man. If it were asserted otherwise, that man is perfect, then there would be no proposition of law needed because in our most perfect state, man would never be imperfect. Whiles the Humanist produces moral standards from an imperfect being; the Christian lives by moral standards from a perfect God. The infallibility of God allows the Christian to believe and live by moral standards that are not moveable.

Many of the Biblical moral standards that Christianity lives by are adopted by the Humanist (even if 'he' refuses to admit as much).

Basic criminal law worldwide offers penalties against murder, and theft. Those standards in Biblical law are incontrovertible. The Bible has standards against sexual debauchery but here is where the water becomes murky. Most Humanist standards would embrace adultery (which is a sexual crime in the Bible) as 'immoral' behaviour. The Bible outlines other sexual crimes as morally unacceptable, such as; beastiality, incest, paedophilia and rape. Dubiously, the standard which the Bible sets against sodomy and homosexuality as morally unacceptable has been 'realigned' by Humanistic standards to the extent that the Christian standard is considered obsolete as a doctrine and morally corrupt in harbouring homophobic agendas.

Communities by Cicero Wilson pg. 16. http://fatherhood.about.com/gi/o.htm?zi=
1/XJ&zTi=1&sdn=fatherhood&cdn=parenting&tm=686&f=20&tt=2&
bt=7&bts=7&zu=https%3A//www.ncjrs.gov/pdffiles/172210.pdf

Sixty years ago, it would be a fair statement to say that homosexuality was considered a sexual taboo and widely unaccepted as a moral behaviour. The constituents of the LGBT community organized from being obscure individuals with perverted sexual fetishes into a voting block of lobbyist who began to understand the force of law, voting and economic clout. They moved their agenda from being pedestrian to mainstream political juggernauts.

The significance of legitimatizing the 'gay' movement through legal, political and social agendas is that it's moral code (standard) is no-longer adjudicated by an Episcopalian-like impetus but standardized through legislative imperatives which 'rebrand' a Biblical wrong as a legal right.

Leo Tolstoy said in his book, *A Confession* "**Wrong does not cease to be wrong because the majority share in it.**" The profoundness of that statement is that it exposes the inherent fragility of supporting a moral agenda by the LGBT and Humanist; no matter how you support it, it still stands as wrong.

Why? It's exactly like a force majeure; if it occurs naturally once, it gains power and sets a precedent as a standard to occur again. A homosexual activist named Paul Varnell wrote, "*The gay movement, whether we acknowledge it or not, is not a civil rights movement, not even a sexual liberation movement, but a **moral revolution** aimed at changing people's view of homosexuality.*"

What happens when the same precedent is used by an organized constituent of paedophiles? In essence this question has been presented previously in this writing but it is not an aberration of irrelevance.

I must beg the forgiveness of my reader but hope I was able to capture the essence of this excerpt I mostly paraphrased because it provides such a visual practicality of the intended point.

In an amazing story found in the Northern Colorado Gazette[111]in October of 2011, and under the heading, '**Pedophiles want same**

---

[111] Pedophiles want same rights as homosexuals; Jack Minor; Northern Colorado Gazette. **http://www.greeleygazette.com/press/?p=11517**

rights as homosexuals; Claim unfair to be stigmatized for sexual orientation'; the writer begins the article by saying that paedophiles are virtually employing the same 'tactics' as gay rights advocates to pursue rights. They are arguing that their 'desire for children is a sexual orientation no different than heterosexual or homosexuals.'

I have attempted to capture the weight of this report below:

> *In an amazing story found in the Northern Colorado Gazette in October of 2011, and under the heading, 'Pedophiles want same rights as homosexuals; Claim unfair to be stigmatized for sexual orientation'; the writer begins the article by saying that paedophiles are virtually employing the same 'tactics' as gay rights advocates to pursue rights. "They are arguing that their desire for children is a sexual orientation no different than heterosexual or homosexuals."*
>
> *The writer of the article, Jack Minor preceded to produce an astonishing article.*
>
> *He begins his article by setting the tone in contrasting the distinct positions maintained between opponents of homosexuality who subscribe to a theory that legalization of this unconventional way of life would breach absolute barriers and render in a state of 'anything goes' compared to gay sympathizers who find that position insulting and feel certain that this inevitability would not occur.*
>
> *Mr. Minor then settles the reader into the controversy by indicating that there are psychiatrist who are in fact proving the gay proponents wrong since the psychiatrist have begun to reclassify pedophilia in the exact manner that homosexuality became legitimised.*
>
> *He states as a fact that the declassification of homosexuals in 1973 by the American Psychiatric Association (APA) is the very same approach taken by psychiatrists from 'B4U-Act[112]' (organization of psychiatrist with mandate to*

---

[112] http://b4uact.org/about.htm;

assist in the psychological development of minor-attracted individuals).

In glaring detail the author presents the agenda of the APA which in 1998 produced a statement which undermined the prevailing assumption that sexually abused children experience 'negative sexual effects' due to abuse. The APA contended that the abuse was 'overstated' and that a high percentage of victims did not register any negative traits.

More shocking in the writers report is that the Federal Governemnt has put in place the James Byrd, Jr. Hate Crimes Prevention Act lists into force which essentially protects a class of sexual deviations of which pedophilia would fall into.

What the author has conveyed is the dubious fact that this bill, whiles important in protecting against hate crimes, has the ominous distinction of extending the very same characterization of 'sexual orientation' to pedophilia which is the language used to legitimize homosexuality.

In the article the Democrat Rep. Alcee Hastings is quoted using language that should cause any discerning individual to give pause for extreme concern. The representative said, "'This bill addresses our resolve to end violence based on prejudice and to guarantee that all Americans, regardless of race, color, religion, national origin, gender, sexual orientation, gender identity, or disability or all of these 'philias' and fetishes and 'isms' that were put forward need not live in fear because of who they are."

To say under any circumstance that 'philias' are only charactizations of who these people 'are' is a gross misrepresentation. It literally raises the issue of prejudice against a legitimate class of people who should have a right to participate in society based on their intrinsic and inate birth right.

If the authors point was thought to be an exaggeration he quotes a retired (but seemingly revered) psychologist[113] who when addressing the Canadian Parliament told them that paedophilia are basically of the same nature as heterosexuals and homosexuals. This obviously implies that the three orientations have the very same basic proclivities that are all natural.

I took the opportunity to take a closer look at the statement by the professor. Although he defends his statement as 'mis-interpreted'; I also noted from his very own site that he considers many pedophiles as having an "irreversible" nature. This for me does not retract from the premise because any behaviour that is an orientation which is considered irreversible means that it is only a representation of who the person was born to be.

In his own words the author quoted him to say;, "True pedophiles have an exclusive preference for children, which is the same as having a sexual orientation. You cannot change this person's sexual orientation. He may, however, remain abstinent."

Again the author of the article showed how this dangerous trend of thinking is gaining traction by listing other prominent psychologist who are hailing this theory as a practical truth. One such person went so far as to say that there was "no evidence" wich can suggest to the contrary that a predilection to child sex can be treated to change that individuals natural preference.

The article pointed out Linda Harvey of Mission America who made a statement that asserted that the more LGBT groups gain normalcy in our society, there will be a

---

[113] Van Gijseghem; retired professor of the University of Montreal; http://www.hubertvangijseghem.com/nouvelles/173-pedophilie.html

concerted push by advocates to equal rights for padophiles to become normalized.

In fact, her claim is not without merit. The writer demonstrates this by quoting a "distinguished lecturer for the Institute for the Advanced Study of Human Sexuality (IASHS) in San Francisco" who as it turns out advocates that 'child pornography could be beneficial to society because, "Potential sex offenders use child pornography as a substitute for sex against children."

The esteemed professor, Milton Diamond, is quoted where he proceeds to espouse his philosophy that as long as individuals are free from any act which may be non-consensual, sexual freedom should encompass the liberty to explore all avenues. Although he does not say children there is a clear inference asserted when he states that individuals should have "the freedom of any sexual thought, fantasy or desire" and should not be "disadvantaged because of age."

For me, this article by Jack Minor was a damning reality check on where 'gay rights' is headed as a precedent.

Many antagonist would probably argue that this article is 'spot-on'. It highlights the inherent faults with a system that has no moral absolutes. Imagine, if you will, **the irony that Christians and Homosexuals would perhaps agree on the nonsensical value of liberating the sexual appetite of paedophilias**. The collaboration ends there; the whimsical arguments and moral fibre of the Humanist/LGBT agenda is spurious at best.

"Right is right even if no one is doing it; wrong is wrong even if everyone is doing it." These are the words of Augustine of Hippo who was a Latin philosopher and theologian from the Africa Province of the Roman Empire. He was generally considered as one of the greatest Christian thinkers of all times.

His words stand as sound reason today. The morality clause in life is no different than understanding the line that draws a difference between wrong and right. When we skew the line of what is wrong we enter into a temporal nexus of capriciousness. That is; we change the whole dimension of understanding what a standard is by introducing uncertainty. Imagine in years to come if murderers are classified as having 'justified rage hormones' where the offender should pay a fine for not seeing a doctor? That scenario sounds very crazy but as an attorney, I can state that there are legal arguments that could be adopted as precedents to make this a standard criminal defence. The only way that it would not happen is if we stand our moral grounds against this type of moral impracticality.

The moral dilemma is that one cannot assert morals if the standard that is relied upon is compromised. Standards must have a foundation that is unshakable. One can't believe that an elephant can walk on eggs without breaking them. Standards must be made of material that can be stood upon no matter the circumstance.

CHAPTER 6

The Dark-side of Love

"An evil soul producing holy witness, Is like a villain with a smiling cheek, A goodly apple rotten at the heart". [114]

There is nothing more fruitful in life than embracing the rewarding subtleties of love. Unfortunately, embracing love without understanding what true love is, can be compared to biting the apple without seeing the poisonous core.

True Love through sacrifice

In the previous chapter I highlighted a quote from Reverend Haffner where she spoke of love being 'sacred' which impliedly constitutes the word love to a deistic existence.

Perhaps the most duplicitous and confusing premise which is alluded to in the debate on gay rights is the statement of a 'loving God'. Imagine speaking to an atheist who resorts to the most bizarre form of issue deflection by giving credence to a precept for which they have no belief, in a sordid attempt to sway the conversation.

Among Humanist and the LGBT community there is a debate retort which is another universal defence mechanism; 'God is a God

---

[114] William Shakespeare (1564–1616), British dramatist, poet. Antonio, in The Merchant of Venice, act 1, sc. 3, l. 99-101.

of Love; not Hate!' When all else fails, that statement is the superlative trump card to play. It is virtually undeniable by the Christian standard. Humanist sing refrains from that statement such as, 'how could you serve a God of love when you hate so much'. Here is a direct quote from a self-proclaimed gay priest; **Fr. Phillip**[115]

> *As a gay Catholic priest, I want to echo the words of encouragement and say that **God loves each and every one as the beloved**. No matter who you are, where you're from or who you love, **God loves you**! You are special in God's eyes and never let anyone make you feel less than because of your sexuality.* **The gospel reminds us of Jesus' mission to spread the love of God to all we meet**. *You are all amazing!*

The 'one, two punch' of God and love is used even more concretely in a declarative creed[116] (it can be read through the link provided) which has been circulated and said to be endorsed by over 6200 religious leaders. It states basically that God is listening to the pain coming from all those who have been disenfranchised by the wider 'religious' community who have not properly addressed the issues relative to human sexuality. The creed takes a position to call out for the protection of all individuals under the LGBT as well as individuals who suffer from HIV. I made particular note of this part of the creed:

> ***God rejoices*** *when we celebrate our sexuality with holiness and integrity. We, the undersigned, invite our colleagues and faith communities to join us in **promoting sexual morality**, justice, and healing*

---

[115] http://www.risingvoices.net/ site created by **Fr. Gary M. Meier** Author, 'Hidden Voices, Reflections of a Gay, Catholic Priest'

[116] http://www.religiousinstitute.org/staff/the-rev-debra-w-haffner Religious Declaration on Sexual Morality, Justice, and Healing; RELIGIOUS INSTITUTE. Reverend Debra W. Haffner

The creed surreptitiously uses the term '**sexual morality**' which is surprising considering that the LGBT agenda particularly rejects the implications of the same terminology when used by Christians because it places moral parameters on their actions.

Thus far, we have stringently attempted to qualify the words 'morals', and 'truth'. Using the same logical transition, let's attempt to qualify 'who' is the God of Love being referenced? What is the reason why we belief he is God? What are the consequences and conclusions of that belief?

A.   Revealing the true God and love.

Previous dialogue in this book has referenced and clarified the position that this debate is focused on the philosophical precepts of Christianity versus the precepts of the Humanist/LGBT community. For this reason, that dichotomy will remain the same but there is an interesting footnote[117].

With perhaps a miniscule reference to the Muslim religion, the debate on gay rights and marriage has seldom focused on an adversarial level, any of its' rhetoric towards other religious 'gods'. Whether there is an assumption that a level of agreement or acceptance exist with the other religions is curious. Besides vague expressions in the Hindu religion, there has been no major literature found which suggest that Islam, Buddhism, Taoism, Judaism, Scientology, Rastafarianism or Baha'i (to name a few) support homosexuality.

Why would Christianity be the focal point of attack or discord with the Humanist/LGBT? The answers migrate from the rather complex[118] to the more obvious[119] and are perhaps better left for another debate; but on the surface, it appears that highly provocative and public vocal

---

[117] This religious point has been somewhat addressed previously in this text but is very relevant for discussion here.

[118] Ephesians 6:12, For we wrestle not against flesh and blood, but against principalities, against powers, against the rulers of the darkness of this world, against spiritual wickedness in high places. King James Version

[119] Christianity is the largest religious group currently in the world. https://en.wikipedia.org/wiki/Major_religious_groups

dissention by Christian religious leaders[120] as well as strict standards employed by the Bible are two very feasible answers.

Accepting that the Humanist/LGBT are fixating or 'speaking of' the Christian 'God', means that greater understanding should be brought to statements which emanate from that community. Essential to the discussion is clarity because the Christian community must understand the divisive nature of the LGBT community using the name of God as a tool to justify sin. At the very same time; it is vitally important that Christians understand how very significant love is and recognizing the need to foster that 'true' attribute.

Statements emerging from this community should not be made in the void but placed under scrutiny. Therefore; I will attempt to present an exegetical analysis of who God is in relation to the truth of His purpose and His character of love. My aim is to bring light to statements made by the Humanist/LGBT so that we can dispel the notion that God supports gay marriage.

Alluding to love as a belief system should be attached to the referencing of the Christian God by the Humanist/LGBT.

1.   The Christian 'God' that is referenced is a very distinct God. Christianity separates and becomes distinctive from all other religions and religious references to 'a god' by embracing 'who' God is as an articulation of the 'Living Truth' in the person of the Holy Trinity[121]. If the Humanist/LGBT make a 'truth' claim to God being a 'God of love'; the full understanding of who God is should be illuminated in accordance to His true purpose.

The pundit for the protagonist has made a very shrewd manoeuvre. As opposed to castigating the God of Christianity, they have made a bold

---

[120] Pope Francis Against Gay Marriage, Gay Adoption The Huffington Post | By Cavan Sieczkowskihttp //www.huffingtonpost.com/2013/03/13/pope-francis-gay-marriage-anti_n_2869221.html

[121] Hinduism does hold the belief in polytheistic or monotheistic. http://en.wikipedia.org/wiki/God_in_Hinduism

attempt to align themselves to Him to assert a compatibility impression. The ingenious language of 'God is love', which is irrefutable, allows them to place Christians on the defensive by devising a congenial stance which suggest that anyone against the action (which that language is attached to) is impliedly not walking in love.

Most interestingly is the syllogistic implication of the sentence, 'God is love'. It is a declarative imperative truth. It answers the question of who, what, why and when and establishes an irrevocable fact. **Who** is God; God is Love. **What** is God; God is love. **Why**; because He is. **When**; He is, yesterday, today and forevermore. Whatever is, exist, and is irrefutable.

How then is this status of God defined in the Bible.

a) God is love - 1 John 4:8 says; *'Whoever does not love does not know God, because **God is love***'. This is an intrinsic statement of who God is in His testimony, the Bible. There is no separation of God and love in the declarative sentence. It is a type of Christian eschatological statement because it sets a finite and irrevocable standard on how men are to act in knowing God and His nature.

b) God loves mankind – John 3: 16 says; *'**For God so loved** the world that He gave His only begotten Son, that whoever believes in Him should not perish but have everlasting life.'* This is the quintessential sacrifice and expression of love but it has implications that there are punitive measures which flow naturally from rejecting the sacrifice. The verse tells us that the 'Father' sent His Son to dwell among us as deliverance and fulfilment (in life and death[122]) of the Word to man; any rejection of that truth has the **penalty of a spiritual death.**

---

[122] Romans 10:9-11; If you confess with your mouth, "Jesus is Lord," and believe in your heart that God raised Him from the dead, you will be saved. For with your heart you believe and are put right with God, and it is with your mouth that you confess and are saved. As the Scripture says, "Anyone who trusts in Him will never be put to shame."

This becomes immediately important because it shows that who God is in relationship to love is not separated from consequences which flow from actions that reject the truth contained in the premise.

2. In a natural transition of understanding the love of God, we would have to define the reason why He showed such love towards mankind. That love was demonstrated in the elucidation of John 3: 16 which not only speaks of His love but annunciates a variance shown by the use of the adverb, 'so'. This gives a full picture that His love was of great circumstance; it was so great that He did something that all parents can relate to. There is no parent that does not understand the degree of love that comes with sacrifices for a child. It is the greatest love. So God gave the greatest love sacrifice that He could, which immediately brings light to the subject of His love. He sacrificed His Son/Himself for the love of mankind.

3. What was the purpose of this love sacrifice? The saddest part of the equation in understanding the God of love is the prevailing fact that many Humanist/LGBT persons live in a created utopia where there is a false sense of powers given to the sheriff. If a civilian kills, the protagonist community rallies behind the sheriff to say that justice in the law must be carried out. The problem with this town of perdition is that its' standards are compromised. The sheriff only has power based on what they 'think' is acceptable. If the sheriff places a standard on 'sexuality'; that sheriff is fired.

They accept the God of love but have not noticed the attachment which comes with the God of love. They seek the entitlement of love without the consequence of their actions. The last part of John 3:16 says'; **'that whoever believes in Him should not perish but have everlasting life.'** That is a mouthful. It articulates survivorship against impeding **spiritual death** in 'perdition'. It gives a formula and invites all to evade the inescapable perishing from life. It heralds a new existence; a dispensation of eternity.

This is what the sacrifice is all about. It is about confirming a **promise through** one person and **confirmed by** that person. Revelation of this is established by Jesus himself. In the book of Matthew 16: 17 – 18 (NRSV) Jesus and His disciples are assembled when Jesus asked Peter, *"Who do men say that I, the Son of Man, am?"*

At that time, Jesus had performed numerous miracles[123] (by man's standard) and was seen by some as **a prophet** rather than **the Messiah**. When Simon Peter answered and said, *"You are the Christ, the Son of the living God"*; Jesus affirmed and replied, *"Blessed are you, Simon Bar Jonah, for flesh and blood has not revealed this to you, but my Father who is in heaven. I also tell you that you are Peter (Petros), and on this rock (Petra) I will build my assembly, and **the gates of Hades will not prevail against it**"*.

Jesus elevates the truth of the spoken Word in John 3:16 by confirming that **spiritual death** is defeated. This has two truths implied to it; firstly, that there is death beyond the gates of Hades, and secondly that Jesus is the Messiah and not believing in Him will deliver that death.

Any fortress is tested by the strength of its gates. Jesus' death and resurrection is the full representation of who God is. He destroyed the gates of hell and eliminates the strength of death through the resurrected of the Saviour. **This is the pinnacle of God's love; the death of His Son Jesus so that man could live beyond the penalty of spiritual death**.

The lay person is admittedly incapable of believing something that exist on a plain which is incomprehensible except that they have faith which is indicated in John 3:16 as '**believing**'. The Bible recognizes this logical dilemma. In 1 Corinthians 2:14 the Bible teaches that, *'The person without the Spirit does not accept the things that come from the Spirit of God but considers them foolishness, and cannot understand them because they are discerned only through the Spirit.'*

The rationality of the testament of God (the Bible) is that it gives actual **revelations to man through the person of the Holy Spirit**. As shown above, all men will not discern revelations from the word

---

[123] Matthew 14:13 - 21

of God. In His infinite wisdom, God then constructs a pathway for man to follow. That path is a revelation of His majesty and existence through **revelation in prophecy** and **faith in the revealing evidence of God's miracles**.

4.   We already know that Humanist are resigned to 'the best evidence' prospect based on empirical knowledge.

From the very beginning chapter of the Bible, there is beyond a presumptive fluency in the nomenclature which focuses on God revealing His truth through Jesus Christ. It becomes evident that the providential intent of the Word of God is to in fact reveal God to man in the person of Jesus Christ. Character after character is aligned with God as a testament of His existence. Whether we read the story of Moses and his miraculous journey with God or the life and times of King David as the established king of Israel; the one thing that stands throughout the Bible is the interwoven evidence of God's revelationary relationship with man. But who is He really revealing?

There is no doubt that sceptics would cause a whole book to be written in dissention of each historical reference; but there is one story of revelation, which if proven true would change the landscape of the entire debate. The birth, death and resurrection of Jesus Christ is the cornerstone of the Christian belief and the presumptive true testimony of the Bible.

As concise as is realistically possible; let's take a look at the evidence that gives credence to the **revelation of Jesus Christ as God.**

   i.   **Prophecy** – Clarity has been given to prophecy as a truth mechanism. The fulfilment of Biblical prophecy by the birth, death and resurrection of Christ is unprecedented. To negate the fulfilment of the prophecies as unauthentic rhetoric, one would have to dispute the entire content of the Bible. There are 66 books which make up the Bible according to the table of contents of the NKJV. There is not one book that does not speak of Jesus Christ[124]. That fact, in and of itself, is revelation of the truth of the historical birth and resurrection. In the history of anthology it would be virtually impossible to find another figure that has come close to inspiring prophetic revelation such as Jesus Christ. According to Peter Stoner[125]a mathematician who wrote the book '**Science Speaks**'[126]; there are over 300 prophecies in the Old Testament about Jesus. He posits that every prophecy was fulfilled by Jesus. It obviously does not take a scientist to understand how miraculous on the preponderance of that assertion, such a result would be. To give credence to his theory, Stoner astutely devises a series of equations to show the low probability of those prophetic fulfilments occurring by choosing only 8 prophetic fulfilments. He is magnifying the point that even if 8 where accounted as actualized out of 300 prophecies; it would still be a revelation of which the probability is astronomical. His results were astonishing. Whiles Stoner did construct logical perimeters around 8 prophecies; for the sake of time, we will examine one (1) along with mirroring his conclusion.

In the book of Isaiah 53:7, Isaiah prophesied; "*He was oppressed, and he was afflicted, yet **he opened not his mouth**: he is brought as a lamb to the slaughter, and as a sheep before her shearers is dumb, so he openeth not his mouth*".

---

[124] JoyBellBarber. List of books and references to Jesus -http://www.encouragers4you. com/poems/jesus_in_every_book_of_the_bible.htm

[125] **Peter Stoner** (June 16, 1888 – March 21, 1980) was Chairman of the Departments of Mathematics and Astronomy at Pasadena City College until 1953; Chairman of the science division, Westmont College, 1953–57; Professor Emeritus of Science, Westmont College; Professor Emeritus of Mathematics and Astronomy, Pasadena City College. http://en.wikipedia.org/wiki/Peter_Stoner

[126] Science Speaks, Scientific Proof of the Accuracy of Prophecy and the Bible; Peter W. Stoner, M.S. and Robert C. Newman, S.T.M., Ph.D. http://sciencespeaks. dstoner.net/Christ_of_Prophecy.html#c9

To deconstruct this verse and extrapolate its significance there are pertinent variables that should be observed.

- According to chapter 1 verse 1 in the Book of Isaiah; Isaiah was a prophet who gave his 'vision' of things he saw concerning Judah and Jerusalem. He would have lived and prophesied during the reigns of Uzziah[127] (783BC) to the death of Hezekiah[128] (687BCE) both kings of Judah. The timeline stands as significant because his prophesies are over 700 years before the birth of Jesus Christ[129] in 3 to 6 BCC according to the Catholic Education Resource Centre.

- Isaiah has over twenty significant prophecies about the birth, life and death of Jesus. The significance of his predictions is the anatomical covalence of time. Isaiah actually tied pre-life, life and death together.

  a) Pre-life prophecy: Will be born of a virgin (Isaiah 7:14) Confirmed; Was born of a virgin named Mary (Luke 1:26-31)

  b) Life prophecy: "He was despised and rejected by men, a man of sorrows, and familiar with suffering. Like one from whom men hide their faces he was despised, and we esteemed him not." Isaiah 53:3. Confirmed; Was not accepted by many (John 12:37, 38)

  c) Death: Will be buried in a rich man's tomb (Isaiah 53:9). Confirmed; He was buried in the tomb of Joseph, a rich man from Arimathea (Matthew 27:57-60; John 19:38-42)

Specific to the verse, Isaiah 53: 7; prophecy is fulfilled by several verses in the New Testament.

---

[127] http://en.wikipedia.org/wiki/Uzziah

[128] http://en.wikipedia.org/wiki/Hezekiah

[129] In What Year was Christ Actually Born? ZENIT http://www.catholiceducation. org/articles/facts/fm0004.html

- Isaiah prophesied that Jesus would be brought before His oppressors, but even with the affliction of condemnation at the hands of His oppressors; he remains silent. In the New Testament book of Matthew 26:63 the plot is hatched by the chief priests and the elders of the people as they "***schemed to arrest Jesus secretly and kill him***". The plot thickens against Jesus as Judas Iscariot (a disciple among the twelve) agrees to betray Jesus and "***deliver him over***" to the chief priest. Jesus is brought before the Sanhedrin council who, with their hidden agenda, had set out to have 'false witnesses[130]' testify against Jesus. Jesus is accused of saying, 'I am able to destroy the temple of God and rebuild it in three days.' When asked if He will defend Himself; Jesus fulfils prophecy and **remains silent.**

  1. It's interesting that Jesus remains silent in this moment of stark debauchery because according to Luke 9:22, Jesus knew what the council had planned. Very clairvoyant to the moment, He revealed to the disciples; "*The Son of Man must suffer many things and be rejected by the elders, the chief priests and the teachers of the law, and **he must be killed and on the third day be raised to life.**"* It is a remarkable self-revelation and confirmation of what was prophesied.

In the book of Acts 8:26-38, Philip the Evangelist is led by an Angel of The Lord to "Go south to the road--the desert road--that goes down from Jerusalem to Gaza." There, Philip encounters a eunuch of great influence under the queen of Ethiopia, Candace. **Philip realizes that the eunuch is reading Biblical scripture from the book of Isaiah.** The fact that the eunuch is a royal official authenticates why he would have exposure to expensive reading material and the education to read[131].

---

[130] Matthew 26: 59 The chief priests and the whole Sanhedrin were looking for false evidence against Jesus so that they could put him to death. NKJ

[131] Wiliam A. Johnson, *Readers and Reading Culture in the High Roman Empire: A Study of Elite Communities* (Oxford University Press,

Philip seizes the moment to enlighten the eunuch on the meaning of what he has read. The eunuch does not understand the true implications of the **prophecy**. A little historical social excavation and one begins to understand why Philip was very effective in evangelising to the eunuch who would have been deeply encroached in paganism. At the time of the ministry of Philip, **Saul of Tarsus** had also just been converted to Christianity and was now known as **Paul the Apostle[132]**. **Jesus** had been crucified within their lifetime. **The death of Jesus would have been highly publicized in Jerusalem**. Many persons would have been aware of the details surrounding His life, miracles and the proclamations He made. Once Philip explained the 'prophetic exactness' of **Isaiah 53** with the circumstance of 'How' Jesus died; it was a **powerful moment of revelation to the eunuch <u>from the prophecy</u>**. The information was so trenchant as the truth, that the eunuch immediately placed his life in the hands of the Christian faith. It is a quintessential moment for Christian Evangelism as *Philip said, "If you **believe** with all your heart, you may." The eunuch answered, "**I believe that Jesus Christ is the Son of God.**"* **This is an affirmation of the prophetic words of Christ** in Matthew 16: 15 -16, when Jesus ask, "But what about you?", "Who do you say I am?" and Simon Peter answered, "You are the Messiah, the Son of the living God."

What the scientist Stoner was trying to achieve based on his experiment, was to illustrate the near impossibility of one person fulfilling just 8 prophecies when in fact, 300 are said to have been fulfilled. His deductions on probability showed that 1 man in 1.7 sextillion, a number of cosmological comprehensions, (from the time of the prophecy to the time of the experiment), would have had the mere chance to fulfil the 8 prophecies.

2010), pp. 17–18. via http://en.wikipedia.org/wiki/User:Cynwolfe/literacy_and_education_in_the_Roman_Empire#cite_note-12

[132] Sanders, E.P. "Saint Paul, the Apostle". Encyclopædia Britannica. *Encyclopædia Britannica Online Academic Edition*. Encyclopædia Britannica Inc., 2013. Web. 08 Jan. 2013 via https://en.wikipedia.org/wiki/Paul_the_Apostle#cite_note-Sanders2-6

Stoner's experiments on the probability of prophecy are faithful reasons why Christians believe in God. His concise wording is a proper conclusion to his experiments; *'Now these prophecies were either given by inspiration of God or the prophets just wrote them as they thought they should be. In such a case the prophets had just one chance in 10^{17} of having them come true in any man, but they all came true in Christ.' 'This means that the fulfilment of these eight prophecies alone proves that* **God inspired the writing of those prophecies** *to a definiteness which lacks only one change in 10^{17} of being absolute.'*

   ii. **Faith in the revealed evidence** – Without any doubt, the aforementioned is a miracle in and of itself but the path that God laid had more ways than one to see the truth of His majesty.

Eyewitness testimony is usually considered a primary tool in solving a mystery. The question of who shot President Kennedy on a conspiracy level; the answer will live in infamy. Nobody actually saw Lee Harvey Oswald shoot the president but on the preponderance of evidence gathered from persons[133] working in the Depository; the suspect was narrowed to Oswald. On an evidentiary level, credibility would be the real enemy of eyewitness testimony but it still does not negate the direct value of the evidence. Various employees from the Depository had divergent opinions on seeing Oswald that day but the evidence was enough to focus on Oswald.

The Ford Theatre were Lincoln was shot had at least 1700 persons in attendance which was a capacity[134].Based on direct evidence there was little doubt that the suspect was John Wilkes Booth and that it was he who assassinated the president in the Presidential Box[135].

---

[133] Warren Commission Hearings, Testimony of Roy Sansom Truly via http://en.wikipedia.org/wiki/Lee_Harvey_Oswald#cite_note-157

[134] "Frequently Asked Questions - Ford's Theatre National Historic Site". Nps. gov. 1932-02-12. Retrieved 2012-09-28 via https://en.wikipedia.org/wiki/Assassination_of_Abraham_Lincoln#cite_note-22.

[135] Weider History Group, History net; http://www.historynet.com/abraham-lincoln-assassination

The easiest way to negate the Bible would be to eliminate the story of the lead character. If history could show that Jesus either never lived or that His crucifixion and resurrection were fictionalized by zealots; the Bible would become the most farcical and contemptuous book of lies ever written. That level of prevarication would turn the Bible and its followers into cult charlatans with an unbelievable commitment to an unprecedented lie. For Christians, that characterization is not unfounded. There are persons living today who have inherently followed the centuries old Egyptian cult (by Christian standards) of Isis[136] and maintained that faith, despite the lack of any prevailing evidence to significantly qualify a coherent belief of Isis as a benevolent and real god.

The importance of verifiable facts of historical significance through the eyes of persons who would have experienced the life and times of Jesus can't be understated. **If there is no Jesus; or if the arrest and crucifixion did not occur; or if there is no witness to His resurrection; the God of love and the proposition of John 3:16 are just an urban legend with a quote perhaps only fit for print on t-shirts (as opposed to a bible testament).** Even worse; **it would mean that there is no limitation or standard to how we can live our lives because the penalty of spiritual death would be vitiated by fraud.**

Who witnessed the death and resurrection of Jesus and was that testimony credible?

(1) **Historical witness of 'the People' before death** - Consideration has to be given to the full context of events leading up to the death of Christ. After reading through the book of Matthew, it becomes evident that the crucifixion of Christ was not a simple domestic event where the local authority of the Sanhedrin Council[137] prevailed. It became much more politicised because

---

[136] The Mysteries of Isis: Her Worship and Magick; Fellowship of Isis; deTraci Regula

[137] The Great Sanhedrin dealt with religious and ritualistic <u>Temple</u> matters, criminal matters appertaining to the secular court, proceedings in connection with the discovery of a corpse, trials of adulterous wives, tithes, preparation of Torah Scrolls for the king and the Temple, <u>drawing</u> up the calendar and the solving of

the council turned the case over to Pontius Pilate[138], who in turn involved Herod. Their involvement alone gave greater visibility on a political level to the events leading to the crucifixion. The crafty voice of the council helped to further politicize the situation when in John 19: 12 they said to Pilate; *"If you let this man go, you are no friend of Caesar. Anyone who claims to be a king opposes Caesar."* Pilate recognized the implication of the cunning words. In the book, 'Confessions of Pontius Pilate[139]'; Pilate is quoted in a conversation with his confidant Albinus as saying, '*Some threatened to accuse me to the Emperor. Thereupon, foreseeing the coming conflict, I reported* the whole affair to the Council in Rome, and asked for military assistance, in case of an uprising taking place among the people, so I would be able to easily quell it.*' (Whether this book is completely factual or not; I do believe that it is great insight into the incredible pressure that Pontius Pilate would have realistically come under to adjudicate the trial of Jesus.)

The Sanhedrin Council was comprised primarily of Jewish religious leaders called Sadducees who relished their position in society as upperclassmen[140]. They enjoyed the hierarchal system of class and control in the Roman Empire and felt threatened[141] by the exaltations that Jesus was the Messiah; the king of the Jews. Pilate also provides

---

difficulties relating to ritual law. **The Sanhedrin; By Shira Schoenberg: Jewish Virtual Library**

[138] The man who heard these charges was the Roman prefect, Pontius Pilate, who ruled over Judea, Idumea, and Samaria. **A Night of Trials and Hearings; http:// www.welcometohosanna.com/LIFE_OF_JESUS/047_NightOfTrials2.htm**

[139] First written, as alleged, in Latin, by Fabricius Albinos, a playmate Pilate; of translated into Arabic by Jerasimus Jar^d, late Bishop of Zahleh, in Lebanon and finally translated by Shehadi, Beshara, East Orange, N.J., Printed by Matthias Plum, inc.; 1917

[140] Political and religious background at the time of Jesus' Ministry; Bible Heritage Foundation http://thestoryofjesus.com/politics.html

[141] John 11: 47 - 53

further witness to this fact; *'Let us now return to Jesus of Nazareth. (Pilate said this, and heaved a deep sigh.) The straightforwardness of this man and the publicity of his teachings and the reprovings of the faults and bad deeds of many, aroused jealousy in the hearts of the chief priests, the learned men, and the wealthy people, the aforementioned sects especially'.*

According to Matthew 26:5, the council had a plot in place which they were obviously ready to carry out but they were limited in executing the plot because Mosaic law, warranted that no 'work' should take place during the Feast of the Passover[142]. In the book, 'Passover[143]' the writer cites passages from Titus Flavius Josephus[144]who has traditionally been acknowledged as an accredited historian of Roman and Jewish history during the 1st Century. Josephus estimates that the city of Jerusalem had around 'two million, seven hundred thousand, two hundred' persons in it during 'Passover' ceremonies. The writer then offers a contrasting account of that figure given by E.P. Sanders[145] who elucidates that the figure is actually 300 to 500,000. Why the figures are of interest is due to the social picture it paints of the significantly high amount of persons who attended Passover each year in Jerusalem. That creates a very large 'witness pool'. One can conclude that those numbers would have remained constant leading up to the crucifixion.

Jesus and His disciples entered Jerusalem approximately 6 days[146] prior to Passover. The night before, they stayed in Bethany. What cannot be lost in the passage is the following of people that Jesus garnered because of the miracle with Lazarus. People were naturally curious and wanted to see for themselves whether Lazarus was alive. Imagine the spectacle this would have created. In John 12:19 we are made aware that Lazarus had been dead for 4 days so many Jews (as is customary) had already visited the sisters of Lazarus to pay their respect. This means

---

[142] Passover - Pesach: History & Overview http: Tracey R Rich; //www. jewishvirtuallibrary.org/jsource/Judaism/holidaya.html

[143] **Thematic Concordance to the Works of Josephus by G. J. Goldberg**

[144] Louis Feldman, Steve Mason (1999). *Flavius Josephus*. Brill Academic Publishers.

[145] *Judaism: Practice and Belief 63 BCE - 66 CE* (p. 126)

[146] John 12:1 KJV

that by word of mouth, many people in the area of Bethany going to Jerusalem, bore witness to and knew about the miracle of Lazarus.

What can be credited to the Gospel of John[147] is the intimate oratory of the events it records leading up to the crucifixion. It explains that Jesus had dinner in Bethany which must have been more of a feast because the disciples, Lazarus, Mary, and Martha (serving) were in attendance. John further states that Jesus travels into Jerusalem on a donkey from Bethany the next day. Bethany is less than two miles from Jerusalem but according to the synoptic Gospels and John[148];

> *[12] The next day the great crowd that had come for the festival heard that Jesus was on his way to Jerusalem. [13] They took palm branches and went out to meet him, shouting, "Hosanna"*
>
> *"Blessed is he who comes in the name of the Lord!" "Blessed is the king of Israel!*

For a crowd to line the streets from Bethany to Jerusalm; there had to be a substantial presence, most likely in the hundreds of thousands. The Bible tells us in John 11:18 that the distance was close to two miles between the two cities.

That large 'presence' of people who shouted 'Hosanna' did not leave after Jesus entered Jerusalem. As a foot note of great interest; In John 12:20, an account is given of 'certain' Greeks coming to see Jesus. One has to preserve the historic and miraculous content of specific Greeks wanting to see Christ. These were no ordinary seekers of Jesus. Passover is mainly a Jewish holiday under Mosaic law so any involvement of Greeks was culturally extraordinary.

The Greeks had broad religious influence over the Roman culture as many of their gods (Acts 17:16) were adopted into Roman theism. Judaism and Christians considered the Greek culture as pagan in

---

[147] John 21:24
[148] John 12:12

their belief system so when verse 20 speaks of certain Greeks; they are fervent followers and believers in the ministry of Jesus Christ. Acts 17:4 shows that the message of Jesus Christ as the Messiah was permeating throughout foreign societies (perhaps helped by indigenous missionaries who left to seek Jesus then returned with His Word of truth).

We see that Paul is preaching the message of 'Jesus as the Christ' to Greeks in Thesalonica and a 'great multitude of devout Greeks' receive, believed and followed Paul and Silas. This story is significant because many independent historians from the Romo-Greek-Jewish community made a point of documenting these developments as witnesses to the times. Why? Like any good journalist or reporter; the headline news of the day becomes relevant. Paul and Silas were evangelising and radically changing the belief system of a pagan society. That was big news. Independent stories from Phlegon of Tralles, Cornelius Tacitus[149], and Lucian of Samosata[150] (to name a few) have from then to now, authenticated in some form the life and death of Jesus Christ.

As Christ is captured and prophecies are fulfilled of His physical bondage (this small period in the life of Jesus also referred to as **'the Passion'[151]** from the Greek word meaning to 'to suffer'); thousands of people lay **witness** to the spectacle of His martyred person, with a crown of thorns walking through the streets on His way to the final resting place of the cross atop Golgotha.

(2) **Witness of the people after death** – When Charles Dodgson[152], a mathematician at Christ Church, Oxford first relayed the story of 'Alice in Wonderland' and wrote it under

---

[149] Cornelius Tacitus was a Roman historian, born A.D. 52-54; http://www.newtestamentchurch.org/html/Christian_Evidence/Historical_Evidence.htm; Historical Evidence for the Accuracy of the Bible By Dennis Crawford

[150] Josh McDowell's "Evidence" for Jesus Is It Reliable? Jeffery Jay Lowder http://www.infidels.org/library/modern/jeff_lowder/jury/chap5.html

[151] Matthew 17:12

[152] http://www.goodreads.com/author/show/8164.Lewis_Carroll

the pseudonym of Lewis Carroll; it was lauded years later as a children's classic. A much closer analysis of the story and one may find the unpleasant hint that his literary devices held secret meanings directed at a psychotropic trip that a person takes when using drugs. The illustrations[153] of mushrooms, smoking caterpillars and grinning cats is enough to evince a clear image that Alice was (possibly) in a drug induced state.

Why would I paint such an awful analyses of the beloved characters? I am illustrating that reading is more about understanding a 'full' possibility by looking deep into the circumstance. Considering the vivid picture of the cultural scene before the trial of Jesus; I will continue to bring to life the story of the past.

Testimony in the Old and New Testament are very vivid when understood from societal perspectives. To verify the situation of **witness testimony** let's first paint a picture of the policing and political structure of Rome at the time of Jesus' death. In just the instant of characterizing the last days and death of Jesus through the periscope of the political and military infrastructure; we can understand the fluidity of time in relation to credence of witness testimony.

Pilate and The Soldiers – There is sufficient historical data which indicates that modern marines are a composite of what started in the Roman culture.[154].There is substantive value in understanding the discipline of the Roman system. Discipline is a key component and the Roman system is one of the first sophisticated styles of governance that adapts 'accountability' as a prerequisite of governing. The security system of Rome is a sophisticated 'hierarchal system' of which the Emperor himself is at the helm.[155]

---

[153] http://www.bbc.co.uk/news/magazine-19254839
[154] The UNITED STATES MARINE CORPS FACTS http://www.usmarinesbirthplace.com/United-States-Marines-facts.html
[155] Roman Army Ranks; http://www.tribunesandtriumphs.org/roman-army/roman-army-ranks.htm Linda Alchin is an author primarily specialising in history. Linda Alchin has been the Director of Education at Siteseen Ltd since 2006. She has

Let's offer a few assumptions in retrospective analogy of the situation at Golgotha. If we assume that Pilate is an astute leader as the 'fifth Prefect' of the Roman province of Judaea'[156]; he would have had that title bestowed upon him from the authority of Tiberius Claudius Caesar Augustus, Roman Emperor from 14 AD to 37 AD[157]. Such a title came with acclaim and great responsibility to maintain order in the Roman kingdom. History[158] shows that this area endured numerous revolts as tensions between the Jews, other cultures and Romans constantly broiled over.

Pilate had to be astutely aware that religious zealots could stir up emotions and use the Passover to conjure anti-Roman sentiment; after all, Passover was a celebration of God delivering the Israelites out of the hands of their enemy. It is understood that Pilate knew how contentious the crucifixion of Jesus would be.

In John 19: 7 – 8: 7 Pilate is told by the insistent *Jewish leaders, "We have a law, and according to that law he must die, because he claimed to be the Son of God."*. Within that understanding, the question is presented; Pilate knowing that Jerusalem had as high as 500 thousand to 1 million pilgrims in the city, how many Roman legions would Pilate have utilized in securing the city, guard duty over the processional and crucifixion, and the tomb of Jesus?

If Pilate wanted to maintain the rule of law and avoid chaos it is submitted that he would have deployed a substantive force of legions to keep law and order in the city. It is further posited that even if Pilate was low on security capital (men), he would have sent his best men to maintain order and to ensure that the empire was not embarrassed.

From the base that I have built, let's construct the remainder of the witness story.

---

acted as consultant on history-themed radio and TV programs in both the UK and USA.

[156] "Britannica Online: Pontius Pilate". Britannica.com via Wikipedia.

[157] Suetonius, *The Lives of Twelve Caesars*, Life of Tiberius 5 via Wikipedia

[158] A History of Rome, LeGlay, et al. 100 via Wikipedia.

Assuming that Pilate understood fully how significant it was to manage the situation with Jesus and the Sanhedrin council; we find in the book of Matthew 26:47 that Judas has approached Jesus in the Garden of Gethsemane to assist with identifying Jesus as the target of arrest. It says', that *'a great multitude with swords and clubs, came from the chief priests and elders of the people'* accompanied Judas.

This is our first true insight into the volatility of the situation. It appears that the council either formed a mob with soldiers or they had completely armed themselves as a mob against Jesus.

As we proceed to Matthew 27: 20 the council now has Jesus before the governor Pilate. Considering the mob crowd a day earlier it would be astute to assert that the council would have had a larger crowd before Pilate. What they needed to accomplish was to ignite the atmosphere in a mob frenzy to convince Pilate beyond any doubt that Jesus was indeed guilty. Verse 20 affirms the crowd when it states; *'But the chief priests and elders persuaded the **multitudes** that they should ask for Barabbas and destroy Jesus'.*

Imagine this; Pilate is sitting before a delegation of the top council membership who is making a public appeal. I can envision the level of showmanship as egos' become involved and the demands become more boisterous. Would anyone imagine that Pilate would not have established military protocol by asserting the presence of the Roman army? I posit that Pilate would have made sure that the prerequisite security detail would have been in place to demonstrate the full control of the mighty Roman force.

That brings me to my salient point. I submit that Pilate would never risk, as representative of the Roman Emperor, losing control over custody of Jesus. From Matthew 27: 27 – 66 there is evidence that Jesus is surrounded by soldiers from the time He is before the 'kangaroo' court to the very point that He is buried.

Why is this point so very significant? With reference to my conversations with protagonist, I have illustrated and implied through this book that there is a number of retorts that they will repeat. It will be asserted either that there is no God; Jesus was only a man; Jesus did not rise from the dead or that if there is a God, He is a God of love with no implications to the life and death of Jesus Christ. How in any circumstance you examine these possible retorts; they all eliminate the purpose and function of love as recognized in John 3: 16.

The true significance of the witnessed actions of Pilot and the witness of the guard detail attached to events associated with the trial, death, and resurrection of Jesus, is that it gives credence and full support to John 3:16 and the true revelations found in Genesis 3:15; Job 14:14; Job 19: 25 -26; Psalm 16:9-11; Hebrews 11:17-19. Each one of the aforementioned scriptures illustrate the purpose of love being the death and resurrection of Jesus Christ to save mankind from spiritual death as a result of sin.

At the end of Matthew 27 we learn in verse 63 that Pilate is asked to seal the tomb of Jesus because it was '**prophesised**' that the Messiah would die and rise after three days. Pilate acquiesces and has a seal placed on the tomb along with a guard. At this stage, Pilate may have been a little sceptical about the story of Jesus rising; after all, this was not pertinent to his pseudo-empirical view of accepting Caesar as regent to God. Whiles the urgency of security may have lessened, there is still 'eyes' placed on the tomb by Roman soldiers. The significant development shown in Mark 15: 43 – 45 is that when Joseph of Arimathea approaches Pilate to retrieve the body of Jesus; Pilate does not release the body until it is affirmed by the Roman Centurion that Jesus is in fact dead. That means that the state of Rome and Pilate were still in control of the situation and death was officially proclaimed by the release. The fact that a centurion reported to Pilate illustrates that a squadron of 100 men called 'Centuria[159]' had been assigned to the crucifixion site.

I will admit that there is some historical prevarication as to the exactness of the number of soldiers and whether they are common

---

[159] http://en.wikipedia.org/wiki/Centuria

auxiliaries[160] as opposed to the elite guard but I would further prognosticate that the seal of the Roman Empire was not to be taken lightly and was yet a further sign that Pilate was acting to protect the security integrity of Rome. If the unit was reduced to a 'Contubernium[161]' squad at the tomb of Jesus, it would mean that no less than 8 to 14 men were stationed; and as indicated previously, the discipline of soldiers was a hallmark of the Roman Army.

We have a witness account from Matthew 27:54 that the soldiers had already experienced a traumatic event at Golgotha[162]at the exact time that Jesus died. It is recorded and perhaps reflected upon as one of the most bizarre miracles in the New Testament. If any reader is curious as to where inspiration comes from for movies like 'The Walking Dead'; read verses 51 – 53. Literally it is said that the death of Jesus released from the tombs, 'saints' or believers who had died believing in the revelation of Jesus Christ. This is in direct correlation with the prophecy that Jesus spoke in Matthew 16: 17 – 18 (which was highlighted formerly) where he ends by saying'; "….**the gates of Hades will not prevail against it**".

The supernatural power that was exhibited during the death of Jesus, opened the gates of Hades in a literal context as it is said in verse 53 that many in the city of Jerusalem were witness to this miraculous phenomena.

How do you think the 'disciplined' soldiers were after being witness to this supernatural event? In verse 54 (TLB) it states; '*The soldiers at the crucifixion and their sergeant were terribly frightened by the earthquake and all that happened. They exclaimed, "**Surely this was God's Son**'.

That point is made to set the tune for what would follow at the tomb. I would suspect that the soldiers on assignment as guards to the tomb were not the happiest group. After a day of paranormal activities, I

---

[160] http://www.historylearningsite.co.uk/roman_army_and_warfare.htm
[161] http://en.wikipedia.org/wiki/Contubernium
[162] Mathew 27: 33

would guess that any soldier would have been uneasy and still frightened about being around the tomb. For this reason on the third day when there is another earthquake and the seal is broken along with the heavy stone being rolled back from the door of the tomb; the soldiers 'naturally' ran away and made a bee-line to the Sanhedrin council.

The incident is another extraordinary event as we are told in Matthew 28 how an Angel appeared with such a celestial field of brilliance that the soldiers actually pretended as if they were dead in His presence. For me personally; that story makes sense. If I had such an encounter outside of my cognitive field of expectation; I would guess that I would react the same.

I submit that the soldiers were so bewildered not only by the sight of the Angel but by the fact that they intuitively knew an explanation of such exigent circumstance needed to be better than, 'we saw a ghost'.

The soldiers desperately needed to account for the seal being violated so they went to the council first, before going to Pilate (who probably would not have believed them) and devised a plan in collusion which would implicate the followers of Jesus as opposed to the implied ineptness on their behalf.

From this point on; Jesus is recorded by witnesses on at least twelve occasions to have appeared after His death. Here are a few.

The appearance record (using the Living Bible)

1) 1Corinthians 15:6-8 - After that he was seen by more than **five hundred Christian brothers** at one time, most of whom are still alive, though some have died by now. Then **James saw him**, and later all the apostles. Last of **all I saw him** too, long after the others, as though I had been born almost too late for this.

2) Matthew 28:8 -9 - The women ran from the tomb, badly frightened, but also filled with joy, and rushed to find the disciples to give them the angel's message. And as they were running, **suddenly Jesus was there in front of them!**

3) Luke 24:13-34 - two of Jesus' followers were walking to the village of Emmaus, seven miles out of Jerusalem. As they walked along they were talking of Jesus' death, when suddenly Jesus himself came along and joined them and began walking beside them. 16 But they didn't recognize him. 31 when suddenly—it was as though their eyes were opened—they recognized him!

4) John 20.26-31 - Eight days later the disciples were together again, and this time Thomas was with them. The doors were locked; but suddenly, as before, Jesus was standing among them and greeting them. **Jesus' disciples saw him do many other miracles besides the ones told about in this book, but these are recorded so that you will believe that he is the Messiah, the Son of God, and that believing in him you will have life.**

5) Luke 24: 50 - 53 - Then Jesus led them out along the road to Bethany, and **lifting his hands to heaven, he blessed them, and then began rising into the sky, and went on to heaven.** And they worshiped him, and returned to Jerusalem filled with mighty joy, and were continually in the Temple, praising God

6) The one testimony that I saved for last is consequential to the most significant testimony for me personally. Although I believe all the testimonies, I realize that it would be rather simple for the average sceptic to reason them away as just inane wishful thinking by disciples who would have a 'game plan' to exaggerate the truth. What tips the scale for me is the testimony of Paul because of the depth of his story. Beyond the fact that Paul becomes a devote apostle is the uniqueness of his witnessed testimony. What makes his story so different is the recording and illustration of radical reform to an 'unbeliever'. We are cognizant that his name was previously Saul of Tarsus[163]. His presence in scripture is onerous in the first instance and can be viewed as an earthly 'angel of death'. He persecuted Christians

---

[163] http://www.biblestudytools.com/encyclopedias/condensed-biblical-encyclopedia/saul-of-tarsus.html

and was notoriously recognised as efficient in so doing. His conversion to Christianity came as he was on the road to Damascus to carry-out his edict of annihilation. Jesus appeared to him and virtually placed the sword of light (my words) into his eyes, which blinded him for three days.

What amazes me about this story is that Saul was well regarded in the Roman society, so his betrayal of allegiance and his conversion, subjugated him to extreme prejudice and torture. As a matter of fact; I would posit that the Caesar, Nero[164], persecuted and tortured Paul specifically because of his conversion to Christianity.

I recognized through my reading here that this is one of many radical conversions that has occurred in the Bible of which the subject becomes an 'enemy of the state'; Moses being the most relevant example of drastic transformation to following Christianity.

Paul was so radically convinced after meeting the resurrected Christ that he endured the most tumultuous existence thereon to preach the word of God. More astonishing to the story of 'Saul the persecutor' is the conversion story of Paul the evangelist who must have been heavily blessed by the Holy Spirit. His writings are prolific in the New Testament over a relatively short period before his death. In Acts 9:13 we can begin to untie the mystery of why Paul is so gifted. A new disciple by the name of Ananias who is also made aware of the resurrected Christ, when he is told by Jesus to go to Paul and lay hands on him whiles he was in penance. Pauls' reputation preceded him and Ananias was afraid to do as instructed. Jesus then informs him of Pauls' special dispensation as an apostle. **In Acts 22: 14 – 16 we have the revelation of Pauls' life and his *witness* before God**; *'The God of our fathers **has chosen you** that you should know His will, and see the Just One, and hear the voice of His mouth. For **you will be His witness** to all men of what you*

---

[164] Paul died in the Neronian persecution in 64-65 AD http://www3.telus.net/trbrooks/12groups.htm

have seen and heard. And now why are you waiting? Arise and be baptized, and wash away your sins, calling on the name of the Lord.

Through the litany of evidence I would submit that Jesus is the resurrected Son of God; the Messiah and God incarnate. The evidence presented does not give credence to those facts alone but it also establishes the position that what He says in the text of the New Testament must be received as truth from God.

Earlier in this chapter I presented two verses which are like the constitution of God's love; one from 1 John 4:8 and the other from John 3: 16. The former gives essentially the essence of what love is and the latter is the key attachment to the purpose and operation of God's love.

I John 4:8 has become the refrain for many persons who seek the love of God. It is stated as if it is a magical elixir that has all the healing properties for the soul. I can understand that sentiment. Who would not want to simply state that 'God is love' and automatically have the ensuing grant of peace and joy. The danger of this belief is that it uses the truth of the implied proposition to dismiss the implication of their actions and level of responsibility.

That premise makes no sense to me, considering that God went through such an extraordinary process to reveal His love to us. How would it be logical that God tells us that His Son was sent to earth to die for our sins so that the forgiveness of those sins would be realized through our penance and personal commitment to believing in Jesus Christ; yet, we eliminate our responsibility to follow the instructions?

We are told that Jesus' death and resurrection brings about the purpose of Gods' love through this exact act.

The question is; are there any penalties or standards associated to God's love or are there no moral absolutes attached so that we experience a plurality of benevolent love based on our own subscriptions?

It seems to me that the most logical way to understand God's love would be to follow the words of Jesus since we have established that Jesus accomplished the mission of God's ultimate expression of love to man.

To explain this final part of the puzzle which will reveal what God's love consist of; I will use a few striking verses of scripture.

1) Let me start with 1 Peter 3: 17 -18 (TLB). What the lay person may not understand in reading about God's love is that the action of John 3: 16 happened primarily due to sin. Here is another philosophical juxtaposition; when the Humanist of LGBT speaks about God and love, does it make sense to assert God but not accept that He says that we are sinful? Again; it only points to our arrogance, but we can be sure that the words of 1 Peter confirm the fact that Jesus died primarily for our sins.

> *'Remember, if God wants you to suffer, it is better to suffer for doing good than for doing wrong!*
>
> *Christ also suffered.* ***He died once for the sins of all us guilty sinners*** *although he himself was innocent of any sin at any time, that he might bring us safely home to God. But though his body died, his spirit lived on,'*

2) Why did God have to express His love by Jesus being placed to death?

Sometimes getting the point across takes a different angle. The story of Adam tells us that all of mankind was doomed to a physical and spiritual death due to the original sin of Adam in Genesis. All of mankind has the scar of sin because of the one act by Adam. This will be expanded further in the chapter following but what we are to understand is that the Act of Adam was influenced by satan. The Bible speaks of satan from the very beginning but the protagonist place this figure in a greater role of fantasy than even being atheistic to God. Our sin is a result of disobeying God through listening to satan. Romans

3: 23 – 26 (TLB) expresses how God feels about disobedience and His solution for it.

> *'Yes, **all have sinned; all fall short of God's glorious ideal**; yet now God declares us "not guilty" of offending him **if** we trust in Jesus Christ, who in his kindness freely takes away our sins. **For God sent Christ Jesus to take the punishment for our sins** and **to end all God's anger against us**. He used **Christ's blood and our faith** as the means of saving us from his wrath. In this way he was being entirely fair, even though he did not punish those who sinned in former times. For he was looking forward to the time when Christ would come and take away those sins. And now in these days also he can receive sinners in this same way because Jesus took away their sins.'*

3) Is it enough then, to simply believe in Jesus so that we would be without sin? This is another problem that the protagonist has. They are willing to place their interpretation of faith before the testament of the Bible. Demonstratively the Bible has illustrated that believing is about faith and in the whole first chapter of Hebrews 1 we learn about the substance of faith. We are told as the chapter begins that faith is, *'the substance of things hoped for, the evidence of things not seen'*. But is faith enough? We are sure that Jesus said that we **must** believe. It is an imperative statement. Jesus does not say that we can rely on our good natures or believe in the Methodist or Baptist or Catholic church.

He is the only way offered to attain 'life' by believing in Him.

Here is the caveat; your belief cannot be a product of fraud. It is not a commitment that is sugar coated with who we know in society. It is a belief that comes with checks and balances. It is qualified by various verses from James 2:14-26 (TLB).

14 Dear brothers, what's the use of saying that you have faith and are Christians if you aren't proving it by helping others? Will that kind of faith save anyone?

*17 So you see, **it isn't enough just to have faith**. You **must** also **do** good to prove that you have it. **Faith that doesn't show itself by good works is no faith at all—it is dead and useless.***

*19 Are there still some among you who hold that "only believing" is enough? Believing in one God? <u>Well, remember that the</u> **<u>demons believe</u>** <u>this too—so strongly that they tremble in</u> <u>terror!</u> 20 **Fool! When will you ever learn that "believing" is useless without doing <u>what God wants you to</u>**? Faith that does not result in good deeds is not real faith.*

21 Don't you remember that even our father Abraham was declared good because of what he did when he was willing to obey God, even if it meant offering his son Isaac to die on the altar?

*22 You see, he was trusting God so much that he was willing to do whatever God told him to; **his faith was made complete by what he did**—by his actions, his good deeds.*

*24 So you see, **a man is saved by what he does, as well as by what he believes**.*

4) If works are simply needed to inherit this gift of life; then it stands to reason that any philanthropist will go to heaven who says that there is a God or says that there is someone by the name of Jesus who existed. That is perhaps possible but the Bible makes a rather external and visible effort to dispel the notion that God is easily tricked into a grant of salvation through false words and actions.

Galatians 6: 7 – 9 states:

> **Don't be misled**; *remember that you can't ignore God and get away with it:* **a** *man will always reap just the kind of crop he sows!* **If he sows to please his own wrong desires, he will be planting seeds of evil and he will surely reap a harvest of spiritual decay and death**; *but if he plants the good things of the Spirit, he will reap the everlasting life that the Holy Spirit gives him. And* <u>*let us not get tired of doing what is right*</u>, *for after a while we will reap a harvest of blessing if we don't get discouraged and give up.*

5) How do we know what works are good and which are 'bad'? This is the pinnacle question. What I have tried to illustrate is that the protagonist who at the very least creates a false paradigm of 'God' and may even reject adherence to the usual doctrine of evolution or atheism, are blinded by the fact that God has delineated between a true way to life and a false way. This standard creates a line between accepted behaviour and unaccepted.

Let me draw the reader's attention to a situation that Christ addressed in the book of Mark chapter 3. The setting of the story is akin to a modern (within context) evangelical revival where thousands have attended and the faith of many has been ignited through the miraculous work that they have seen. We get a picture of the evangelist Jesus who has worked tirelessly among a population that is 'hungry' for healing. We can't lose sight of the fact that this is not a time where the medical community thrived. With the story of Jesus healing the ten lepers[165]; His curing the woman with a blood disorder[166]; His restoration of sight to the blind man[167]; it becomes obvious that there is a great

---

[165] Luke 17:11-19
[166] Luke 8:43-48
[167] Mark 8:22-25

appreciation and need for a 'healing' ministry. The carnage of disease and life threatening ailments would have been wide spread among the people.

We can tell that Jesus has maintained an exhaustive schedule; for even His disciples in verse 21 are quoted as thinking that Jesus is 'out of His mind'. It shows the sheer exasperation they must have felt in the moment when understanding the amount of persons that where demanding the time of Jesus and the fact that He was accommodating so many.

What catches my attention is verse 22 where the 'scribes' are quoted as acknowledging that there has been miraculous works but they attribute the work done (by Jesus) to that of 'Beelzebub' (satan). In the Living Bible the scribes are identified as the '*Jewish teachers of religion*'. Of further note is the immediacy with which Jesus addresses this accusation in verse 23.

The urgency with which Jesus brings correction to the situation depicts the deep importance of the matter. These men were no ordinary men. They were men of understanding such that they taught 'religion' to the Jewish people. As I will demonstrate deeper into this writing; God has always taken the transference of His truth very seriously. We know that these men are aware of the complicity of words they use because the Bible indicates that Jesus specifically speaks to them using parables or proverbs that they 'understand'.

I posit that it is for a reason. That reason being that He is placing their backs against the wall to be held accountable to what they are saying. The implication of what they have said is a deep theological warning to the Christian community. Why; Because Jesus brings condemnation to their knowledge.

Jesus tells them that of all the sins that man can commit; all will be forgiven (if we seek forgiveness) except the sin of "blasphemy against the Holy Spirit".

Jesus tells them that it is irrevocable as a condemnation against their soul.

The question of 'Why' arises again.

a) The work that Jesus was doing in healing people was work that satan was attacking constantly in those days as there was a plethora of cult religions. The fact that the very teachers assigned to the transference of knowledge from the Torah and other books of the Old Testament and the fact that they were aware of the work of Jesus, yet would choose to speak against His work as 'demonic'; this contravened the ministry of truth that Jesus was establishing. So let's place it in perspective. What could be more injurious to an organization than the very people who are to serve, contravening the purpose and truth of that organization?

Think about priests today who say they serve God but are committing blasphemy as their actions speak against the ministry through acts of paedophilia, adultery, homosexuality, covetousness or even theft. How about pastors who speak against the work of God (the Bible) by declaring that homosexuality is accepted and God blesses this union. I posit that any Christian that reads the Bible and knows what it says but speaks against the word of God (not in ignorance) is blaspheming the Holy Spirit. This is why Jesus spoke to the scribes in proverbs that they knew; because they intentionally and knowingly spoke against truth and the '**true work**' of God.

b) In Matthew 7: 15 – 17 it is written; *"Beware of false prophets, who come to you in sheep's clothing, but inwardly they are ravenous wolves. You will know them by their fruits. Do men gather grapes from thornbushes or figs from thistles? Even so, every good tree bears good fruit, but a bad tree bears bad fruit."*

The implication of this verse with what Jesus said in Mark 3 exceptionally demonstrates Jesus conviction to justify 'good works and bad works'. What Jesus accomplishes in verse 22 to

27 of Mark is demarcation between the work of satan and God. In essence Jesus is saying that there can be no contradiction because satan would never circumvent his own nature of evil. Satan would never cast out a demon from a person. It is nonsensical and antithetical to his true intention.

The very same way that satan is against 'casting 'out his own nature would be analogous to Jesus being against any person declaring that the work of the Holy Spirit is akin to the devil; it is "blasphemy" and injurious to one who speaks it.

It is clear that Jesus indicates how we can determine what is good work and bad. The real problem is not in the fact that there is a standard per se; because there is wide acceptance of the general rational that things like murder are wrong. It is the fact that the protagonist attempts to create a standard that is outwardly rejected by scripture.

Consider the very blunt words by the prophet Isaiah in chapter 20: 18 - 20 and his conclusion in verse 24. He is quoting (prophesising) a promise by God towards the action of those who would mock God's way.

> *'Woe to those who drag their sins behind them like a bullock on a rope. **They even mock the Holy One of Israel** and dare the Lord to punish them. "Hurry up and punish us, O Lord," they say. "We want to see what you can do!" **They say that what is right is wrong and what is wrong is right**; that black is white and white is black; bitter is sweet and sweet is bitter.'*

This is the dilemma! The protagonist insists that they are correct in assessing a 'fair' standard to live by based on their love and a loving God. What the word is telling them is different from what they are saying.

1 Corinthians 6:9-11(NKJV) states:

> *'Do you not know that **the unrighteous will not inherit the kingdom of God? Do not be deceived**. Neither <u>fornicators</u>,*

> nor <u>idolaters</u>, nor <u>adulterers</u>, nor **homosexuals**, nor **sodomites**,
> nor <u>thieves</u>, nor <u>covetous</u>, nor <u>drunkards</u>, nor <u>revilers</u>, nor
> <u>extortioners</u> will inherit the kingdom of God. And such were
> some of you. But you were washed, but you were sanctified,
> but you were justified in the name of the Lord Jesus and by the
> Spirit of our God.'

A somewhat cheeky response that I have heard to this verse is that 'heaven will have nobody' based on that strict standard. I'm not prepared to debate the facility of being a 'born-again' Christian and the process of walking in faith but I will say that the Bible is not hypocritical. It does not separate homosexuals from adulterous or thieves from drunkards. What the Bible is showing is that God has a standard that adheres and does not change.

I agree with anyone that proclaims that God is love. I am sure that His love extends to all of humanity whether homosexual or heterosexual. The inevitable truth though, is that it is simply impossible to characterize one's existence merely on God's love (again within context). That would be like walking on the road with a car bumper in your hand but not heeding the warning that a 'Mack' truck is heading towards you; the bumper is simply not sufficient. There was no prevarication of words by Jesus which imputes to me that His words suggest a different 'truth'. When He says' in the Book of John 14: 6 "**I am** the way and **the truth** and **the life**. No one comes to the Father except through me"; I believe those words because they are a prophetic confirmation of the words Moses received from God in Exodus 3:14 which states that God is "**I AM**'. The book of Revelation is attributed as '<u>**The**</u>' revealing testimony of Jesus. John is given holy guidance to record the prophecy of Jesus. In Revelation 21:8 (NKJV) Jesus says'; "***But the cowardly, unbelieving, abominable, murderers, sexually immoral, sorcerers, idolaters, and all liars shall have their part in the lake which burns with fire and brimstone, which is the second death.***"

This final footnote before moving to the next chapter; it is obvious, I would assume, that the effort to establish the validity of truth to the reader is not an extraneous effort. It is a fundamental precept to life that man would know truth. The conclusion of believing in 'I AM' as established in the Bible is an unmovable 'post' and points to why logic and truth are so very important to be established. Knowing the establishment of truth grants to us the surety of knowing the truth of love and true love.

Christians must know what they believe. It must be unshakable. When in Isaiah 48:16 we read, "*I have not spoken in secret from the beginning; From the time that it was, there am I; and now the Lord God, and his Spirit, hath sent me*"; it establishes the prerequisite of individual faith and allows us to understand the logical truth of the Bible.

Christians can't believe in God 100% but not believe that the Bible is His 100% inerrant **word**. It would amount to an illogical syllogism and give credence to the half-truths of salvation by simply knowing a God of love. Imagine this contention as a type of inductive reason:

> ➤ GOD TELLS MAN IN THE BIBLE - '**I AM**' as proof of existence in Exodus 3:14 (Man believes 100%)
>
> JESUS (as the '**word**' defined in John 1:1) TELLS MAN IN THE BIBLE- John 14:6; "**I am** the way and **the truth** and the life. No one comes to the Father except through me." (Man believes 100%).
>
> Conclusion ∴ GOD TELLS MAN IN THE BIBLE – that '**All**' of His **WORD** (the Bible) has been inspired and given by Him (God the Father and God the Son) and sets the standard for how His Word is to be used in 2 Timothy 3:16; "**All** Scripture is breathed out by God and profitable for teaching, for reproof, for correction, and for training in righteousness".

How could we then believe 50% or 99% or 20%? The Bible is either 100% false or 100% true. Christianity cannot take a tangential route and declare any part of the 'Word' incorrect because it would vitiate each premise of infallibility and inerrancy resulting in a pernicious affect to the foundational conclusion of Christianity. There is no room for half-truths in Christianity. Wrong is wrong and right is right!

Understanding that God makes the ultimate statement in, 'I AM THE WAY, THE TRUTH' (John 14:6) is to understand the ultimate complexity of the statement.

An exacting view of the verse is to comprehend the value of the answer in relation to the question posed by Thomas who asked Jesus, '....how can we know the way?' Jesus is not offering a metaphor but literally saying that the way to God the Father is through 'the Word' which is Christ Jesus. In the book of John where '**the Truth**' becomes '**the Word**'; it shows an embodiment of the two as one and the same. The Truth is in the Word and the Word is the Truth. John 1:14 says'; *"And the Word became flesh and dwelt among us, and we beheld His glory, the glory as of the only begotten of the Father, full of grace and truth."*

CHAPTER 7

The True Essence of Marriage

"Both men and women today see marriage not as a way of creating character and community but as a way to reach personal life goals. They are looking for a marriage partner who will 'fulfil their emotional, sexual, and spiritual desires.' And that creates an extreme idealism that in turn leads to a deep pessimism that you will ever find the right person to marry."

— Timothy Keller, The Meaning of Marriage[168]

In Essence, people are creating an audition environment to seek the 'perfect' partner but the superficiality of such prospects where money, sex and even spiritual compatibility is involved, is that the suitor to love is blinded from what the true essence of marriage is.

Spiritual Marriage

There are many people including Christians who feel that marriage should be allowed between homosexuals (LGBT) because there is no harm in allowing individuals to come together in 'love'. I would be the

---

[168] The Meaning of Marriage by Timothy Keller; http://www.goodreads.com/work/quotes/16321346-the-meaning-of-marriage

first to admit that I was not sure why civil unions should not be allowed. I thought that civil marriage was just a simple ceremony, which allowed or gave rights to a **legal union** between a man and woman. However, as I started to understand marriage in relationship to the Bible; I realized that God attributed a very serious burden upon marriage because it was and is established as a fundamental spiritual institution within the **legal testament** of the bible.

I discovered that God went through absolutely extraordinary measures to protect the institution. Christians who surrender this institution to the justification of gay rights advocates are committing a travesty against a holy legal institution that was not established by legal decree of man but was created by the divine decree of God the Father. For this reason, I am attempting to bring spiritual clarity to their knowledge of marriage and expose the satanic scheme which seeks to weaken the true intention and purpose of it.

This language is not meant to offend but I do intend to pull the veil of factual and spiritual ignorance away so that an honest understanding can emerge.

Although I learned that the institution of marriage was more complex than I imagined, the foundation of it is not convoluted and is in fact very logical. As said; I found that God took great steps to set up and protect the institution, so it was that very procedure and action by God that alerted me to how serious marriage is. He built it on precedents which were literally the proverbial 'rock' as the foundation[169].

Walking through the maze of information made me apprehensive at times because there was clearly a chance that I would lose myself in the myriad of evidence and research but as I ventured on through text I was able to discern a spiritual conundrum which paved the way for where I knew I should start my reasoning.

I was reading through the books of first and second Kings along with Malachi and it became clear that God was not pleased with the nation of Israel; even more so, God was very disappointed with His

---

[169] Ephesians 2: 20 - 21

servants, the priest. I viewed this as important because all the profound implications are relevant to conditions predominant in today's church where marriage is concerned. I learned that priest and prophets in the Bible maintained a pivotal role in the establishment of spiritual marriage. There is no better way to place this quandary into perspective than to quote from 2 Kings 17: 13 – 20 (NIV). It is a bit lengthy but it thoroughly captures the scope of God's position and prepares the start point towards understanding spiritual marriage and its relevance to present society. Here's what is written:

> *The Lord warned Israel and Judah through all his prophets and seers: "Turn from your evil ways. Observe my commands and decrees, in accordance with the entire Law that I commanded your ancestors to obey and that **I delivered to you through my servants the prophets."***
>
> *But they would not listen and were as stiff-necked as their ancestors, who did not trust in the Lord their God. **They rejected his decrees and the covenant** he had made with their ancestors and **the statutes he had warned them to keep.** They followed worthless idols and themselves became worthless. They imitated the nations around them although the Lord had ordered them, "**Do not do as they do."***
>
> *They forsook all the commands of the Lord their God and made for themselves two idols cast in the shape of calves, and an Asherah pole. They bowed down to all the starry hosts, and **they worshiped Baal.** They sacrificed their sons and daughters in the fire. **They practiced divination** and sought omens and **sold themselves to do evil** in the eyes of the Lord, arousing his anger.*
>
> ***So the Lord was very angry with Israel and removed them from his presence.** Only the tribe of Judah was left, and **even Judah did not keep the commands of the Lord their God.** They followed the practices Israel*

135

> *had introduced. **Therefore the Lord rejected all the
> people of Israel**; he afflicted them and gave them into the
> hands of plunderers, until he thrust them from his presence.*

The transition of God's attitude towards this situation is then captured in the last book of the Old Testament; Malachi. We find that **the priest** are being reminded and commanded to follow and obey the **Levite Covenant,**[170] which they are partnered to. God has decided to curse the ecclesiastical power intrusted to them.

What stands out is that their reprimand is specific to their neglect of duty. That is a startling revelation towards the beginning of my understanding of spiritual marriage because God justified His punishment of the tribes of Judah and Israel through the negligence of duty placed onto the priest.

Picture this scenario; parents leave home to attend a function and relay exact instructions to the oldest child to watch over the house of siblings. The oldest child is charged with the responsibility of everything which transpires thereafter until the parents return. If the younger siblings destroy furniture or even burn down the house; the oldest child charged with responsibility gets the blame. That is exactly what is happening in the book of Malachi. God held the Levite priest to a standard because their responsibility was to carry out the edict of the covenant. Whiles God was 'away' from the physical and spiritual realm of man (due to the separation from Adam); the priests were charged with keeping law[171] and order; being the messengers[172] and the message keepers. When Judah profaned the 'holy institution[173]', which God loves, the Levite priest received the rebuke and the whole nation suffered.

I will tie together the intriguing relationship between God and spiritual marriage later, but first a complete composite analysis and understanding of the factors which build spiritual marriage must be

---

[170] Malachi 2: 4
[171] Malachi 2:7- 8
[172] Malachi 2; 7-8
[173] Malachi 2:11

considered so that the final conclusion will reflect the sheer importance of the institution of spiritual marriage. Discernment must first be brought to the contents of Malachi 2 so that there is understanding to, **the introduction of marriage under a covenant; the covenant; the Levite Covenant of Peace; Levite covenant of Priesthood; Purpose of the New Covenant; The Mystery and the 'Mysteries' revealed.**

1.   Introduction of marriage under covenant

Malachi 2 is the only place in the Bible where a covenant is directly implied in relation to the marriage of a man and woman but also intertwined with the church. The real value of the covenant is the imposition or charge which surrounds it and the results which flow from such an obligation.

It states in Malachi 2: 13 -14 (NIV): *Another thing you do: You flood the Lord's altar with tears. You weep and wail because he no longer looks with favor on your offerings or accepts them with pleasure from your hands. You ask, "Why?" It is because the Lord is the witness between you and the wife of your youth. You have been unfaithful to her, though she is your partner, **the wife of your marriage covenant.***

The mere fact that there is an association of the word marriage with the word covenant means that we should examine and understand the significance of that affiliation.

We find in the book of Malachi 2, first mention of the word 'covenant' in verse 5 which says', ' *My covenant was with him of life and peace; and I gave them to him for the fear wherewith he feared me, and was afraid before my name'.* What I understood and derived from the introduction of the word in the first five verses is the **charge of responsibility** which God places on the priest from verse 1 on to verse 5. This charge (I will show) is essential to God's marital relationship to man. The charge was in continuation and fulfilment of what God had already placed into motion over 900 years[174] prior (Numbers to

---

[174] http://bibletimeline.info/

Malachi). We find in the book of Numbers that God has issued a devastating edict to the priest that their lack of responsibility to carry out their charge, has resulted in severe consequences. That charge was set as a covenant beginning in the book of Numbers 25:12 where we find God conveying to 'Phinehas son of Eleazar, the son of Aaron, the priest', a **covenant of peace** and a **covenant of priesthood.** This covenant also called the **Levitical covenant** was split into two parts but both had unconditional promises attached. The covenant of peace in Ezekiel 37:26 is called 'an everlasting covenant' and the covenant of priesthood is termed 'a lasting ordinance' in Exodus 27:21.

What we will achieve by examining the covenant, (the covenant of peace and the covenant of priesthood) is a thesis on how God was advancing a legal precept to protect the spiritual institution of marriage. Just as we will come upon knowledge which imputes that priest had responsibility for the actions of Judah, we will learn that the role of the High priest is to also protect the institution of marriage.

It will be made clear that marriage within the context of the Bible breaches the barriers of traditional thought and the definitions will maintain spiritual cohesiveness under a covenant which sets 'irrevocable' legal standards and guidelines.

2. <u>The covenant</u>

The word covenant is more commonly associated with land. It is a legal instrument, which allows one party (the covenantee) to benefit from a binding obligation held against the covenantor who is normally the dominant owner[175]. One of the factors prevalent in land covenants is that the obligation can be viewed as negative to the covenantor.

From a Biblical perspective, that definition implies varying degrees of truth. Of the major covenants found in the Old Testament, (the covenant with Noah; the Abrahamic covenant; Mosaic covenant and the Levite covenant) only the Mosaic covenant is a conditional contract

---

[175] Elements of Land Law, Freehold covenants, covenants at law 13.26, pg. 1352

which does not 'bind' absolutely (in a negative legal sense) God the owner to His obligations.

When examined as a whole in the Old Testament, covenants between God and man mostly appear as monopleuric[176] unilateral acts (agreements) of God where the **terms are set and initiated** by God. Some can be considered bilateral in the sense that there is a mutual relationship between God and man; this means that man can agree by obeying or reject in revolt. The intrinsic worth of God's covenants with man is that the obligation from God is always perpetual because fulfilment of the obligation runs perpendicular to man's existence, performance and God's purpose. The covenant stays in existence based always on God's set terms.

a. <u>**The general purpose of the covenant**</u> –I believe that God had a divine blue-print plan which was executed through the provision of covenants. The groundwork of legality and strict adherence to the statues justified the plan, which under the law of the Old Testament placed God in a punitive position. The covenant was also a means to an end, to achieving God's legal purpose for marriage. Here are parts of God's blue-print plan utilized under covenants.

1) God's Rule of Law

Perhaps the major reason that God implemented the legal system of covenants was to enforce His very own rule of law.

I am not sure if there is any other legal concept that sets up the proper dissemination of established rules and guidelines such as the theory, 'Rule of Law'. When applied properly, the theory gives the framework under which all governments, leaders and people are

---

[176] THE CONCEPTS OF CONDITIONALITY AND APOSTASY IN RELATION TO THE COVENANT - Dennis A. Bratcher; 4th paragraph. http://www.spindleworks.com/library/bratcher/Chapter_Two.htm#1

protected by recognised law. It reminds them of their responsibility to adhering to written law and provides a standard that does not allow persons or institutions to operate above or outside the law.

The applications of God's covenants with humankind are preambles, which guide the legal relationship between both God and man. Any contravention of the rules is unallowable due to the strict adherence of operating under the rule of law.

Whiles it is important to place this point on the 'rule of law' at the beginning of this conversation on covenantal purpose, to inundate the thought process; the idea will be fundamentally expanded under explanations on the covenant of peace. It is also worthy to note that if the premise, of God being restricted under His own established 'rules', is proven true; it would indicate how God uses the constitution of law in-synch and analogous to His nature of order. The explanations under the covenant of peace will also draw the readers to the facts and reasons why God hates divorce and revers marriage. It will become obvious that He expects <u>every</u> party to the contract to fulfil their legal obligations by adherence to the rules.

2)   Ministry of Death

A very difficult concept for men in general to understand is God's articulation that the law under covenant is akin to a ministry of death. The difficulty to fully comprehend this concept is manifest by the Christian and Jewish community; who even after receiving and being aware of grace through Jesus Christ, continue to misinterpret and live by the work of the law.

I believe that the ministry of death is akin to spiritual adultery which removes man (man removes himself by his own actions) 'legally' from the committed relationship with God.

When the Israelites were delivered from the repression of Pharaoh and travelled into the desert, God made every effort to give the Israelites **fulfilment of His sustaining grace**. What was most evident was God's presence with them as an assurance that they were being led by the God of their forefathers. Reading through the great exodus gives an inescapable image of God virtually standing in front of the Israelites and leading them under a theocracy.

Why was God so present under the exodus from Egypt?

This scene definitely has to be set for the full appreciation of the historical social context. In Genesis 15:13 God tells Abram that his descendants will be in captivity for four hundred years. As we move into the story of Moses in Exodus 12:40–51, the children of Israel have been delivered from that captivity. Great contextual sensitivity must be dispersed in understanding the social environment of this deliverance from captivity which further justified the necessity for a covenant.

   i.   After Moses escaped from Egypt as the former heir to the throne and lived over a passage of time in a wilderness type existence; he is found tending sheep for his father-in-law deep in the desert.

God appears to Moses and immediately identifies Himself through a very specific legal reference; He says', *"I am the God of your father, the God of Abraham, the God of Isaac and the God of Jacob"*. Naturally we would think that a voice in the desert emanating from a burning bush would need no identification as God, but it is insight to the spiritual reality of where the Israelites are. Moses grew up in a culture which thought him to worship pagan gods from the Egyptian culture. Besides the fact that Moses has a sense of morality, as exhibited in his act to save an Israeli slave from the whip of an Egyptian lord, there is no indication that Moses has any 'practiced' affinity towards Judaism. Because Abraham and his lineage have such a tangible story within the Jewish community, his name is highly revered. When God introduces Himself to Moses by referencing Abraham, it establishes a repoire of respect and acknowledgement.

ii. When Moses has accepted that he is in fact speaking with 'The God' of his forefathers he still wallows in self-doubt concerning his task because he also understands where the people are spiritually. Moses is fully aware that convincing the tribes of Israel to follow him will be a gargantuan task to accomplish. He asked of God a rather logical question from a man who is pessimistically influenced. In Exodus 3: 13 – 15 (NIV) the conversation is recorded as follows:

> *"Suppose I go to the Israelites and say to them, 'The God of your fathers has sent me to you,' and they ask me, 'What is his name?' Then what shall I tell them?" God said to Moses, "**I am who I am**. This is what you are to say to the Israelites: 'I am has sent me to you.'" God also said to Moses, "Say to the Israelites, '**The Lord, the God of your fathers—the God of Abraham, the God of Isaac and the God of Jacob**—has sent me to you.*

God's answer to Moses can be likened to providing a starving man with a full meal. The phrase in Hebrew is a derivative of the letters 'YHVH' which we pronounce Yahweh on a postmodern interpretation[177]. In revealing this name to Moses, God is basically giving a personal assurance to His people through Moses that He is the transcending God of all. He is the God who will be with them throughout history as their foundation and source[178].

That revelation to Moses along with the same heritage association to Abraham further indicates to the people that God is their past source. He is also confirming His covenant with Abraham.

iii. Moving through the passages of Exodus allows for greater confidence to the explanation of God creating a covenant

---

[177] http://www.agapebiblestudy.com/documents/the%20many%20names%20of%20god.htm

[178] http://www.hebrew4christians.com/Names_of_G-d/YHVH/yhvh.html

through Moses. In Exodus 4 God indicates to Moses that the people, as well as Moses, will know that He is God through the 'signs[179]' and guidance.

The infinite wisdom of God was present in these series of conversations between Moses, Aaron and the people of Israel. It seems certain that God was omni-aware of the spiritual plight of the Israelites. It almost seems as if God takes up the idiom, 'fight fire with fire' as a relative antidote to combat the level of disbelief and demi-god indoctrination among the Israelites. The Israeli people have been so steeped in a culture of Henotheism worship in Egypt that it becomes obvious that they foster scepticism about who is the 'real' God. The Egyptian culture was known to have embrace polytheism (can be seen as interchangeable with henotheism) including the four sons of Horus[180](Isis, Nephthys. Neith, Serket).

The manifest result of the influence is magnified in several accounts but in Exodus 32 where God is speaking with Moses; He instructs Moses to return to the people because they had quickly turned to their old ways and made an idol to worship. What gives us confirmation of the spiritual state of the people is the conversation between Aaron and Moses in verses 21 to 22 where Moses in exasperation inquiries of Aaron why he would allow the people to commit the sin of idol worshiping. Aaron answers; "Do not be angry, my lord. **You know how prone these people are to evil**".

To answer the question; **The reason that God was so prominent during the exodus from Egypt is because the people were exceptionally wayward**. God knew that the people had a very corrupt nature. They were called a 'stiff-necked[181]' people. In versus 7 to 8 He informs Moses of their corrupt nature and bemoans the fact that even

---

[179] Exodus 3: 12 & 4:30
[180] Aufderheide, Arthur C. (2003). *The Scientific Study of Mummies*. Cambridge: Cambridge University Press via http://en.wikipedia.org/wiki/Four_sons_of_Horus
[181] Exodus 32: 9

with His divine presence; the people have accorded their freedom from slavery to the gods of their making.

I posit that for this very reason, the law (**the ministry of death**) which was incapable of being fulfilled due to the rigors of it, was placed under covenant to validate God's justice. In other words; God gave the people laws which governed them based on their own proclivities instead of the Grace of God himself. This is why in 2 Corinthians 3:7-9 (NIV) it states; '*Now if **the ministry that brought death**, which was engraved in letters on stone, came with glory, so that the Israelites could not look steadily at the face of Moses because of its glory transitory though it was, will not the **ministry of the Spirit be even more glorious**? If the ministry that brought condemnation was glorious, how much more glorious is the ministry that brings righteousness*'.

The people chose the law and condemned themselves as opposed to choosing the faithful guidance of God's presence. **This was a precedent to show man that in all his avails, he could never accomplish justice or righteousness by himself and without the presence of God's grace in 'his' life.**

We find further reasoning in Deuteronomy 31 why God predicts the death of Israel under their covenant which they have failed to follow. It states in verses 16 through 18 (NIV); '***They <u>will</u> forsake me and break the covenant*** *I made with them. And in that day I will become angry with them and forsake them; I will hide my face from them, and they will be destroyed. Many disasters and calamities will come on them, and in that day they will ask, 'Have not these disasters come on us because our God is not with us?' And I will certainly hide my face in that day because of all their wickedness in turning to other gods*'.

God is justified through the covenant in turning His face from them because <u>they have turned to other gods</u>. This is the very same action which they committed preceding Moses' return to them with the covenant and the laws governing the covenant. As I will state again later; we can't lose sight of the fact that from the time of Adam to the time of Moses the people have not been under any written standard.

Realigning them to a 'GOD' standard would prove to be a task only accomplishable by a 'supreme' intervention.

3) A legal conduit

It will be demonstrated further on that God and Adam had a type of marriage relationship; but, built on that premise is the assertion that God needed a legal conduit to advance his relationship with man.

After the fall of man, it can be said that the 'marriage software' of God was no-longer compatible with the marriage hardware of man. God's nature was completely 'out-of-sync' with man. God needed a way to reconnect to man. He had to bring order to the disorder of Adams fall so that His purpose would be fulfilled.

Any behavioural apologist should be able to demonstrate that humankind is generally classified according to The Myers-Briggs Type Indicator[182], which indicates our innate quality of psychological norms. God, as the Creator, has systematically designed man with recognizable personality traits. If this premise holds true, God as the progenitor of all personalities has the unique quality of being **systematic and orderly**. It is easily demonstrated in His adherence to time on Earth. The entire Milky Way system runs in a precisely time oriented and systematic fashion.

The covenant is in fact a legal conduit, which facilitates God's orderly nature. It has the parameters of a contract that assigns a legal duty on the parties involved to fulfil their obligations.

The strategy to consistently demonstrate the orderly nature of God is important because it shows that His plans are not sporadic and unpredictable but intelligently designed and purposeful.

In Exodus 9:16 (AMP) God tells Moses, *'But for this very purpose have I let you live, that I might show you My power, and that My name may be declared throughout all the earth.'* We see from the verse above

---

[182] The Myers & Briggs Foundation; Online, http://www.myersbriggs.org/my-mbti-personality-type/mbti-basics/

that God brings awareness to His orderly plans, which are cogently set through-out the Bible. So extensive are His plans that He has even measured considerations for the conclusion of the wicked according to Proverbs 16:4; but further in Isaiah 14: 24 (AMP) God says', *"The Lord of hosts has sworn, saying, Surely, as I have thought and planned, so shall it come to pass, and as I have purposed, so shall it stand"*.

Having established this premise, it can be shown that God laid a very meticulous plan for establishing covenants. He used it as an orderly and legal way to justify His actions.

In other words; God established the legal framework and **orderly conditions** to allow His work to be carried out under strict principles of law.

The covenant was like a legal software that allowed God to maintain order and harmony with man.

4)   God's lawyer or Legal intercessor

God's conceptualization and implementation of the covenant with man (Noah) set up a consistency of precedent which was followed in all subsequent covenants.

Just as that precedent was established, God orderly customized a blue-print plan for a facilitator or legal counsel who would receive instructions. God needed to facilitate instructions through specific men who were His covenantors or beneficiaries.

The master software facilitator to the hardware of man is an **intercessor**. The ultimate intercessory relationship, which is moulded in the New testament under the New Covenant, is through Christ Jesus. This can be determine from Ephesians 4: 11 – 13 (NIV); '*So Christ himself gave the apostles, the prophets, the evangelists, the pastors and teachers, to equip his people for works of service, so that the body of Christ may be built up until we all reach unity in the faith and in the knowledge of the Son of God and become mature, attaining to the whole measure of the fullness of Christ*'.

The blueprint intercessor or master precedent was established by God through his relationship with Adam.

Adam was the first spiritual and literal marriage, as well as the first spiritual and literal divorce. As a precedent, Adam had all the essential elements which justify God's use of a covenant.

Intuitively following the story of the 'creation', we know that Adam was created in the image of God[183], so we can safely assume that Adam knew no sin. His righteousness was engrained in the very fact that he was the master creation before sin filtered in.

In Genesis 2: 9 we are made aware that there are two trees in the Garden of Eden; one is the tree of life and the other is the tree of the knowledge of good and evil. When Adam made consideration to eat, and ate of the tree of knowledge, it was a spiritual death. He committed sin and a whole new spiritual dispensation was created.

God was no-longer able to simply walk in the garden and communicate with man. This was a physical and spiritual divorce for God because He could not be in the presence of sin. When Adam sinned, he saw his nakedness which was actually the era of his way. He actually felt ashamed to be in the presence of perfection (God) because he (Adam) had now become imperfect[184].

Adam was removed from the garden and sin was born into the world through him as a curse[185].

God now needed a precedent intercessor to flourish His master plan which was to re-enter into full communication with man. He needed an intercessor to act as an intermediary that embodied all the traits necessary for God to continue communicating to His people. The intercessor had to have the characteristics of a person willing to:

> ➤ Risk and sacrifice; boldly defend; volunteer; seek mercy; have humility; be a prophet; serve; pray; lead and receive favour.

---

[183] Genesis 1: 26
[184] Genesis 3:10 -11
[185] Genesis 3: 17 - 19

From the onset, many people will contend that Adam did not exhibit these qualities but I theorize differently. There is a conceptual fact that needs to be understood about existence before Adam.

If we say that God is a God of purpose, then Adam could not have been a random thought. God did not create Adam as an afterthought or random differential among living species; that is the evolution model not the creation model. In 2 Tim 1:9 (KJV) it reads, *'Who hath saved us, and called us with an holy calling, not according to our works, but according to his own purpose and grace, which was given us in Christ Jesus **before the world began**,'*. It shows us that the Apostle Paul was spiritually aware in revelation that God had purposed saving man through the Grace of Jesus Christ before the world was even created. He makes a powerful statement of this fact in Ephesians 1: 4 – 5 (NKJV) by saying, *'just as **He chose us in Him before the foundation of the world**, that we should be holy and without blame before Him in love, having predestined us to adoption as sons by Jesus Christ to Himself, according to the good pleasure of His will'*.

Paul's spiritual intuitiveness was a part of the unveiling of '**the great mystery**[186]'which will be addressed further on.

> ➢ This may be hard to understand but it can be said that the fall of Adam was a fulfilment of a part of his purpose. God already knew that satan had a plan. I posit that God was always ahead of any plan by satan. He was completely aware that satan was about to change the dynamics of all His creation.

The Hebrew name satan is not surprisingly, 'adversary[187]'. It was brought to my attention[188] that this progresses the purpose of satan in only one direction; to be against every purpose of God. Once I understood the contentious nature of the enemy to God; I realized

---

[186] Ephesians 3: 1 -7

[187] http://www.biblestudytools.com/dictionary/satan/

[188] Words derived from or paraphrased from sermon by Dr. Myles Munroe on 25/08/13

that the Angel Lucifer had already fallen when he spoke to Eve in the Garden. God's plans predestined any plan of satan. This we know because two great prophets of God spoke (I only choose to highlight these two but there are further revelations about satan throughout scripture) about satan in context that defines God's intention for satan and God's awareness of satan's plans. In Isaiah 14 there is a prophetic revelation of how satan fell from Heaven because God knew what was in his heart/mind[189] and God spoke of his ultimate demise. Daniel 4: 31 -34 is confirmation of God's divine purpose found in Isaiah 14: 24 – 27 (NIV). God has purposed that there shall be an everlasting dominion. Once God spoke His purpose into existence it became an immutable fact. For this reason, Isaiah poses this rhetorical question at verse 27; *'For the LORD Almighty has purposed, and who can thwart him? His hand is stretched out, and who can turn it back?'*

> ➢ Relying on a logical syllogism; If Adam is the original specie of man, he would have to be the master contributor for the gene pool and the personality banks. It follows logically that every trait of man flowed from Adam (as engrained from God). It also would hold as logical, that if God is the creator; Adam being made in the image of God means that Adam had the blue-print of God's DNA in him upon creation. He had intrinsic values instilled. Adam had to feel and know everything that man experiences today. My leap of reasoning is that Adam had to have been a genius based on his special endowment.

Adam knew risk and sacrifice exhibited in the way that he took the risk to eat of the tree of knowledge which resulted in sacrificing his relationship with God. From that point on, Adam knew the value of having knowledge towards what should and should not be sacrificed. Adam boldly defended himself in the face of God when asked by God

---

[189] Isaiah 14: 13

how he was aware of being naked in Genesis 3: 11. Adam told God that it was the woman whom God had given to him; she was at the heart of his disobedience. This is certainly not the type of spiritual boldness displayed by Abraham who was willing to suffer God's wrath by boldly negotiating with Him in Genesis 18:22; but again and within context, it is all a learning curve for the first man. Genesis 2: 19-20 states that God brought the animals to Adam 'to see', (notice that God did not demand Adam), what he would call them. Adam volunteered names to every animal.

I can continue with this analysis of the attributes an intercessor must have but I don't want to stray much further from or convolute the importance of having a **precedent intercessor**.

If Adam is the precedent or blue-print plan for an intercessor then all subsequent intercessors will follow the ordered plan of God. This plan is how we cross-section into the covenant of priesthood

Whiles I am sure that parts of this will be difficult to follow for non-believers, the premises are in line with the logical proposition that if Christians follow and believe in an omnipotent God, then it becomes rational that God can prosper any plan through His divine providence. The word says', *And he is the radiance of his glory and the* **exact representation of his nature**, *and* **upholds all things by the word** *of his power. When he had made purification of sins, he sat down at the right hand of the Majesty on high* (Hebrews 1:3 NASB). Jesus confirms this truth in Matthew 19:26 (NRS) 'But Jesus looked at them and said, *"For mortals it is impossible, but for God* **all things are possible**".

The conclusion is that God used the covenant as a tool through which He accomplished the goals of establishing, the rule of law, the ministry of death, a legal conduit and a legal intercessor or counsel. Each one of these tools is either analogous or metaphorically important to spiritual marriage as will be demonstrated.

3. Why a Covenant of Peace

Now that we understand the construction of what a covenant is, we can facilitate the specifics of why God conveyed a covenant over the Levitacal priesthood. One part of the covenant is designated as a Covenant of Peace. God is so very ordered in His nature that He purposes exact reasons, like by-laws, into the need for the establishment of the Levitical Covenant.

We find the word 'peace' used in Numbers as part of the covenant conveyance, which is the same word used in Malachi 2:5. The covenant of peace must be placed into perspective. At the beginning of the chapter (Numbers) we recognise that the men of Israel have progressed into sexual immorality with the Moabite women who lived in Shittim.

It's obvious, if we follow stories from Noah to Moses, that cross cultural problems are afflicting the Israelite. This has become a recurring and spiritually plaguing problem which can also be attributed to the Israelites spending 400 years in service to the Egyptians. Notice should be born to the fact that **Malachi 2: 11-12 references this sexual immorality as an abomination committed <u>against God's Holy institution</u>**. The reason it is an abomination for God is that it is diametrical to His nature.

a) God's Nature

As previously implied, God's nature creates the need for a covenant. During the period of historical cultural development from Noah to Moses in the Old Testament, one thing becomes very evident; the Israelites are very obstinate if not rebellious as a people. God actually tells Moses this much in Exodus 32:9 where he calls them 'stiff-necked' people. This term is referenced towards the Israelites on 20 other occasions.

Throughout the early cultural development in Genesis, God has continuously shown the people that He cannot relate to man whiles he is steeped in wickedness; it is an aversion to his very nature.

In simply reading the Genesis account of history before the flood and after the flood; one forms a picture that man has become rather depraved in his thinking. God had to provide a resolve to this dilemma. In the Garden of Eden, we see that God had such an intimate friendship with the first man that he took strolls in the garden to speak with him. I posit that after Adam sinned God desired to re-establish a personal relationship with man but man's sin nature was abhorrent to God. This is another fundamental point in understanding the genesis of covenants. God's very nature placed man in jeopardy when in His presence. Consider Exodus 19 (WEB) where God issues His conditional covenant whiles speaking with his leader Moses. He tells him in verse 5 through 6 that he is to tell the people (in a messenger position) of Israel *'Now therefore, if you will obey my voice and keep my covenant, you shall be my own possession among all peoples; for all the earth is mine, and you shall be to me a kingdom of priests and a holy nation'.*

After Moses has obeyed God's instructions as a messenger between God and His people; a very curious thing happens. It is as if God is tired of using an intermediary. He is desirous of speaking directly to the people to lay yet another spiritual marker of His omnipotence. There is a problem here; God cannot simply be in the domain of His people without them being consecrated because of His holy nature. He needs to have the people rededicate themselves. The words consecrate or sanctify means to make holy by separation from the world which garners or results in a relationship with/to God. In verse 14 to 15 (Exodus 19 NIV) it says, *"After Moses had gone down the mountain to the people, he consecrated them, and they washed their clothes. Then he said to the people, "Prepare yourselves for the third day. Abstain from sexual relations."* All indications are that the people had to even abstain from sex because it made them unclean; and they had to bath themselves both physically and spiritually.

The picture that needs to be painted here is how drastically opposed to sin God's nature is. When He simply sat in observation of man from heaven[190] and observed what man was doing on earth; he was prepared

---

[190] Genesis 6

to 'wipe' man from the face of the Earth. It's important to understand this position because we see that God's nature contrasted to man's sin nature is like oil and water; they simply don't mix. More perilous for man in the Old Testament is that God continuously considers destroying man as He observes or comes into contact with man's sin nature.

I posit that full comprehension of God's nature demonstrates why God had to utilize legal covenants in general and a covenant of peace; he had to guarantee that no matter how repulsed He became by us, he would not destroy us. If my assertion is incorrect, I doubt that the word 'life' would have been used in correlation to the word peace in Malachi 2:5 (NKJV). It states; "My covenant was with him, *one* of **life** and **peace**..." That connection is placed into contextual value to the Levitical covenant in Numbers 25:11 where God has withheld His anger (which would have resulted in the destruction of Israel), simply due to the faithful and 'jealous' actions of Phinehas. He secured a reprieve of God's wrath due to his own anger against those who would worship other gods. The action of Phinehas brings '**life**' to Israel; to have life was to have peace. God protected the life of Israel from His wrath by a grant or covenant of peace.

In other words; God set a standard of commitment for Himself. An example of this is with Noah; God set a restrictive standard on Himself not to ever flood the Earth again. To add a flare of human understanding to this, I would say that in God's thought process; He wanted to create a 'rule of law' to govern His own instincts.

Let's look further at God's nature.

In Genesis 1: 27 God Himself says that He has created man in His image. If this is the case; why would He appear to man as he did in Exodus 19: 18? The verse says' that when Moses led the people out to the mountain, '*Mount Sinai* [it] *was covered with smoke because the Lord descended on it in fire*'. I recognize that God wanted to show the Israelites His power to continually enforce His divinity and to encourage them not to sin[191] but there is also a key understatement here. As we read on through verse 22 (NIV) God continuously enforces a prime directive to Moses. He says', *"Go down and warn the people so they do not force their way through to see the Lord and many of them perish. Even the priests, who approach the Lord, must consecrate themselves, or the Lord will break out against them."*

This is the second time that God has reminded Moses to keep the people at bay. Even after the Israelites have consecrated themselves, they can't approach beyond the barriers that Moses has set up. Moses tells God, in reply and almost in a tone which implies that he emphatically understands the directions; *"The people cannot come up Mount Sinai, because you yourself warned us, 'Put limits around the mountain and set it apart as holy."*

To be honest; if I were Moses I would have been paranoid about the situation because even after telling God this, He issues yet the same instruction. The only variance this time is that God has invited the other High Priest of Israel who will lead the people, Aaron, to join Moses on the Mountain. Not even the other priest can approach the mountain.

If I could inject a bit of linguistical-swagger, I would say that the words used in Exodus, *'or the Lord will break out against them'*, is equivalent to a person telling another that they will get a 'beat down'.

Why would God resort to such harsh language? I posit that it is proof of His divine and Holy nature against sin. God has no choice but to destroy sin when it is in His presence without fettered instructions and God's direct authority. The closest that anyone has come to being in God's presence is Moses and even in those instances we see that God places a barrier. In Exodus 3: 4-6 (NKJV) when Moses first comes in contact with God, it is written;

So when the Lord saw that he turned aside to look, God called to him from the midst of the bush and said, "Moses, Moses!" And he said, "Here I am." Then He said, "Do not draw near this place. Take your sandals off your feet, for the place where you stand is holy ground." Moreover He said, "I am the God of your father; the God of Abraham, the God of Isaac, and the God of Jacob." And Moses hid his face, for he was afraid to look upon God.

---

[191] Exodus 20: 20

It is not enough that Moses is the chosen leader and has a righteous demeanour. He still is unable to be completely in God's presence and observe God's true spirit body.

In Exodus 33:18–20, Moses has specifically ask God to see His Glory, and God replies; **"You cannot see My face; for no man shall see Me, and live"**.

I believe there is somewhat of a deeper meaning here also. We have seen that God is very order driven. In Genesis 3: 21 God makes 'tunics of skin' and cloth Adam and Eve. I personally believe that the spiritual symbolism of this moment is that when Adam was in his perfect spiritual body, he was allowed to walk with God. When God placed the tunic of skin on Adam he immediately removed him from the garden. I believe that skin is symbolic to God as spiritual death. Notice that Moses was wearing sandals which he had to remove. The sandals are more than likely made of dead flesh. This I believe is why Romans 3:19-20 says', *'Now we know that whatever things the law says, it says to them who are under the law: that every mouth may be stopped, and that all the world may be liable to punishment before God. Wherefore, by works of law there shall* **no flesh be justified** *in his sight; because through law is the knowledge of sin'.* Flesh had to be living, consecrated and justified (righteous) as acknowledged by God to approach His presence.

Follow through to chapter 32 of Exodus and we find the most telling characteristic of how God's nature reacts to sin.

In Exodus 20: 23 God has given explicit instructions to Israel which says', *'Ye shall not make with me gods of silver, neither shall ye make unto you gods of gold.'* A short time later in chapter 32 Moses is before God receiving full instructions on setting up the Holy Tabernacle along with all the laws. Whiles he is in communion with God the people fear that he has gone lost to them and set out to create another god that they can follow[192].

---

[192] Exodus 32: 1

Here I would hope that the religious zealots would forgive me for injecting a light-hearted moment because the real truth is that this is a very serious incident where the people so quickly turn away from God. Imagine a fight between parents of a child that has gone wayward and committed an act which reflects poorly on the reputation of the parents. We can just imagine the father disowning the child and placing the burden of the child onto the mother. We have heard this joke before; when a father says', 'that's your child; not mine!'

Here is the conversation between Moses and God. It is a pejorative reaction by God when He indicates to Moses that something is inappropriate in the camp. He says'; *"Go, get down! For **your** people whom **you brought** out of the land of Egypt have corrupted themselves. [8] They have turned aside quickly out of the way which I commanded them. They have made themselves a molded calf, and worshiped it and sacrificed to it, and said, 'This is your god, O Israel, that brought you out of the land of Egypt!'"* God goes on to say to Moses, *"I have seen this people, and indeed it is a **stiffnecked** people! [10] Now therefore, let Me alone, that My **wrath may burn hot against them** and I may consume them. And I will make of you a great nation."* One can hear the hurt, anger, betrayal and threat of retribution against sin that God feels; so much so, that he temporarily disowns the people and is ready to destroy them. He goes so far as to indicate that He is prepared to create a new race through Moses [Very important to note Isaiah 54 here because we know that God is accountable to His actions through the covenant.] He acknowledges His **nature** by saying in verses 7 – 8; *"**For a mere moment I have forsaken you**, But with great mercies I will gather you.[8] With a little wrath I hid My face from you **for a moment**; But with everlasting kindness I will have mercy on you," Says the Lord, your Redeemer."* More importantly, I will point out that this chapter is a prophetic reconciler to God's words from the OT to the NT.

Moses reply is filled with wisdom and righteousness because he gives to God, His very own words which God cannot contradict based on His nature. Moses says in verses 11 – 14 (ESV), *"Lord, why does Your wrath burn hot against **Your people** whom **You have brought** out of the land of Egypt with great power and with a mighty hand? [12] Why should* the Egyptians speak, and say, 'He brought them out to harm them, to kill them in the mountains, and to consume them from the face of the earth'? Turn from Your fierce wrath, and relent from this harm to **Your people**. *13* **Remember Abraham, Isaac, and Israel, Your servants, to whom You swore** by **Your own self**, *and said to them, 'I will multiply your descendants as the stars of heaven; and all this land that I have spoken of I give to your descendants, and they shall inherit it forever.'"* Moses reacts to God in such a way that His wrath is removed from the people.

This is similar to what occurred in Numbers 25. When connecting the story of Phinehas in Numbers; insight to the reaction of God shows another primary responsibility of the Levite priest. In verse 10 God tells Moses that the reaction by Phinehas has turned His anger away from the Israelites. **I believe that God used the righteous reaction of priest to atone for the sins of the people which shielded them from His wrath.**

To answer the question of why a covenant of peace; I theorise that the **covenant of peace** allows man to live with knowledge; (1) that God will not vanquish him in His anger (2) that God will protect man (3) and that God will bestow a benefit on man to increase him if man adheres to the terms. The nature of God gives understanding why there was infinite wisdom in creating a rule of law through covenants. God literally protected Himself and man.

4.   Why a Covenant of Priesthood

The theory on the covenant of peace becomes a bit more complex when combined with the covenant of priesthood. Shared with the fact that God required and utilized an intercessory relationship with various individuals; God also used the important position of priesthood to prosper His divine purpose. The covenant of priesthood was the 'do' aspect of how the Covenant of Peace would be achieved but it also had a composite value that I refer to as the 'duality of purpose'.

Insight to the purpose of the covenant starts with relying on the previous premises that God had a master plan.

Evolution of the Purpose

The plan in the covenant has essential components where God effectively utilizes the Levitical priest. Reading into the central theory of God's master plan which defines His nature of order; we find that in Exodus 2:1 the story of Moses is about to begin. The spotlight focuses on the fact that the verse begins explicitly showing that Moses came from the union of parents who traced their lineage to the House of Levi. This is the first clue that God was purposing a future priesthood.

Although Moses has direct heritage to Abraham, his genealogy is not progenic where he is in-line to the blessings of the 'promise' passed from Abraham to Isaac and Isaac to Jacob/Israel who in turn blessed Joseph. That line of blessing eventually passed directly to Ephraim who was the progenitor of the Abrahamic covenant. Moses line of succession is from Jacob and Leah (Jacob's first wife) which eventually births Levi.

God '**purposes**' the life of Moses according to the usual wisdom of his **plan of heritage**. We know that there is a direct genealogy from Noah to Abraham and Abraham to King David. We also know that the lineage of King David is traced to Jesus. This genealogy arose based on the covenant with Abraham, which I prefer to call 'the seed covenant', because Abraham was promised by God that his seed would be blessed such that a great nation would be produced and land would be inherited. This is an unconditional covenant from God to Abraham; there are no prerequisites for man to fulfil. Abraham justified the appointment of the covenant blessing upon his life through his faithfulness; so the only requirement left to achieve on the covenant is God being faithful to the words He spoke to Abram. God said in Genesis 22:18; "*In your seed all the nations of the earth shall be blessed, because you have obeyed My voice.*"

Interestingly, God has removed the Levites who are also Israelites from the blessing of land heritage. The curious nature of that separation is offset by a tithe paid to the priest by requirement of law from all the other tribes (which will be expounded on further). The fact that security in land ownership would jeopardize, distract and place limitations on the fervour of their (priest) marriage to the tabernacle work and evangelism, seems to be at the heart of that separation.

After searching the contextual aspects of various chapters and books in the Bible, the most revealing and persuasive answer that I could find in understanding the relationship between the establishment of the Abrahamic and Mosaic covenants, occurred all the way in the book of Galatians 3 where Paul is giving counsel to the Galatians. Paul has built a persuasive argument for the effectiveness of grace through faith and not the works of the law. In developing his argument, Paul succeeds in demonstrating why the Mosaic covenant was conceived and he demonstrates the prophetic nature of the **promise**, which is based on genealogy.

In verse 19 Paul insightfully pries into his audiences minds by asking why the law was introduced under covenant. It is somewhat rhetorical as he provides his own answer. It says', '*Well then, why were the laws given? They were added after the **promise** was given, to show men how guilty they are of breaking God's laws.....*' In using the Living Bible translation we find distinct clarity which is also referenced as affirmation in Romans 3:20 which reads; '***Now do you see it? No one can ever be made right in God's sight by doing what the law commands. For the more we know of God's laws, the clearer it becomes that we aren't obeying them; his laws serve only to make us see that we are sinners.***'

The interpretive value of the two verses demonstrates that the Mosaic Law was presented to serve as an illustrated and justified standard that man could not achieve righteousness on his own volition. What God achieved in implementing the Mosaic laws was a 'man in the mirror' affect. This covenant was a way to orderly give a standard of righteousness justified under the law of God, whiles at the same time reflecting the sin nature of man, such that we could (at some stage) recognize our inability to meet those standards through our own efforts.

We find further at the end of Galatians 3 verse 19, the symbolic and interdependent 'promise' similar to the aforementioned blessing in the line of Abraham to Moses; it states, '*...But this system of law was to last* *only until the coming of Christ, the Child to whom God's* **promise** *was made.'* This verse is symbiotic and transitional because it illustrates the connection between the promise of fulfilment in the seed of Abraham through the laws of Moses and the promise of the seed of righteousness born through faith in Jesus Christ.

What is even more pertinent to the understanding of this section is that the Levitical covenant acted as a catalyse to standardize the law. God needed to ensure that Israel would not rewrite their own standards as collaborators of a new unitarian belief system. Certainly we find that the very implementation of the Levitical covenant comes about based on the spiritual subterfuge being committed as Moses receives the law from God; the Israelites are at that very moment attempting to create their own theocracy by creating a golden calf to worship. **God needed to have a zealous designated mediator (Levites) to enforce and protect the laws and the standards therein.**

Why is this important within the context of spiritual marriage? The practicality of the Levitical covenant is that it has two branches working in a harmonious marriage relationship such that God indicates it in Numbers 25:10-13. Although the foundation of the purpose for the marriage starts with the promise to Abraham; the first recognized implementation of that promise begins with the prophet Moses as the first High Priest of Israel and held on covenant through Aaron and his sons.

The premise that is being prospered is that the 'priesthood 'was initiated as a married concept to propagate and orderly manage the plan of God which was to inevitably fulfil the Abrahamic '**promise of the seed**'.

Duality of Purpose

The priesthood can be viewed as a procreation tool with duel or **duality of purpose,** by which God is able to birth a '**nation of priest**' and a '**holy nation**' under the conditional promise made in the Mosaic covenant; this ultimately affirms God's unconditional promise from the Abrahamic Covenant.

Relying on the established premise that the Levites are progenies in the line of Moses; Exodus 19:3 -6 gives special insight of instructions being passed from God to His mediator Moses. Verses 5 and 6 states (NKJV); '*Now therefore, if you will indeed obey My voice and keep My covenant, then you shall be a special treasure to Me above all people; for all the earth is Mine. ⁶And you shall be to Me a **kingdom of priests** and a **holy nation**.*' This illustrates that God has given clear instructions to the Levite priest Moses, who is mandated to deliver and produce results towards the nation of Israel. Because God spoke of and designated an 'everlasting priesthood' in Numbers 25:13 the intertwined nature of those words becomes progressive with the purposes of 'kingdom priest' and the achievement needed to produce a holy nation.

Here is how God achieves His goal of spiritual marriage under commitments to fulfil the obligations of the Abrahamic, Mosaic and Levitical covenants through the priesthood.

Kingdom of Priest

A. Understanding the important positioning of the priest by God can start in Malachi (NIV) 2: 1 - 2. It says', "*And now, you priests, this warning is for you. If you do not listen, and if you do not resolve to honor my name,*" *says the Lord Almighty,* "*I will send a curse on you, and I will curse your blessings. Yes, I have already cursed them, because you have not resolved to honor me.*"

God has issued this stinging edict against the priests who are in contempt due to their dishonour of the name of God. Verses 7 and 8 of Malichi implies and explains the exact reasons why the priests are considered to be in contempt. They have '**corrupted the covenant of Levi**' which was entrusted to them to uphold. The priests, as messengers, were entrusted to be congruent with the mandate of Moses by keeping the knowledge of God alive through the transference of His message to the people. That entrustment started and came through Moses.

Before going further, let's take a quick look at the mandate of the priest which if followed properly, would produce a nation of priest and a holy nation.

In Malachi (NIV)2: 5 - 6 it states:

> "My covenant was with him, a covenant of life and peace, and I gave them to him; this called for **reverence and he revered me** and stood in awe of my name. **True instruction was in his mouth** and **nothing false was found on his lips**. He walked with me in peace and uprightness, and turned many from sin."

According to these two verses God gave the covenant to the Levi priest to accomplish (4) four primary things under the law.

i. To establish Reverence – this word in the Hebrew has two denotations. It is derived from the words Yare', which essentially means "fear" and it also signifies the word 'Shachah' which depicts a bowing or "falling down" of the body before God as superior to us.

The contextual implication of the covenant is not to place God in a position of piousness or arrogance but it was implemented to regiment the necessary standards of respect and discipline (for priest) which would adhere to God's purpose under the law for Israel. His purpose under the law for Israel is found in Exodus 19: 5 -6 where God tells Moses that His covenant with the people of Israel will make them His *'treasured possession'* and a *'**kingdom of priests'** and a holy nation'*. Further insight into what God meant is found in Isaiah 49:6 (NAS) which etches an analogous meaning between priest and the word 'light'. It says,

*"It is too small a thing that You should be My Servant To raise up the tribes of Jacob, And to restore the preserved ones of Israel; I will also give You as a **light** to the Gentiles, That You should be My salvation to the ends of*

the earth.' Keeping in mind that the reverence of the priest is akin to Old Testament doctrinal discipline to keep their charge; what is gathered here is that the priest are given an extended mission beyond simply fulfilling the charge of holding the tribes of Judah and Israel under the law. Their mission has much larger implications. The priests are to be the 'light' to the Gentiles. We are already aware that the priest are charged with carrying the testimony of God and that responsibility entailed having the doctrine kept on their lips as knowledge; so being the light was an analogy of carrying forth the word of God to the Gentiles.

The exegetical nature of the word is built on logical premises such as Psalm 119:105 where David says', *"Your word is a lamp for my feet, a light on my path"*. Placed into complete context it becomes evident that God intended for His word, which is instilled into the knowledge of the priest, to become a light for which Jews and Gentiles alike would see that path of salvation.

When we transition to the New Testament; we find the culmination of the prophetic mission towards salvation addressed by the apostle in 1 Peter 2:19 (KJ). It states, *"But ye [are] a chosen generation, a royal priesthood, an holy nation, a peculiar people; that ye should shew forth the praises of him who hath called you out of darkness into his marvellous light:"*.

I have shown that the Israelites where constantly wrestling with various forms of debauchery. God wanted the priest to have **reverence** to His decrees to accomplish the covenant established with the nation of Israel. Even further, that reverence was to protect the institution of marriage so that the people would not disfigure and divorce God's intentions.

ii. The priests were to speak from their mouths, 'true instructions'. Reference to Ezra 7:10 illustrates that the purpose of a priest knowing the law was to impart that knowledge in truth and completeness to the Israelites. This was in keeping once again with the intentions set forth in the Mosaic covenant. These true instructions were important within the deliverance of marriage because the priest stood as an example of marriage. Marriage for a priest was in knowing the law in truth; speaking the law in truth and being 'attached' to the work of the law in truth. This is confirmed in Leviticus 21: 12 – 15 (LIV) which sets out the true instructions for priest with regards to marriage. It states; "*He shall not leave the sanctuary when on duty,* **nor treat my Tabernacle like an ordinary house,** *for the consecration of the anointing oil of his God is upon him; I am Jehovah.* **He must marry a virgin.** *He may not marry a widow, nor a woman who is divorced, nor a prostitute. She must be a virgin from his own tribe, for he must not be the father of children of mixed blood—half priestly and half ordinary.*"

I believe that God was telling the priest to marry the unadulterated 'true' word of God to the Israelites and that such a union must be kept pure and outside of the defaming nature of other pagan cultures which is analogous to sin.

iii.   The priests were to walk with God in '**peace and uprightness**'. This defined term of peace is presented as an essential part of what the priest helped to establish but only if they walked in righteousness. Peace was attributable to those who had favour with God according to Luke 2:8 - 14. In this story we come upon a scene where shepherds are in the presence of God's glory in the form of an angel. The men are very afraid but are told, "*Do not be afraid, for behold, I bring you good tidings of great joy which will be to all people*". A few verses later we are highlighted to the reason for such joy; the baby Jesus is revealed and the host of angels rejoice in delivering the revelation of great joy, which is; the birth of the Son means, "Glory to God in the highest, and on earth **peace**, goodwill toward men". The birth of Jesus brought favour among men to have peace with God through salvation.

iv.   They were to **turn many from sin**. Evangelism was another essential function of the priest. It is obvious from the Mosaic covenant that God desired Israel to be a nation that behaved and upheld the laws as a 'holy nation' but God also wanted them to prosper the righteousness of the law as priest.

Essentially, the role of the priests was to produce a by-product from their very own actions that would be consistent with producing a 'Nation of Priests'. The very fact that the priests were to act zealously to protect the 'Hoy Institution' triggers the effects or results that were intended by God. The zealousness of the priests would necessitate the importance of being holy in their role with God, which would inevitably place them in good moral standing to transfer the knowledge that was entrusted to them, such that the people would inherit that wisdom and reproduce it in their lives.

A Holy Nation

Understanding the duality of the Priesthood requires a great appetite to digest the depth of information. There is a challenge to connect the reasons why the Levitical covenant has such complexities. It's not the structural complexity of the covenant that offers evidence on the road of reasoning but the term of the agreement that clarifies why this part of the covenant is aptly viewed as symbiotic. It has relationships that are inescapable and required if we are to gain a full appreciation of revealed knowledge and purpose.

The term of the Abrahamic Covenant is uniquely unconditional (as stated above) because it places no direct stipulations upon Abraham, which follows the nomenclature of a conditional covenant that states, '**if** you will, **then** I shall'. The Mosaic Covenant is in fact conditional; it states in Exodus 19:5-6, '*Now therefore, **if** you will indeed obey My voice and keep My covenant, **then** you shall be a special treasure to Me above all people; for all the earth is Mine. And you shall be to Me a kingdom of priests and a holy nation*'.

The Levitical Covenant is unconditional. At face value, it appears pruned to failure. It relies on the imperfectness of the priest to reach its' goals. The danger of this legal precept becomes obvious because the priests seem to understand that the construct is perpetually binding. How else would one explain their bold defiance? They act impervious to their sin and refuse to acknowledge their responsibility to account for their actions.

This is where we see the indelible ink print of why marriage is not detachable from God. The dependant relationship within the covenant of priesthood is a covalent bond between the 'do' element of the priesthood (which is the work) and the offspring or result of that work, which is the 'Holy Nation'. The Holy Nation is directly correlated to the unconditional promise given to Abraham; but, it is only brought to fruition through the marriage relationship of the priest.

The mere fact that the Abrahamic covenant is unconditional but has to go through the conduit of the conditional Mosaic covenant and the unconditional Levitical covenant to be achieved, allows us to understand the complexities involved in marriage. We can imagine the turbulence of a contract of marriage that is meant to be irrevocable but one partner violates the '**if then**' syllogism and commits adultery. Place that thought into perspective of the whole framework of the Levitical Covenant and we can see the powerful blueprinted of how important marriage is to God. Throughout the whole passage in Malachi 2 there is no mention of God signing the divorce decree. He makes it very clear in verse 16 that 'He hates divorce'; but like any marriage where there is an unfaithful partner, the marriage suffers through results that inevitably arise from the treacherous act of adultery.

Indeed, it does not go unnoticed that the priests cry before God like an adulterous partner who has been caught; then, 'they' tell lies in a vain attempt to deny 'their' responsibility to the contemptible act. The priests bring cheap flowers and gifts of offerings like a scorned suitor but God has made His case and He is prepared to righteously apply justice for the betrayal.

This is where the imagination gets dark because the link between the work of the priest and the result is that the result is the figurative analogy of a child. The child is Israel found in Exodus 19:3-6. This child is the superlative example of neglect and abuse, which occurs in divorce; but that neglect is essentially charged to the actions of the priest. It is a child that has a common darkness inherited from the debased minds of priest that seek to avoid the righteousness of a prevalent God. What this child represents is the collective; the worldly hive mentality. This child is the failure of the priest to produce a righteous mentality among the nation of Israel that would produce as a collective, a 'Holy Nation'.

The question is, what happens in a marriage when one partner walks away and abandons the terms of the marriage? In reading this passage, it would appear as if God walked away from the priest and deserted His unconditional decree. This is faulty thinking. In fact, the abandonment occurred at the very moment that the priest 'dealt treacherously' and committed an abomination by profaning the 'holy institution', which is the marriage. Abandonment (in this context) is not a physical act per se; it is a spiritual act where the priest neglect 'the way' (as stated in verse 8 of Malachi 2) 'and cause many to stumble at the law.'

We then recognize the benevolent love of God and how that love characterizes the unconditional plan of God set forth in the Abrahamic Covenant because in chapter 3 of Malachi God shows the way towards restoration of the relationship by sending 'the Messenger of the covenant'. This indicates two key developments within the significance of spiritual marriage:

1. God never divorced from the Levitical covenant, which proves that it is in fact unconditional. He refined it through the perfection of the Messenger who is Christ Jesus. The marriage actually started with the unconditional bond to Abraham and became a perfected bond through the Messenger.

2. Even with the 'air' of convictions hanging over the head of the priest; we have assurance that God extends mercy and grace to their lives. This speaks to the redemptive nature of the marriage. The marriage itself is just. The acts by the priest or partners were wrong but God is willing to bring restoration to the institution He loves (Malachi 2:11). He brings restoration because the purpose is still intact; the purpose is to produce 'godly offspring'(Malachi 2:15 NKJV) which then produces a 'Holy Nation'.

Metaphors and Allegory: binding poetry for a complex theory

As if there is a pink elephant standing in the room, the obvious and looming question is why did God attach such depth of metaphorical and allegorical meanings to characterize marriage within the Levitical Covenant?

That answer is sufficiently demonstrated in the conclusion but what is evident upfront is that the complexity of the entire subject matter from the Abrahamic covenant through to the New Covenant, requires allegories and metaphors to avoid the appearance of abrogation between the covenants.

A very deep look into these allegories and metaphors will help to pull the whole equation together on why the covenants and more specific, the Levitical Covenant, is so very important to understanding spiritual marriage.

1. As stated previously, Malachi 2 presents the tumultuous marriage relationship between God and the priest. We are shown that the priests are rather disturbed by God's rejection of their offerings. This is an allegorical sign that the priests have lost their moral fortitude and have broken the holy link of communication with God. By losing holy communication with God, the second aspect of their purpose (a holy nation) can't be achieved. God reminds the obstinate priest that He is not fooled by their false worship and offerings. In Malachi 2:14 it states, *'**Because the Lord has been witness between you and the wife of your youth, with whom you have dealt treacherously; yet she is your companion and your wife by covenant.**'* The pertinent aspect of this verse steeped in allegory and metaphor is the intimacy of God reminding the priest that He has a patrimonial relationship with the covenant where He is aware of every aspect of its' functionality; it's beginning and it's end.

2. In verse 14 of Malachi 2, where it speaks of 'the Lord' being witness; this is a type of comparative metaphor to reference the Covenant

of Priesthood and Peace, which God has acted as covenantor (God maintains this position with all covenants) between Himself and the Levi Priest. However, as we have oft seen; the meaning is far more expansive. There is another event that God has been witness to which is metaphorically implied. Where God has been witness between 'you and your wife of your youth' is an allusion to the nurtured physical relationship of marriage.

The complexity to exculpate meaning from this verse, so that the logic of it can be digested with clarity, teeters on whether the sceptic will accept the truth of such revelation or condemn it as ecclesiastical heresy.

Stepping back and observing the verse from a broad sense reveals the masculine addressee intended in the verse. It has significance because it follows an 'Adam-like' orderly synergy that one would expect if speaking to a husband and wife; Adam was addressed first then Eve.

We observe that the first recipient is the male who is indicated as having dealt treacherously with the wife of his youth, and has left the covenantal relationship.

The logic of the conversation confirms and stands up to (at the very least) two truth propositions from the Bible. It also shows (once again) God's orderly nature.

i. Malachi 2: 14 indicates that God holds the head of the church responsible, which is reflective of the hierarchy of responsibility in marriages. This synergises with the story of how Adam was held responsible in Genesis; and how all men are held responsible to the keeping of the covenant relationship in marriage. This is in agreement with 1 Corinthians 11:3 which states; *'But I want you to know that the head of every man is Christ, the head of woman is man, and the head of Christ is God.'*

ii. Just as the ignorance of the priest will move them towards divorce the wisdom of a man will save him from the adulterous woman; God also adds balance because a man's wise decisions will preserve his choices in marriage. This is reflected in Proverbs

> 2: 16 – 17 (NIV); *'Wisdom will save you also from the adulterous woman, from the wayward woman with her seductive words, **who has left the partner of her youth and ignored the covenant** she made before God.'*

3. We find further clear evidence of the metaphorical and allegorical implications to marriage in Malachi 2:14-15. The composition of both verses has a transitional purpose as it moves away from the married state of the church and priest and alludes' to the literal matrimonial relationship between a man and woman.

One is forced to see the vivid sense of responsibility and prominence God attaches to the institution of marriage between the priest and the church by a comparison to the intimate, conjugal connection of the man and woman who are joined as one flesh.

This indication takes us one step closer to completing the ligature of why spiritual marriage is important to God.

Verse 15 begins by quoting; *'But did He not make them one, having a remnant of the Spirit?'*

My initial understanding of this complex allegory, 'remnant of the Spirit', comes from gluing the contextual use of the terms in Revelations 12: 17 along with an extended meaning in Revelations 19:10. In the Amplified Bible the word remnant is substituted with the word remainder. It states; *'So then the dragon was furious (enraged) at the woman, and he went away to wage war on the **remainder** of her descendants—[on those] who obey God's commandments and who have the testimony of Jesus Christ [and adhere to it and [a]bear witness to Him]'*. Defining the attachment of the term *'testimony of Jesus Christ'* with the word remainder gives a plausible subtext that this verse is a simple definition of subsisting people who are following the testimony of Jesus Christ; but like many scriptural verses, one comes to understand that there is normally a greater meaning on words than first revealed.

Each time the word remnant is found in the Bible, we find that it has a mission such that someone or persons are fulfilling the greater and extended purpose of the Lord under extreme circumstance. The word tends to show **intrinsic faith**, so taken at its' higher value, the word in this passage is indicating that 'the dragon' must wage war against spiritual warriors or stalwarts of the faith. These are people who are **unshaken in their belief and the testimony of Jesus Christ**. For me, this brings to mind the zealot nature identified earlier in Levite priest.

Most recognizable to the adherence of covenantal rules as it pertains to the Mosaic covenant is how strict God is in His own governance. If taking note of 1 Chronicle 15: 1 – 15, we would realize that David was King of all Israel but he was careful to follow the law of God by not allowing anyone but the Levite priest to handle the Ark of the Covenant or to make sacrifices. In the story of King Saul, when he tried to offer a sacrifice for the nation, he lost his kingship and was later killed based on his neglect to follow the law.

This would mean that the prophet Elijah was either a Levite or a Levite priest because in 1 Kings 18: 36 we find him making a sacrifice to God on behalf of the nation of Israel. The connection of Elijah to the priesthood is not underplayed in its significance. From 1 King 18 to 19 there is a great story of faith and perseverance unfolding. Elijah had received instructions from God to let King Ahab know that a drought[193] of several years would take place primarily because the King and his wife Jezebel introduced the worship of a foreign deity, Ba'al, to Israel. **Elijah exhibited the type of zeal and faithfulness that is synonymous with covenantal obligations**. Elijah stood before the King with authority and challenged his faith. In verse 21 of chapter 18 Elijah says', *"How long will you falter between two opinions? If the Lord is God, follow Him; but if Baal, follow him."* In following the story that developed from the miracle of God destroying the alter of Ba'al; a deeper story emerges that speaks to the frailty of the human psyche. It is the

---

[193] 1 Kings 17:1

exact same psychological challenges that Moses faced. Elijah has just stood before the nation of Israel and God has demonstratively shown without dispute that He is God. Elijah has also delivered as the oracle of God, the end to years of drought. Certainly now, the people would turn from their evil ways and whole-headedly follow the precepts of God. Instead, Elijah receives news that Queen Jezebel is pursuing him to revenge the death of her prophets of Ba'al and have him placed to death.

It's easy to see into the passage and imagine the exasperation from Elijah, recognizing the blatant rejection of God even after the victory at Mount Carmel; so with a broken spirit he goes on the run for his life and takes up a nomadic condition. It is in this context that we see the word '**remnant**'. God is speaking with Elijah in verse 10 and we hear the frustration from Elijah. He is quoted as saying, *"I have been very **zealous** for the Lord God of hosts; for the children of Israel have forsaken Your covenant, torn down Your altars, and killed Your prophets with the sword. I alone am left; and they seek to take my life.*[194]" God responds by revealing to Elijah that he is not the only prophet left. In fact, He tells Elijah that He has *'reserved seven thousand in Israel*[195]'. This verse is co-referenced in Romans 11: 4 – 5 which evidences the word remnant. It quotes: *'But what does the divine response say to him? "**I have reserved for Myself** seven thousand men who have not bowed the knee to Baal." Even so then, at this present time there is a **remnant** according to the election of grace.'*

I believe that the significance of the correlation lies in the fact that Elijah had temporarily lost faith and believed that the mission of God was defeated. I posit that God revived his spirit by showing him first that the unyielding faith of the 7000 was strength enough to save Israel against the work of Ba'al worship. What God was interested in was not the persons fixated on large demonstrations of power [**God had already shown through Moses before Pharaoh that Ba'al worshippers could perform miracles but the faith of the people to follow Him who**

[194] NKJV
[195] 1 Kings 19: 18 New King James Version

rescued them from sin was His goal]; <u>He wanted a holy nation (priest)</u>
<u>who adhered to His word through zealous faith.</u>

We have confirmation that God still wanted to prosper His purpose
straight into the diaspora of the New Testament by the mere fact that
Paul in Romans 11 uses the story of the remnant to justify his ministry
to the Gentiles. He in essence establishes **God's providential purpose,**
which was to have salvation come to the Gentiles through the Jews as
confirmation of God's covenant with Abraham.

Elijah had assumed that the display at Mt. Carmel would revive
Israel after seeing the might of God but in fact it was the stalwart
resilience of those priests who stood on their faith regardless of what
the enemy (Ba'al) showed them that exulted the righteousness that
God sought. Elijah also assumed that he was the only prophet left to
carry out God's work. Notice that he knew that part of the work which
needed to be done was in the temple. He stood before God as if to say,
'I am the only one left who could carry out the covenantal mission'
because *'the children of Israel have forsaken Your covenant, torn down*
Your altars'. I believe that God showed Elijah the successive nature of
His covenantal grace. He immediately chose another Levite who would
be the successor of all that Elijah had done. Elijah's work was important
but it was his faith that God needed to remain grounded.

This was all a precursor to why the priest became divorced from
the bride of their youth. **<u>They had lost the remnant of the spirit.</u> The**
priest had neglected their faith and the spirit of the covenantal
relationship to not worship other gods such as Ba'al.

In Revelations 19:10 (AMP) the testimony of Jesus is called *'the*
substance (essence) of the truth revealed' and is *'the spirit of all prophecy'*. To
place this verse along-side Malachi 2:15 which says', *'But did **He** not **make***
***them one,** having a **remnant of the Spirit**'*; we can find a comprehensive
understanding of how significant the phrase is based on the defined truth
of what the 'spirit represents. The amalgamation of the two verses can

suggest that the question in Malachi 2:15 can be read in the following context, which does present the rhetorical; 'why has the husband **dealt treacherously with his wife** that he is **joined to by God**, when **the truth [in Jesus] of the unyielding and zealous prophetic testimony** which is infallible and 'unshakeable[196]', **has already been revealed**.

In asking this first question, 'But did He not make them one, having a remnant of the Spirit'; the author from Malachi, further synergizes prophetic truth in Matthew 19: 4 – 6 with the truth of spoken word from Genesis 1:27; Genesis 5: 2 and Genesis 2:24.

Matthew 19: 4-6 (TLB) says'; *"Don't you read the Scriptures?"* he replied. *"In them it is written that at the beginning God created man and woman, and that a man should leave his father and mother, and be forever united to his wife. The two shall **become one**—no longer two, but one! **And no man may divorce what God has joined together.**"*

Genesis 1: 27 and 5:2 are prophetically amalgamated to Matthew through the affirmation that God has created man and woman whiles Genesis 2: 24 symbiotically attaches by stating through God's edict that, *'a man [shall] leave his father and his mother, and shall cleave unto his wife: and they shall be one flesh.'*

These verses are further confirmation of the use of metaphors and allegory to pull together **duality of meaning** between the physical and spiritual fallibility of the Levi priest and husband and wife. The marriage nature of both is shown through the bond the priest must have to the church through prospering the teachings of the law, whiles also being under covenant to not contravene or divorce themselves from the contract with God and the truth derived from that contract. This is virtually the same for a husband and wife.

Proceeding further into this exposition, we then see that another rhetorical question is placed to our attention in the same verse; it ask, **'and why one?'**

---

[196] http://www.bibleinfo.com/en/topics/remnant

Keeping in mind and on the path of recognizing the requirements of the priest, we are made to remember that God said to the Levites and Israel through the covenantal agreement that they were to be '*to Me a kingdom of priests and a holy nation*[197]'.

We have already illustrated the intended purpose of the priest but the author of Malachi puts forth the clear answer to the question that only God has inspired.

The answer is to accentuate the spiritual and physical accomplishment which only marriage can achieve.

Malachi 2:15 says', '**He seeks godly offspring.**' This is cerebrally placed into context through the referenced interpretation found in 1 Corinthians 7: 14 of the Living Bible which says';

> *For perhaps the husband who isn't a Christian may become a Christian with the help of his Christian wife. And the wife who isn't a Christian may become a Christian with the help of her Christian husband. Otherwise, if the family separates, the children might never come to know the Lord; whereas a united family may, in God's plan, result in the children's salvation.*

The purpose of marriage for the Levi priest and the purpose of marriage for a man and woman are one and the same; to propagate 'holy' off-spring. This is a physical and spiritual procreation.

Firstly and to reiterate; when God says' in Isaiah 49:6 that the work of the Levites (as implied) is to give light to the Gentiles, and that they will help extend God's salvation to the 'ends of the earth', that mandate is only achieved through impregnating the nation of Israel and the Gentiles with the word of God. This is spiritual procreation.

In the book of in EZRA chapter 9, it becomes important to rehash the spiritual significance of the story. It's indicated that the people of Israel including the priest and the Levites have failed God's mandate of refusing intermarriage between themselves and people who have

---

[197] Exodus 19: 6

consistently been identified as cultures which embrace pagan worship. God specifically did not want Israel to intermarry. It would be easy to interpret this as modern genetic profiling but the truth is not derived from this notion; the Israelites were being asked to protect the 'holy seed' of God, which was His word. **God desired that the work of the priest through Israel would produce spiritual copulation of the testimony of God.**

This is the bourgeoning success of God's purpose as also revealed in James 1: 18 which says'; *'He chose to give us birth through the word of truth, that we might be a kind of firstfruits of all he created.* The birth results in children or firstfuits who are also confirmed in Jeremiah 2:3, seen as the natural evolution of God's eschatological intention of 'holy offspring', designed from Genesis to Revelations.

5. Purpose of the New Covenant and marriage

What is the New Covenant? The road to that answer can start in the book of Isaiah chapter 39. We find the prophet Isaiah telling King Hezekiah that God has spoken and that Judah will come into bondage and exiled into the hands of Babylon. We are aware that the people have been continuously rebellious to the law and have repeatedly incurred sever discipline from God. By the Book of Jeremiah the king Nebuchadnezzar has already fulfilled that prophecy where the people have been 'exile from Jerusalem to Babylon[198]'.

In Jeremiah 30, Jeremiah prophesies that God will *'bring my people Israel and Judah back from captivity and restore them to the land I gave their ancestors to possess;* this prophecy would be in fulfilment of the Abrahamic covenant which was unconditional and guaranteed the land to the Israelites. This is another exceptional validation of God's nature to uphold His word even though there is a dismal spiritual failure by the people. Whiles the whole book of the Old Testament is designed to produce the prophetic establishment of the New Covenant; it can

---

[198] Jeremiah 29

validly be argued that the re-establishment of Israel and Judah also signals prophetic progression towards **the New Covenant.**

There is a residual effect of restoring the people to the land in confirmation of the Abrahamic covenant. God cannot simply allow the Israelites and the priest to implement the very same spiritual conditions that they have lived with under the law; that is what resulted in their banishment in the first instance. God has prophetically prospered a new system to administer them under. In verse 29, the prophet says', *"In those days people will no longer say, 'The parents have eaten sour grapes, and the children's teeth are set on edge."* This is a clear indication that God has told Jeremiah that the sins of the father or generation will not fall on the backs of the children. Such has been the case throughout the tumultuous history of Israel, where God has punished one generation and the children spend (as an example) 400 years in captivity under Eygpt[199]. God is prepared to remedy this dilemma with a perfect solution; **a new covenant.**

God declares through the prophet; *"The days are coming,"* declares the Lord, *"when I will make a new covenant with the people of Israel and with the people of Judah*[200]*"* Being consistent and instrumental to His nature; God explains why He is setting a new covenant. In verse 32 we get the **first indication of the divorce** that took place between God and Israel. It is an 'essential' element to understanding the importance of spiritual marriage. God says' that he must create a new agreement because the people of Judah and Israel have broken the old agreement even though 'I was a husband[201]'. Here, **God implies that He was in a marriage to Israel as the husband.** Keep in mind that in Malachi 2:16, God has indicated His disdain for divorce. This again is significant insight into the revelation of spiritual marriage coming together from the Old Testament to the New.

---

[199] Gen 15:13

[200] Jeremiah 31: 31

[201] Jeremiah 31:32

The Lord makes five decrees of what he will establish in the marriage of the New Covenant.

1. He says' that he will 'put my law in their minds'; Jeremiah 31:33. This is a reference of confirmation from Deuteronomy 18:18 and again in Joshua 1:8 through which God has used prophets in the Old Testament to prosper His testament. God will continue in the New Testament to utilize the mouths of prophets to deliver His divine testament.

2. He will 'write it on their hearts'; Jeremiah 31:33. This is a cross reference to the Holy Spirit in 2 Corinthians 3:3 and gives the truth of Hebrews 10: 15 which says that the Holy Spirit shall be witness to us.

3. He establishes His divinity once again over the people and divine ownership as the creator by saying, "I will be their God and they will be my people"; Jeremiah 31:33 and as affirmed and established in Leviticus 26:12 verbatim.

4. God confirms through Jeremiah that His New Covenant will cause His word to be propagated throughout all the Earth so that people will all know who He is; Jeremiah 31: 34. This is testimony to the prophecy of Isaiah in Isaiah 11:9 where he has a vision of the knowledge of God covering the Earth like the sea.

5. God indicates to Jeremiah that this covenant will not need the regimented way of the law which required the Levites to teach the law and the Israelites to learn from each other. The New Covenant established the **authority of the Holy Spirit** where in John 14:26 we are guided on the fact that 'all things' which we will need to know will come from the Advocate of God; the Holy Spirit.

Let's ponder this for a moment. God is setting up a new system but he is still using a covenant to do so; why? This is where the level of deep and critical evidentiary exegesis is justified. Through all that has been shown previously, another consistent factor that stands out in relationship to how God deals with covenants is His '**perpetual bond**' to the covenant. One would take notice of the many analogous usages of the word marriage when God is speaking about an established covenant. **The matrimonial process for God is unconditional and irrevocable by His instance and only conditional and revocable by the actions of the 'Adamic' creation**. It is too obvious that there is a fervent protection of covenants and the implication of or use of syntactical 'adverbs' such as 'forever' illustrates a commitment that is not meant to be broken.

What God is implying in every covenant is that His tacit use of the marriage institution to forge a perennial everlasting relationship is always the intention and whether the covenant is conditional or unconditional is irrelevant to His nature because He hates divorce no matter how it happens. If this were not so, God would not have enacted a New Covenant. His divorce would have been final. This is also why the Abrahamic covenant is unconditional; it allows God to justify from that precedent His actions under a conditional covenant where adjustments must occur to rectify man's eras. God is then able to redeem those actions (eras) under the perpetual justification of the unconditional covenant with Abraham. An example of my reasoning is illustrated in the instance of Genesis 17:8 NKJV where God tells Abraham under the unconditional covenant that He will *"give to you and your descendants after you the land in which you are a stranger, all the land of Canaan, as an everlasting possession; and I will be their God."* However, what we find in an earlier verse from Genesis 15:13-16 NKJV, is that God also conveys to Abraham the fact that his people the Israelites will be in bondage and servitude for 400 years away from the land that is promised to them. Whatever purpose God is achieving through His ordered nature by having Abrahams descendants in slavery, will still be justified yet forgiven as a debt through a reversion to God's irrevocable words as laid out in the covenant with Abraham.

Heritage through lineage

Understanding the various mechanisms, examined under the Old Testament and intrinsic to establishing spiritual marriage; ultimately helps us to bridge the gap, which concludes the rather complex theory as it transitions into the New Covenant. Suffice to say again, the Old Testament is in fact a transitionary doctrine to the final purpose of God. The comprehensive extraction of meaning to understand the various elements from the OT has been and is necessary for the proper assimilation of the theory of spiritual marriage into the New Covenant.

One of the first important elements in the transitionary stage of understanding is the **prophetic, ancestral and spiritual lineage** established throughout the Bible and concluded in the New Testament. This may seem like a mundane perusal of fact (which actually evades many readers of the Bible), but there is a pervasive and consistent effort made by the different writers of the Old Testament (OT) books to show cogency in lineage. Take note that there is no distraction from the fact that all scripture is also prospered by the supernatural; this is according to 2 Timothy 3:16 which states, *'All Scripture is given by inspiration of God, and is profitable for doctrine, for reproof, for correction, for instruction in righteousness.'* Hidden deep in this significance is the obscurity of thought and logic, which should be obvious in understanding **the importance of proving lineage,** but the attention to detail where these facts are presented is also missed in the larger historical context. Consider this; every recognised monarchy which exists today has historical significance based on bloodline (lineage). In fact, it is said that the Queen of Britain can trace her heritage back to King Alfred the Great[202]. Effectively, that makes the Queen the 32nd great granddaughter and **legitimate heir** to that kingdom.

God's adherence to heritage is consistent with the logic of kingdoms being established through historical lineage. **Fulfilment of heritage is a key mandate in the purpose of the New Covenant because it restores men as the legitimate heirs of God's original purpose and marriage**.

Somehow the precedent nature of the aforementioned fact eludes the rationalist in understanding the transitional truth and nature of the

---

[202] http://www.britroyals.com/faqs.htm

Bible as it relates to the heritage and life of Jesus. More importantly, the historical heritage of Jesus becomes the cornerstone towards the final elements in understanding spiritual marriage.

i. **Prophetic lineage**

Earlier in the composition of this book, I endeavoured to establish the logical relevance found in confirming the consistency of prophetic syllogisms in the Bible.

What was shown is that a vast amount of prophecy is directed at the birth, life and death of Jesus Christ which shows prophetic lineage. This is not a peripheral fact. It is salient towards the significance of the impact that those prophecies have in spiritual marriage.

The prophetic birth, life, death and resurrection of Jesus the Christ as demonstrated earlier in this book remains prophetically pronounced and consistent from Genesis to Malachi. The obsessive use of prophesy and the subjectivity of person is clearly an indication that Jesus is the personification of the transitional complexity of the Old Testament.

If we were to then view 'Jesus' as the focal element of the New Testament (NT), the question of 'why' would still have to be answered. Why was Jesus the focus of the NT?

For me, there is no answer that is more succinctly appropriate than two chapters found in the NT; John 3: 18 and1 Peter 1: 18 -21.

The first exemplifies God's purpose through Jesus and it states; "*The one who does what is sinful is of the devil, because **the devil has been sinning from the beginning**. The reason the Son of God appeared was to destroy the devil's work*.

The second reveals another purpose which also compliments the first, where it is written; "*For you know that it was not with perishable things such as silver or gold that you were **redeemed** from the empty way of life handed down to you from your ancestors, but **with the precious blood of Christ**, a lamb without blemish or defect. **He was chosen before the creation of the world**, but was revealed in these last times for your* *sake. Through him you believe in God, who raised him from the dead and glorified him, and so your faith and hope are in God".*

The two very dynamically interwoven purposes are to destroy the work of the devil and to redeem mankind through the death and resurrection.

The reason that the verses appeal to my sense of rationality is because man continuously fails to understand the depth of what I call 'life containment'.

In the first instance, **the law,** which is described as sin and death[203], was given to show man that we are incapable of self-fulfilment and the rigidity of the law allows us to reflect on the era of our way. The reality of that reflection is essentially an element of life containment that remains evasive to the consciousness of man; which is, the devil contains man's life in a state of oblivion towards the existence of his ultimate schemes. The Bible reveals in Ephesians 6:12 that *"…. we wrestle not against flesh and blood, but against principalities, against powers, against the rulers of the darkness of this world, against spiritual wickedness in high places."* This is a clear indication that the particularities of our life's discretions are **contained** within a spiritual battle between 'good and bad'. The protracted view of this is played out through the entire length of the Old Testament. In essence, satan is attempting to reverse the curse against him in Genesis 3:15 in which God states; *"And I will put enmity between you and the woman, and between your offspring and hers; he will crush your head, and you will strike his heel."* **Satan is attempting to counter-attack that curse by placing enmity between man and God!**

What God was/is accomplishing as a road map or transitional logical equation was/is to bring balance to what happened in Genesis 3 where we are introduced to 'the craftiness' of the serpent. That event (the fall of man from the 'Garden') is the cataclysmic perpetuation of divorce between God and man.

---

[203] Romans 8:2

We are told in Ephesians 2 how God has shown mercy to mankind by synergizing with 1 Peter 1: 18 – 21 where we find redemption. The fall of man is a presumptive allegory connoting the expansive nature of sin, which consumes humankind by the act of Adam. His 'sin' act released him from the protected covering of marriage to God and the ensuing divorce gave satan access to man who was no-longer in the veil of Heaven (Garden of Eden) but had fallen into the world. That dilemma became apocalyptic for God. The reason it is apocalyptic is because God purposes prophesy to reveal His coming mystery from before the point of the 'fall' in Genesis to the resurrection of Jesus Christ in the NT. How do we know it was before the fall? Aforementioned; in 1 Peter 1:20 God revealed a divine plan by saying that Christ 'was chosen **before the creation of the world**'. That would predate satans' plotted tyranny against man.

The word apocalypse is normally associated with the 'fiery' end of the world but in essence it is more biblically[204] associated with something such as **a mystery** being revealed. What is being constantly revealed in the Old Testament is the **prophecy** of the coming life, death and resurrection of Jesus Christ and the authentication of those prophesies occur in the NT. God's apocalyptic view therefore, had to be transitional because in the last book of His testimony, 'Revelations', He reveals in the very first verse the authentication and confirmation of Jesus Christ through to the 5th verse, (using the New Living version for emphasis); '*This book unveils some of the future activities soon to occur in the life of Jesus Christ. God permitted him to **reveal these things** to his servant John in a vision; and then an angel was sent from heaven to explain the vision's meaning. John wrote it all down—the words of God and Jesus Christ and everything he heard and saw.*'

Verse 5 (which syntactically ends in verse 6) has a solid star annotated to it in the New King James Bible. This is a classification to indicate the verse is a complete fulfilment of prophesy. The verse states; "......*and from Jesus Christ, the faithful witness, **the firstborn from the***

---

[204] http://www.thefreedictionary.com/apocalypse

*dead, and **the ruler over the kings of the earth**. To Him who **loved us
and washed us from our sins in His own blood**, ⁶ and has **made us
kings and priests** to His God and Father, to Him be glory and dominion
forever and ever. Amen".*

The way that this relates to spiritual marriage is that through
the prophetic confirmation in Revelations 1: 5 *redemption of the
'original sin' of Adam*, which caused man to be divorced from God,
is now corrected and forgiven through the 'washing of our sins' which
is brought about by the resurrection of Jesus Christ. **This process
remarries us to God.**

The prophetic lineage is supremely responsible for breaking the
curse, which occurred in the Adamic Covenant of Genesis 3: 15 - 19
and pronouncing confirmation of the defeat of satan.

Here is what Genesis 3: 15 (AMP) says' prophetically; *'And I will
put enmity between you and the woman, and between your offspring and
her Offspring; He will bruise and tread your head underfoot, and you will
lie in wait and bruise His heel.'*
The true depth and prophetic meaning of this statement is commonly
defined as proto-evangelium in its' nature. That means that theologians
of the Bible view it as the true first gospel[205].
The word 'gospel' is interesting because in some more liberal
theoretic affiliations[206] the word is ascribed to being the 'revelation
of Christ'; whereas other more conservative definitions[207] refer to it as
a combination of a Greek noun and verb which when used together
produce the derivative, 'messenger of the good news'.
If we accept the first definition it would mean that Genesis 3:15
is a revelation of Christ. We know that the Canonical gospels are

---

[205] http://www.catholicculture.org/culture/library/dictionary/index.cfm?id=35865
[206] http://wiki.answers.com/Q/What_does_the_word_gospel_mean
[207] https://bible.org/question/what-does-term-%E2%80%9Cgospel%E2%80%9D-
mean

primarily evangelical truths about the birth, life and resurrection of Jesus as revealed by the Apostles through guidance of the Holy Spirit. So what inspired the 'Gospel' in Genesis 3:15? The answer would have to be reflective of God's divine will to show the revelation of Christ as certain hope within the pits of the curse against satans' scheme. This is referenced through to Romans 16:29.

In the second instance we would derive virtually the same context but with wider scope. It would mean that God sends a message of His good news prophecy that the plan of satan is defeated. **Satan's plan was to deceive man and divorce him from God forever through the spiritual death which occurred in the 'fall of man'.** This is therefore the **'good news' Gospel of remarriage** and that Satan is defeated in that effort. Furthering confirmation is in Revelation 20:10 where satan will be thrown into the lake of fire and destroyed. The verse refers to the 'deceit' of satan and attaches the penalty of death.

ii. <u>Ancestral lineage</u>

Within the purpose of the prophecy about the coming of Jesus Christ, we find that God uses heritage to determine the Earthly linage of Jesus Christ in three ways; **marriage to Jerusalem; marriage to Judah** and **the ancestral heritage of leadership over the priesthood.**

Marriage to Jerusalem - In the book of Luke 1:30 - 33 it says', '.......*Mary; you have found favor with God. You will conceive and give birth to a son, and you are to call him Jesus. He will be great and will be called the **Son of the Most High**. The Lord God will give him the **throne of his father David**, and he will **reign over Jacob's descendants** forever; his kingdom will never end'*. This reference to the conception of Christ establishes that lineage of Christ as prophesied through King David and Jacob.

The relationship to Jacob is more easily overlooked in its' importance. In Luke 3: 23-38 the genealogy of Jesus is given from His birth. We are aware that this lineage must be an account from the parentage of Mary because it list Joseph the husband of Mary as the son of Heli but there is clear biblical evidence that Joseph was in fact the son of Jacob (as listed in the book of Matthew) and Mary was the daughter of Heli. The reason for this irregularity is because culturally Jewish history almost always records genealogy through men and not women.

The real proof for me that this is a genealogy through Mary is the fact that the 38 verse ends by stating; 'the *son of Enosh, the son of Seth, the son of Adam,* **the son of God**'. I theorise that the anthropological ending of the salutation 'the son of God' is a prophetic confirmation of what the Angel Gabriel told Mary about the ancestral heir of the son she would conceive; '*He will be great and will be called the* **Son of the Most High**'. This birth is the miraculous culmination of prophetic heritage, spiritual heritage and ancestral heritage.

If the aforementioned is the 'real proof', the true significance of this hierarchal lineage from God is multi-fold but focus will be kept on the salient point.

Jesus was never called the son of Joseph or Mary in the genealogy tracing from the book of Luke. He is referred to as the 'Son of the Most High' and He is implied as the 'Son of David'.

A.   Son of the Most High – This heavenly proclamation as it relates to the heritage of Jesus, places a covering of **ownership** (as I would call it for literal emphasis) over mankind.

Follow me through this voyage of explanation towards the phrase 'Son of the Most High'.

In verse 31 of Luke the first chapter, Mary is told that she will conceive and give birth to a child. She is told that He will be the 'Son of the Most High' and He will be given the throne of David and will reign over the descendants of Jacob. This is a statement of heritage and genealogy.

We are made aware by verse 34 that it will be a miracle birth because Mary confirms to the Angel that she is a virgin. She insightfully asks of the Angel 'how' the pregnancy will happen. He informs her, "*The Holy Spirit will come on you, and the power of the Most High will overshadow you*". This directly implies that through this divine intervention of the Holy Spirit; 'The Holy One' is born.

When Mary is simultaneously told about the pregnancy of Elizabeth she visits with her and stays for three months. The reason for this bit of information is that we are drawn to the fact that although Mary is having a miracle conception, the gestation period for her pregnancy takes place as is normal for giving birth. That would mean to me that the foetal Saviour is growing in an amniotic environment. Medical science has shown conclusively that a foetus/baby does not receive blood from the mother[208] but the insemination of the mother's ovary by a man is needed to transfer DNA and to start the conception. This is the reason why children of HIV positive mothers can be born without the infection; because babies develop their own blood.

It stands to reason therefore, that the conception of the 'Holy One' must be attributed to miraculous insemination from the Holy Spirit; and DNA from God the Father and Mary. But, the 'blood' of Jesus had to be a genetic anomaly accredited to only Jesus. The blood was unique to only Him and no other.

Derivative knowledge must be pulled from I John 1:7 which tells us that "*…the blood of Jesus Christ his Son cleanses us from all sin*" and Revelation 1:5 which says, "*To Him who loved us, and washed us from our sins in His own blood.*" By extracting logical meaning from the two verses we can conclude that the blood of Jesus must have had redeeming powers and it must have been free from sin as blood only attributed to the 'owner'; Jesus Christ.

What then was the clear reason why God used blood to symbolize redemption?

---

[208] Howell's Textbook of Physiology, Second Edition, pages 885 and 886 per; http://www.jesus-is-savior.com/BTP/Dr_MR_DeHaan/Chemistry/04.htm

Taking note of the fact that there is never an instance in the Bible (as far as I know) where a human being is used for a sacrifice, except in pagan cultures; I will glean my assumptions from the nearest instance of human sacrifice written of in the Bible. In the story of Abraham from Genesis 22, God has asked Abraham to take his '**son of the promise**[209]' Isaac to a mountain in the Moriah region to sacrifice him as a burnt offering. We know that Abraham also has a son Ismael but God has chosen Isaac as the son of faith whom the seed of Abraham shall prosper through[210]. What is rather striking about the contextual emphasis in the story of Abraham and his son are the strong metaphorical alliances to the story of Jesus.

Before I venture forward, consider if you will the following anomalies in the story of Isaac that are all metaphors of a mirrored life to Jesus.

Isaac	Jesus
Genesis 15:4 Consider that most theologians accept that Isaac is the child of **promise** which is also in accord with the words of Hebrews 6:13-14 (TLB) "*For instance, there was God's promise to Abraham: God took an oath in his own name, since there was no one greater to swear by, that he would bless Abraham again and again, and give him a son and make him the father of a great nation of people*".	Genesis 3:15; Every prophetic utterance in the Bible about Jesus is a **promise** of His coming and the confirmation of the promise in Christ; assured in Galatians 3:19(TLB) "*Well then, why were the laws given? They were added after the **promise** was given; to show men how guilty they are of breaking God's laws. But this system of law was to last only until the coming of Christ, the Child to whom **God's promise** was made*".

---

[209] Genesis 15:4
[210] Genesis 17:15-21

Genesis 22:2; Isaac is considered by God as the only '**begotten**' son of Abraham.	John 3:16; Jesus is called the only **begotten** Son by God
Hebrews 11:17-19; Abraham exhibited great **faith** and assumed that his son would be raised from the dead to fulfil the faithful promise made by God. *"By faith Abraham, when he was tested, offered up Isaac, and he who had received the promises was in the act of offering up his only son, of whom it was said, 'Through Isaac shall your offspring be named.' **He considered that God was able even to raise him from the dead**"*	Romans 6:4; Christ was raised from the dead which resurrected our sins from death to life in Christ through our **faith.** *"Therefore we were buried with Him through baptism into death, that just as Christ was raised from the dead by the glory of the Father, even so we also should walk in newness of life".*

These spiritual anomalies help to show clear intention by God to direct the path of heritage along an **ancestral precedent**.

The precedent that stands out greatest as a metaphor of the coming of Christ is what occurs in verse 7 to 8 of Genesis 22. Isaac had travelled with his father to the place that God directed them to. He ask of Abraham, *"Look, the fire and the wood, but **where is the lamb** for a burnt offering?"* and Abraham answers him; *"My son, **God will provide for Himself the lamb** for a burnt offering."* Abraham assumed that his son would be the sacrificial lamb for the burnt offering. Unbeknownst to Abraham is that this whole scenario is parallel to the metaphorical attribute of Jesus as the sacrificial lamb described in 1 Peter 1:18-20 and further confirmed in John 1:29. What God took from the assumption of Abraham was a validation of his impenetrable faith. What the reader may not discern from this fact though is that God still allowed the offering to go forth but He had Abraham use a 'ram'.

This, I posit, was because all of mankind had one thing in common from the fall of Adam; **blood that represented sin**. God could not accept an offering which was tainted with sin. Animals are not moral beings so one cannot impute sin or a sin nature to the blood of animals; hence the allowance of an animal sacrifice. Surgically cutting into a few verses allows this conclusion to be inevitable. In Galatians 5:19 it says'; *'Now the works of the flesh are manifest, which are these; Adultery, fornication, uncleanness, lasciviousness.'* If works of the flesh produces these symptoms of sin then it reasons that when God was instructing Moses in Leviticus 17:11 on the sanctity of the blood and said to him, *'For the **life of the flesh is in the blood**, and I have given it to you upon the altar to make atonement for your souls; for it is the blood that makes atonement for the soul';* it further implies that what gives life to the by-products of sin in the flesh, is the blood. The end of this reasoning is that the *'**precious blood of Christ, a lamb without blemish or defect**[211]'*, is the only blood that is capable of being offered for sacrifice and redemption.

Tying this all back to **ownership** through ancestral lineage is the fact that Jesus, who has sinless blood, does not share Mary's blood but He shares her DNA lineage which gives Him ancestral credibility. In the book of Luke, it specifically names Adam as the earliest Earthly blood relative of Mary.

Following the evidence of creation in Genesis; Adam was created in the image[212] of God. Verse 7 of Genesis 2 illustrates ensuing life after God has breathed the breath of life into the nostrils of Adam. It follows therefore that every living being from that point forward inherited the 'breath of life' from the owner or progenitor or first breath (however we can depict the original) who is God. King David in Psalms 24:1 acknowledges the 'owner' by saying that, *'The earth is the Lord's, and everything in it, the world, and **all who live in it**…'.*

---

[211] 1 Peter 1: 18 - 20

[212] Genesis 1:26

What the lineage illustration in Luke achieves is the direct correlation between the creator and the created. It establishes the **ownership** premise logically by implicating a genetic disposition between God, the creator and owner, and all of mankind; and it also prospers true historical ancestry from Mary to Adam in an uninterrupted and accountable fashion.

That single fact, confirms God's relationship to the Abrahamic covenant[213] which the lineage of Mary passes through as progenic. The DNA and Blood of Jesus Christ which results in our redemption is therefore the result of progenic heritage which is confirmed by words of the promised seed found in Galatians 4: 22 – 28; *'For it is written that Abraham had two sons: the one by a bondwoman, the other by a freewoman. But he who was of the bondwoman was born according to the flesh, and he of the **freewoman through promise**....... Now we, brethren, as **Isaac was, are children of promise**'*

The infinite testimony of this progenic lineage is the provisional nature of it towards the ancestral lineage which accomplishes half of the prophetic task to unite Jerusalem and Judah spoken of in Jeremiah 33:16 which says', *'In those days Judah will be saved and Jerusalem will live in safety. This is the name by which it will be called: The Lord Our Righteous Saviour'.*

Symbolically there are many ecclesiastical meanings and representations of blood in the expanse of the Bible but from a heritage point of view 1 Peter 1:18-20 is directly relevant. This ultimately marries God to His people by:

> ➢ **His blood redeems us** because of the price that Jesus paid on the cross. Redemption is figuratively a word, which conveys payment. One can only redeem an item, thing or person by completing a transaction, which gives value to a creditor for a debt owed. The debt of sin,

---

[213] Genesis 12:2-3

which, mankind incurred through the sin of Adam was so great that only Jesus as the new Adam could atone for our sin before God. The blood of Jesus redeemed the nations, which came out of Abraham. First Peter 1:18-19 says, "For you know that it was not with perishable things such as silver or gold that you were redeemed from the empty way of life handed down to you from your forefathers, but with **the precious blood of Christ, a lamb without blemish or defect.**"

➢ **His blood brings Abrahams seed into fellowship with God** which is confirmed by Ephesians 2:13, "But now in Christ Jesus you who once were far away have been brought near through the blood of Christ."

Whiles I would like to think that it would be easy to limit scripture quotation from a purist mind of writing; I am under no illusion of spiritual arrogance to suggest that I would be better set to present (write and reason) the following perching truth. Such is the case in reading through Galatians 4: 1 – 7. It is the exact truth of all that I have written summed up in seven lines.

Paul is speaking to the Galatians and says:

> *What I am saying is that as long as an* ***heir is underage****, he is no different from a slave, although he owns the whole estate. 2 The* ***heir is subject to guardians and trustees*** *until the time set by his father. 3 So also, when we were underage, we were* ***in slavery under the elemental spiritual forces of the world****. 4 But when the set time had fully come,* ***God sent his Son, born of a woman*** *[thus born into the lineage of Jerusalem[1]], born under the law, 5* ***to redeem*** *those under the law, that we might receive* ***adoption to sonship****. 6 Because you are his sons [****OWNERSHIP[2]****], God sent the Spirit of his Son into our hearts, the Spirit who calls out, "Abba, Father." 7 So*

*you are no longer a slave, but God's child; and since **you are his child, God has made you also an heir**.*

Marriage to Judah – Much of what was written above, are peripheral facts which are applicable to ancestry and are relative to the relationship between **Judah** and **Jesus** but there are differences which must be pointed out.

In the Book of Matthew we start with the very first hurdle. The lineage of Joseph is meticulously laid out for 42 generations and culminates with ancestral beginnings from Abraham. One can tell that the focus of the lineage, which is also called the 'Sceptre' blessing (based on Genesis 49:10), was on the direct link between Jesus, King David and Abraham because the very first verse identifies the book as this exact genealogy.

The hurdle that is approached is one of biology because it is recognized that Joseph is not the biological father of Jesus. We read in verses 18 through to 23, that Joseph was approached in his sleep by an Angel after he had already married Mary, who explained the circumstance of her pregnancy. One can tell that Joseph must have been a very just and patient man because he actually took action to protect Mary before the Angel had even reached out to him. The law as written in Leviticus 20:10 certainly would have warranted her death for the crime of adultery; but Joseph chose to shield her from that inevitability. What Joseph does instead is to accept what the Angel has told him. This is confirmed by verse 24 to 25 which states; '*Then Joseph, being aroused from sleep, did as the angel of the Lord commanded him and took to him his wife, and **did not know her till she had brought forth her firstborn Son**. And he called His name Jesus*'. I deem that Joseph action is an acceptance of Jesus as his adopted son and I posit that this adoption results in the full acceptance of heritage into the Judaic line and the **redemption of adoption**. This is a precursor and premise for Galatians 4 which says', '*But when the set time had fully come, God sent his Son, born of a woman, born under the law, to redeem those under the law, that we might **receive adoption to sonship**'* and Ephesian 1: 4 -7 which contains the words, '*In love he predestined us **for adoption to sonship** through Jesus Christ........ In him we have redemption through his blood, the forgiveness of sins.....*'

The second hurdle that must be cleared is the fact that the first book of Matthew relatedly infers that Jesus is the Son of David. In Genesis when **God is giving the promises** to Abram, He makes a particular promise which states, "**Kings shall come out of thee.**" The very same promise is iterated to Sarah, which is quoted as, "**Kings of nations shall be of her**". I surmise that the same basic information being told to both Abram and Sarah is much to do with the procreation of the 'promise' that was made. If we take notice of events following these promises combined with the words that were used; we would get a sense that God placed a mandate on the 'seed' of Abraham as confirmed in Genesis 21: 12 and Hebrews 11:18, "*In Isaac your seed shall be called,*". As told previously, the promise to Abraham and Sarah was given by God when both were very old. They were so old that Sarah actually laughed when she heard God tell Abram that his wife will bear him a son but in Genesis 22, **the promise is fulfilled** as Sarah gives birth to her son and names him Isaac.

The miracle of his birth (Isaac) to old parents who were considered barren is inherited into his life when he himself attempts to have children with his wife Rebekah. We learn that in Genesis 25: 20 – 28 Isaac faithfully prays to God to allow his wife to give birth because she is barren. In these verses we learn that God promises Rebekah that she has two boys in her womb of which only one will be the leader. By verse 26 God makes an identical promise to Isaac as He had made to Abram; '*in your seed all the nations of the earth shall be blessed*'. Isaac and Rebekah have two sons, Esau and Jacob, of which **God's promise** to Rebekah is fulfilled in Jacob who ultimately received the blessing of heritage (I call it) or birthright from Isaac. This line of heritage is important because we are told in Romans 9: 1–13 that God had a 'Sovereign Choice' or a kingly discretion on what the line of heritage would be. It is clarified in this chapter, verses 6 to 8 which says'; '...... *For not all who are descended from Israel belong to Israel, and not all are children of Abraham because* *they are his offspring, but "Through Isaac shall your offspring be named."* This means that it is not the children of the flesh who are the children of God, but the **children of the promise** are counted as offspring'. The 'children of the promise' is fulfilment of the promise made to Sahara.

Esau the first born and Jacob were predestined in the womb of Rebekah. It was foretold by God that: "Two nations are in your womb, Two peoples shall be separated from your body; One people shall be stronger than the other, And the older shall serve the younger" (Genesis 25:23).

The importance of this is that God chose to make Jacob the holy line of heritage because He knew that Esau would be wicked. Genesis 25:24 shows that Esau so despised his birth-right and heritage (something that God had guarded as important for thousands of years) that he was willing to trade it for a bowel of 'red stew ' We find confirmation of how God felt about Esau in Romans 9:11 - 13 where it says'; "*.....though they were not yet born and had done nothing either good or bad—in order that God's purpose of election might continue, not because of works but because of him who calls— she was told, "The older will serve the younger."* As it is written "*Jacob I loved, but Esau I hated.*"

Through God's promise to Sarah and His promise to Isaac; His **divine plan of election is prospered**. God's plan is unchanging. God knows who will 'elect' Him, so He 'elects' them with a purpose in the fullness of His knowledge; this is confirmed in 1 Peter 1: 1-2; '.... ***To God's elect***, *exiles scattered throughout the provinces of Pontus, Galatia, Cappadocia, Asia and Bithynia, who have been chosen according to the* ***foreknowledge*** *of God the Father, through the sanctifying work of the Spirit, to be obedient to Jesus Christ and sprinkled with his blood: Grace and peace be yours in abundance.*'

Understanding that God has a sovereign right to election, helps to paint a clear picture of how Israel received a king. Through the Old Testament, Israel was primarily following a theocracy with various leaders such as Moses acting as mediators to God. By the time that we reach the story of Joseph (son of Jacob) in Genesis 37 we glean that there is great animosity towards Joseph from his brothers who are not all from the same mother. Some are sons[214] of Bilhah and Zilpah (concubines) whiles others were sons of Leah and Rachel (of whom Joseph and Benjamin are from).

Here is where it gets really interesting and the crux of the point towards heritage and spiritual marriage comes into focus.

At this stage, the full lineage of Jacob comes into perspective as the twelve tribes of Israel is established. The reason that there is a dislike for Joseph among his brothers is because he has proven to be the favourite son of Jacob and as if rubbing salt into their wounds, Joseph conveys a dream that he has which implicates servitude by the brothers to Joseph. The brothers plot to kill Joseph but the only sons who do not fully participate in the plot are Reuben and Judah. Whatever insight is brought to the plot against Joseph, one thing becomes certain; it is the intervention of Judah that actually saves Joseph from being killed by the other brothers by suggesting that he be placed into a pit. Now, this is a walk on the proverbial pirates plank (again) but I do believe that this one act by Judah displays the trait that likens him to the wisdom of great rulers and I posit that God blesses him for it. Moving ahead through all that transpired in the life of Joseph, we know indeed that his family does bow down to him. But in a twist of faith, it is Judah that receives the true sceptre of 'kingdomship' when in Genesis 49: 8 - 12 Jacob delivers a prophetic blessing of a lifetime. Jacob tells Judah:

> *"Judah, your brothers will praise you; your hand will be on the neck of your enemies; your father's sons will bow down to you. You are a lion's cub, Judah; you return from the prey, my son. Like a lion he crouches and lies down, like a lioness—who dares to rouse him?*
>
> *The **scepter will not depart from Judah**, nor the ruler's staff from between his feet, **until he to whom it belongs shall***

---

214 http://www.abrahams-legacy.ca/family-tree.html

come *and the obedience of the nations shall be his. He will tether*
his donkey to a vine, his colt to the choicest branch; **he will wash**
his garments in wine, his robes in the blood of grapes. *His*
eyes will be darker than wine, is teeth whiter than milk.

There are a few quick reference points that must be brought to light. Earlier on, this dialogue started by exhibiting the fact that Jesus was called the son of David. If we go to verse 15 of chapter 48 in Genesis, we find that Jacob (who is now called Israel) is speaking to Joseph. He begins blessing Joseph using an idiomatic that I believe is cultural but also inspired by God; he says', "May the God before whom my father's Abraham and Isaac walked faithfully…" We know that Isaac was indeed his father and that Abraham was his grandfather but the successional importance of these two patriarchs is also a key reason he starts by acknowledging them. It is through this line of heritage that God has established His **promises** so this acknowledgement does not go unnoticed.

Also; this is a place of reference where one can see once again how meticulous God is with his prophets that the tree of genealogy reflects the prophetic links to Jesus Christ. Without any doubt the prophecy of Jacob reflects the 'kingly' link to the crown of Jesus.

Still moving towards the point of spiritual marriage and exiting this dialogue from Genesis; there is one final point to be illuminated. When God indicated to Abram much earlier in Genesis that his descendants would be in bondage for 400 years; the story of Joseph and his brothers can actually justify the reason for this. What is easily discerned is that Joseph and his eleven brothers (12 tribes) are not in 'brotherly' harmony. It is fair to say that there is dislike among them. I believe that when God sent them into bondage and showed them that the enemy came not from within or among themselves but from a foreign threat; it was a way of preparing their hearts through persecution to unite them under the justice of one God. What is interesting is God always allows His intention to be seen, even if man fails; I believe that God always wanted the tribes to be united (Revelation 7:4-8) and not at war with each other. This is why we will find that satan constantly attacked the unity between the 'promised' lineage of the tribes but especially Judah and Israel. More proof of this spiritual (demonic) attempt to separate the tribes is found in Judges 19 where a concubine wife from the line of Ephraim who is married to a man from the Levi tribe is brutally raped and murdered by men from the tribe of Benjamin. The crime is so horrendous that the entire remaining tribes unite and succeed in almost vanquishing the entire male population of Benjamin from existence.

Unfortunately when proceeding into the historical account of the prophet Samuel we find the very point where the people of Israel completely divorce themselves from a theocratic existence. In 1 Samuel 8: 5 – 9 Israel ask for an Earthly King to follow and reflect the systems of governance that other pagan cultures such as the Egyptians and Philistines are under. God instructs Samuel to anoint Saul from the tribe of Benjamin as the first king of Israel. At first Saul shows all the attributes of being a very great king but for all his qualities he did the very thing that God did not want from His leaders; he followed his own agenda and disregarded the instructions of God. As said many times before, this is a sore spot for God because He recognizes the many schemes that satan presents into the lives of man and although Samuels failures are seemingly subtle; God in His wisdom knows that satan only needs a subtle start of disobedience to turn it into insurrection.

By 1 Samuel 15, Samuel has informed Saul that he will not be king for much longer due to his disobedience. In verse 27 to 29 there is a demonstrative exhibit God holding fast to His principles. The story reads; *'As Samuel turned to go, Saul grabbed at him to try to hold him back and tore his robe. And Samuel said to him, "See? The Lord has torn the kingdom of Israel from you today and has given it to a countryman of yours who is better than you are. And **he who is the glory of Israel is not lying, nor will he change his mind, for he is not a man!**"* What Samuel is telling Saul is that **God is very principled** and does not simply move away from entrenched policy.

Saul discoverers in 1 Samuel 28:13 - 21 the truth of his faith by seeking out a soothsayer who gives him the prophecy of his impending death; this leads to the first established **kingship in the lineage of Judah.** David is crowned king by 2 Samuel 2: 4 -7 but his chief general Abner absconds to the descendants of Saul.

Here is a fundamental point which I alluded to earlier and although it may seem dragged out there is cogency of truth and logic towards the final point of spiritual marriage. There was several times during the reign of Saul that David had opportunities to kill Saul but refused to do so based on his sense of decency but more fundamental; his sense of faithfulness to the will of God. David did not act on principled things unless directed by God to do so. Through his many faults; David was most noted for his humbleness to God's instructions and will. Each time that a person took it upon themselves to act outside of God's instructions, David would see them killed; 2 Samuel 3:39 and 2 Samuel 4, *'David replied, "I swear by the Lord who saved me from my enemies, 10 that when someone told me, 'Saul is dead,' thinking he was bringing me good news, I killed him; that is how I rewarded him for his 'glad tidings.' 11 And how much more shall I do to wicked men who kill a good man in his own house and on his bed! Shall I not demand your lives?"*

Completely through the book of 2 Samuel and continued through the book of 1 Chronicles we are shown a leader who not only obeys God but consults with him intimately. That line of communication is exactly what sets David apart and makes him the predecessor in the ancestral line who is analogous to Jesus through the phrase *'throne of his father David'*. This is proven in a very effective way. David was from the line of Judah born through Leah.

The only people allowed to enter the Holy Tabernacle were the Levite priest. In 2 Samuel 6: 15 – 18, David is rejoicing because the Ark of the Covenant is being returned home to Israel. During the celebration, the animals stumble and one of the men named Uzzah inadvertently reaches out and touches the Ark (**Uzzah was the son of Abinadab who was an Israelite of the tribe of Judah in whose house the Ark of the Covenant was placed after being returned by** the Philistines; 1 Samuel 7:1) The servant dies immediately. This is very reminiscent of words spoken (and previously quoted) by David in 1 Chronicles 15, '*King David says, "**No one is to carry the ark of God but the Levites…*" This is virtually the same law for entering the 'Holy Tabernacle'. The Tabernacle had an outer and inner chamber, which was called the 'Holy of Holies'. This chamber was only entered by the high priest once a year. In Exodus 28:2 through 43, God is giving Moses instructions on what can be worn in the Tabernacle by the priest. He specifically tells Moses which garment Aaron, who is the High Priest, is to wear; that garment is identified by the name 'Ephod'. Towards the end of the chapter, Moses is also instructed to have garments made for the sons, which are described in verse 40; "*For Aaron's sons you shall make tunics, and you shall make sashes for them. And you shall make hats for them, for glory and beauty.*" God then tells Moses that the clothing is to be worn by the consecrated priest when entering the tabernacle; verse 43 "*They shall be on Aaron and on his sons when they come into the tabernacle of meeting, or when they come near the altar to minister in the holy place, **that they do not incur iniquity and die.**"*

Tying this instruction into the story of the Ark and Uzzah in 2 Samuel 6 there is a tremendous scriptural exaltation of the status of King David. In the first verse it says', '*Wearing a linen **ephod**, David was dancing before the Lord with all his might…*' More revelation is added in verses 17 to 18 which says', '*So they brought the ark of the Lord, and set it in its place in the midst of the tabernacle that David had erected for it. Then David offered burnt offerings and peace offerings before the Lord. And when David had finished offering burnt offerings and peace offerings, he blessed the people in the name of the Lord of hosts.*' Not only did David wear the ephod as high priest; he also entered into the tabernacle as seen in 2 Samuel 7: 18 (TLB), '*Then David went into the Tabernacle and sat before the Lord and prayed*'. **Fundamentally, no other person had ever entered into the Tabernacle that was not from the tribe of Levi; or had anyone, except for a Levi priest, worn the ephod.**

This is why David was the metaphorical father to Jesus. In his actions David became literal king of both Judah and Israel; High Priest over the church and prophet in one person. We know that he was a prophet as verified in the words of Peter in Acts 2: 29 – 30 (NASB); "Brethren, I may confidently say to you regarding the patriarch David that he both died and was buried, and his tomb is with us to this day. 30 "And so, **because he was a prophet** and knew that GOD HAD SWORN TO HIM WITH AN OATH TO SEAT one OF HIS DESCENDANTS ON HIS THRONE[3]".

This is the embodiment of Christ.

> **Prophet** – Moses speaking about Christ said in Deuteronomy 18:15; '*The Lord your God will raise up for you a **prophet** like me from among you, from your 1countrymen, you shall listen to him.*'

> In Matthew 13: 57, Jesus speaking about Himself says'; "*A **prophet** is not without honor except in his 1hometown and in his own household.*"

> **Priest** – Hebrews 6: 20 states; '*.....where Jesus has entered as a forerunner for us, having become a **high priest** forever according to the order of Melchizedek*'.

> Hebrews 9: 11 states; "*But when Christ appeared as a **high priest** of the good things to come, He entered through the greater and more perfect tabernacle, not made with hands, that is to say, not of this creation.*"

> **King** – When appearing before Pilot, Jesus is asked in Matthew 27:11; "Are You the **King of the Jews**?" And Jesus said to him, "**It is as you say**."

> Matthew 2:2 quotes a seeker of Christ; "*Where is He who has been **born a King of the Jews**? For we saw His star in the east and have come to worship Him.*"

The ancestral lineage of Jesus is prophetically confirmed by David in 2 Samuel 7:27 – 29 where he states whiles speaking to God; *"For you have revealed to me, O Lord of heaven, God of Israel, that I am **the first of a dynasty** which will rule your people forever.......... so do as you have **promised**! Bless me and my family forever! May our dynasty continue on and on before you; for you, Lord God, have promised it."*

Through David's line of ancestry Jeremiah 33: 17 – 18 is also confirmed; *'For this is what the Lord says: 'David will never fail to have a man to sit on the throne of Israel, nor will the Levitical priests ever fail to have a man to stand before me continually to offer burnt offerings, to burn grain offerings and to present sacrifices'*

iii. <u>Spiritual Lineage</u>

Galatians 4:28 -31 children of the supernatural

I certainly understand the level of scepticism by those persons who are not spiritually indoctrinated to God's supernatural charge over the process of His will being accomplished. The truth is; the very same disconnect from the presence and work of spiritual relevancy is the reason why 'spiritual lineage' is important to spiritual marriage. The spiritual nature of God as a supernatural being is a physics anomaly which evades the scientific precepts of modern man. The conceptual allusiveness of a spiritual being to the human mind-set has become so metaphorical that God's will to reconnect through spiritual marriage is impeded by man's bulging dis-belief in God and hypocritical exultation of 'the humanist self' as a demi-god. For this reason, many are still today void of accepting or understanding the gift that Jesus spoke of in Luke 11: 13, *"If you then, though you are evil, know how to give good gifts to your children, how much more will your Father in heaven give the Holy Spirit to those who ask him!"*

This has become a circulated problem in man's historic development with God. At every thematic point in the Bible, there is a level of proof that God not only exist but His supernatural presence exudes omnipotent relevance; yet man remains in a **merry-go-round of doubt** from age to age. This doubt has been manifest throughout history whether we speak about Noah and the Ark; Moses in the desert; Joseph in Egypt or the fire from heaven with the prophet Elijah.

The ministry of supernatural work as I would prefer to call it was implemented to distinctly bring truthful balance to the supernatural deceit of satan which is also responsible for **doubt**, and to prepare the way for the redemptive nature of the great miracle. In simple fact; God knew that satan would appear to the people and bring confusion by appearing as 'the god' of supernatural force and that he would also use that confusion to plant seeds of doubt.

Supernatural miracles - The story of **deceit** in Genesis 3 by satan combined with the instructions God gave to Moses in Exodus 4: 1 – 9 reflects what I believe is one of the primary reasons that God imposes His supernatural nature into an organic environment.

The wider scope of the story in Genesis is that satan was also banned from the heavenly realm of God but his banishment brought him as an alien or unnatural being into the cosmos of Earth.

Trying not to fall away from the crux of this point; the depth of this theological dilemma must be conveyed. From the labyrinth of information already presented in this book combined with the representation of Ephesians 6:12, it can be logically attested that satan became the purveyor of worldly opposition to the will of God. The Bible pedantically and without obfuscation points out satan's positioning in the world. That is an important observation because it points to the fact that God acknowledges what satan chooses to hide.

Notice Ephesians 2: 1-3 (LIV) which states; '*Once you were under God's curse, doomed forever for your sins. You went along with the crowd and were just like all the others, full of sin, obeying* **Satan, the mighty prince of the power of the air, who is at work right now in the hearts of those who are against the Lord**. *All of us used to be just as they are, our lives expressing the evil within us, doing every wicked thing that our passions or our evil thoughts might lead us into. We started out bad, being born with evil natures, and were under God's anger just like everyone else'.*

This denotes that God not only acknowledges satan but describes him as the prince of the power of the air. This means that satan has power in this world. That power was seen in Egypt when Moses carried his staff and threw it to the ground in front of Pharaoh. The essential element of relevance is that God in His omniscience told Moses that upon his approach to Pharaoh, he was to perform a miracle guided by the supernatural. It was nothing less than the antithetical supernatural spirit to God, satan, that showed at that moment. Verse 9 tells us that God tells Moses and Aaron that the miracle must be performed because Pharaoh will require a level of proof that Moses is speaking with the authority of God. One would think that upon the staff of Moses turning into a snake, Pharaoh would have acquiesced to the demands of Moses instantly. Think about that. If someone were to approach me and turn a staff into a snake, without any other influences, I would be prepared to do what was beckoned as if a gun were to my head.

Not Pharaoh; Egypt was already a polytheistic[215] society were named gods such as Ra and Baal were being worshipped. The truth about Eygyptian worship is that satan had already established his supernatural power among them but God being always a step ahead of satan's schemes; had already made adjustments in anticipation. Verse 10 to 12 states (LIV); *'So Moses and Aaron went in to see Pharaoh, and performed the miracle, as Jehovah **had** instructed them—Aaron threw down his rod before Pharaoh and his court, and it became a serpent. Then Pharaoh called in his sorcerers—the magicians of Egypt—and they were able to do the same thing with their magical arts! Their rods became serpents, too! But Aaron's serpent swallowed their serpents!'*

The necessity of God's supernatural presence was to negate the deceit of satan who had already used demonic trickery and beguile to convince Pharaoh and his cohorts that they were worshiping the true god.

Satan is the master of deceit and doubt. John 8:44 states; *'You belong to your father, the devil, and you want to carry out your father's desires. He*

---

[215] http://en.wikipedia.org/wiki/Ancient_Egyptian_religion

*was a murderer from the beginning, not holding to the truth, for **there is no truth in him. When he lies, he speaks his native language, for he is a liar and the father of lies.**'* He uses doubt and lies to camouflage his intentions and to conceal the truth of God's purpose.

Spiritual lineage is imputed then, as the establishment of supernatural heritage, which reflects God's spiritual nature to prosper His glory and will on earth and to work against the deceit of satan.

I posit that God revealed his ministry of supernatural work in preparation of man's mind-set towards the greatest supernatural event that would ever occur.

The greatest supernatural miracle was the birth, life and resurrection of Jesus Christ; the purpose for which was to counter the deceit of satan who caused God to divorce His relationship with man.

Redemptive miracle - The miraculous birth and resurrection of Jesus Christ and re-introduction of the Holy Spirit are the physical supernatural confirmation of God's prophetic proclamation of the covenant and the result is the remarriage of man to God.

Consider that Malachi 2 ends where God is speaking of his condescension towards the divorce treachery of the priest. Immediately in Malachi 3 we see the 'New Covenant' answer to that treachery. God begins by prophesying that His '**Messenger of the covenant**' is coming. This is the birth of Jesus. The prophecy of the redemptive miracle which is spiritual remarriage is then spoken of. Malachi 3: 2 - 3 speaks of Christ being like a 'refiner's fire' and like 'launderers' soap' who purifies the 'sons of Levi'; two references to Christ's purposed nature. To refine something is to 'remove impurities or unwanted elements having been removed by processing[216]'; therefore Christ as the refiner's fire is the processor of our sins to have them removed. Christ as the launderers soap is the cleanser who washes away our sins.

---

[216] http://www.thefreedictionary.com/refine

Christ then, as the purifier of the sons of Levi, accomplishes the redemptive union or marriage of 'Judah and Jerusalem' who can then 'offer to the Lord in righteousness'.

The reason that this whole redemptive process is attributed to spiritual marriage is the easily overlooked words of verse 4 which at the end reads, 'Then the offering of **Judah** and **Jerusalem** will be pleasant to the Lord, **as in the days of old, as in former years**'.

Those words are the protracted solution and end of God's wrath against the priest which began in Malachi 2 where the priest had moved away from the covenant and corrupted it. That move away from the covenant created an '**abomination²¹⁷**' whereby Judah profaned the 'holy institution' and Jacob (Jerusalem) was cut off.

Concisely read, one would recall the wording of Malachi 2:9 which says', '......**Because you have not kept My ways....**'. These words are past tense in nature indicated by the past participle 'kept'. What was not kept was God's way as guided by covenant of the fathers. This is another indication of the past as the word 'fathers' is the historical reference to Moses and Abraham. The key link to this historical past relationship is then indicated in verses 14 and 15 both of which speak of '**the wife of your youth**'.

What God is then saying in Malachi 3 is that the Messenger of the covenant (**Jesus**) will purify (**by His supernatural miracle of birth, and resurrection**) the abomination (**sin**) that was committed so that the holy institution is once again reconnected (**as in the days of old, as in former years**) to God such that the relationship of marriage, (**which is the wife of our youth**), is completely restored.

This is the spiritual lineage of Jesus Christ in the Old testament; that Judah and Jerusalem would be spiritually married and united as 'one flesh' under Christ pursuant to Genesis 2:24 and analogously

---

²¹⁷ Malachi 2:11

keeping the focus of the matrimonial ceremony sacred as God intended between a man and woman.

In the New Testament the lineage of Jesus follows through His purpose revealed in Galatians 3: 26 – 29; *For you are all **sons of God through faith in Christ Jesus**. For as many of you as were baptized into Christ have put on Christ. There is neither Jew nor Greek, there is neither slave nor free, there is neither male nor female; for you are **all one** in Christ Jesus. And if you are Christ's, then **you are Abraham's seed, and heirs according to the promise**.*

Here we find that **Jesus has made us all <u>one</u>** through His lineage.

6. <u>The Mystery and the Mysteries revealed</u>

At this stage I would assume that the direction of my intended conclusion is fairly obvious but there still remain a few points that have not been brought to full light.

The Bible can be compared to a treasure map which when read properly and guided by the Holy Spirit, will produce a well-earned bounty. Indeed David was correct in proverbs when he wrote that seeking the word of God like hidden treasure will teach us to revere God and our reward of knowledge and wisdom would be forthcoming.

Unfortunately much of the Bible remains a mystery to the community at large. Today, man seeks to plunder wisdom from places that are only shadows of the truth.

The Bible assures us that there is a clear road map to reveal the stated mystery of marriage but there are some relative mysteries that can only be found through the eyes of the Holy Spirit. For the purpose of this section, I will endeavour to show the mystery of spiritual marriage as stated and the other spiritual mysteries that are discerned through the Holy Spirit in reference to spiritual marriage.

<u>Mysteries revealed</u>

1) Godly Offspring – This fact may not seem as a revealed mystery within the context of this writing because I alluded to it prior to this; but it does not negate the exceptional revelation that this conclusion brings to the conversation of spiritual marriage.

Let's look at the full extrapolation of evidence around this statement made in Malachi 2:15 so as to identify the intrinsic debt of value that God places on this revelation.

Prior to the answer of 'He seeks godly offspring', a type of open-ended question is commissioned to the reader which implicitly gives rationality to the answer. At the very beginning of verse 15 the question that is begged is; *'But did He not make them one, Having a remnant of the Spirit? And why one?'* if we look at this verse in the Living Bible translation it states clearly; *'Has not the one God made you? You belong to him in body and spirit. And what does the one God seek?'* The truth of this translation is derived from the obvious exegesis done from verse 10 which states; *'Have we not all one Father? Has not one God created us? Why do we deal treacherously with one another by profaning the covenant of the fathers?'*

The meaning of the answer in concert with the question fills a very important gap towards Gods 'full' intention.

i. God is critically demonstrating that staying synchronized with Him and His exact plan under the covenant would result in the rationale of His intended purpose for the 'Holy Institute'. His exact plan is spiritual marriage. It indicates that the only way to avoid His intended end is through proselytizing to another way; that way is divorce.

ii. The answer also gives legitimacy to the fact that the only way for offspring to occur is through the copulation of a man and woman (which is also a physical metaphor of the bound between the spirit of man and the Holy Spirit). What God is setting up is the incorporation of the family as intended through the 'Adamic race' and His spiritual kingdom through the perfection of the priesthood. This is a very serious precedent because one can discern that in verse 16 God issues another stern threat against those that pay no heed to His words. He states; *'For the Lord God of Israel says That He hates divorce,* **For it covers one's garment with violence***.'* Notice is brought to the fact that from the beginning of the chapter where God uses the relationship between the priest and the church as a metaphor to the marriage relationship of a man and woman, there are two words that remain consistent with each other; 'treacherously and curse'. The complexity of those two word offerings is that they are resulted from two actions; the priest committing a treacherous act that is an abomination because that act profanes the covenant, and God curing the act and committing the action to various verdicts of sentencing.

What we find from verse 15 then, is that God follows His answer of 'godly offspring' with an immediate verdict to those who do not heed his words.

The fact that God would issue a stern warning directly following gives weight to the premise that He does not take the establishment of the family for the intention of His holy purpose, as an insignificant matter.

iii. That answer opens up the intention of God from the very beginning where in Genesis 1: 28 God says', *'Then God blessed them, and God said to them,* **"Be fruitful and multiply***; fill the earth and subdue it; have dominion over the fish of the sea, over the birds of the air, and over every living thing that moves on the earth."* As stated prior; God wanted man to propagate the Earth with His intention which was to have holy families begetting holy families.

iv. I could see the non-believer yawning at such utopian language but the most amazing fact is that people seem unaware that satan is doing the very same thing. This is the reason why God seeks to maintain so stringently His order of things. Satan seeks offspring also. It is stated directly in Genesis 3:15; *"And I will put enmity Between you and the woman, And **between your seed** and her Seed"*. It is confirmed in revelations 21:8 (TLB) who these seeds are; *"But cowards who turn back from following me, and those who are unfaithful to me, and the corrupt, and murderers, and the immoral, and those conversing with demons, and idol worshipers and all liars—their doom is in the Lake that burns with fire and sulphur. This is the Second Death."*

2) The Great Mystery – Of all the leaps that I have taken to justify my reasoning, I believe that this is the greatest leap of spiritual exegesis yet.

In Ephesians 3: 3 – 6, Paul reveals a great mystery that God has kept hidden from all mankind. The mystery is so revealing that God has given Paul the special assignment to administer the knowledge of this mystery.

I have chosen to quote the Living Bible once again for common language and emphasis of what Paul reveals:

> *God himself showed me this **secret plan** of his, that the Gentiles, too, are included in his kindness. I say this to explain to you how I know about these things. In olden times God did not share this plan with his people, but now he has revealed it by the Holy Spirit to his apostles and prophets.*
>
> *<u>And this is the secret</u>: **that the Gentiles will have their full share with the Jews** in all the riches inherited by God's sons; both are invited to belong to his Church, and all of God's promises of mighty blessings through Christ apply to them both when they accept the Good News about Christ and what he has done for them.*

The intuitive question would be 'why'? Why did God keep such a secret from satan and mankind. The immediate answer is within the verses that follow but I believe that I have been given the spiritual direction to think outside the realm of what was written. My initial inclination to an answer was so radical that I did not know how to write it without possibly offending many people; but here goes.

Firstly; I know that God understands the nature of mankind even before he created us. As an Omniscient God, He knew exactly what types of personalities would emerge among the many cultures of Earth. Take notice in the book of Genesis when God makes his promises to Abraham and Sarah. Every promise that God gives is a prophecy about the future. When He tells Abraham that his generations will be like the stars in the sky; is there any doubt that the maker of such a declarative decree, must have seen with clairvoyance into the lives of each generation of persons to come. Indeed, God told the prophet Jeremiah[218] as much when He said, *"Before I formed you in the womb I knew you, before you were born I set you apart; I appointed you as a prophet to the nations."*

If this is true; take further notice of His continued description of the Israelites throughout Exodus. In Exodus 33 God tells Moses; *"And I will send My Angel before you, and I will drive out the Canaanite and the Amorite and the Hittite and the Perizzite and the Hivite and the Jebusite. Go up to a land flowing with milk and honey; for I will not go up in your midst, lest I consume you on the way, **for you are a stiff-necked people.**"* I alluded to this previously but the jest of what I am conveying now is that the Israelites were defiant to a fault. Most amazingly is that many do not see the by-product of the 'fault' which is actually their strength. Whiles it is easily shown that many in the nation of Israel inexplicably and irrationally rejected the Messiah after the many miraculous revelations placed before them; what is often missed is the level of resilience that they have shown as a people.

---

[218] Jeremiah 1:5

Throughout the Bible, the nation of Israel suffered greatly due to their impertinence to God's will. God delivered them over to their enemy (figuratively and literally) over and over again. It was as if a father stood over his wayward child and spanked that child in discipline each time he would rebel. Israel continuously rebelled but showed a tenacity for survival.

Well; I posit that Israel could be likened to the sacrificial lamb. What was birthed out of Israel was the Saviour Himself. A closer look under the microscope and we can understand perhaps a deep hidden truth. Israel as a nation and people had the resilience and tolerance to bring forth the Messiah. Again, for those who are of the belief that we operate on an ambiguous plain of existence; I draw you back to this much used verse in my writings. Ephesians 6: 12 states; *"For we do not wrestle against flesh and blood, but against principalities, against powers, against the rulers of the darkness of this age, against spiritual hosts of wickedness in the heavenly places."*

What I believe based on my level of bible reading, is that God has a purpose in everything that he does and much of that purpose is revolved around crushing the plan of the enemy; satan. God did not simply choose the Israelites as His people based on a random proportion of thought or irrational favouritism. I posit that God knew these people and their 'zealous' attitudes. The deepest revelation of this thought for me was the premise that God's selection of the nation of Israel was a proverbial curve ball thrown at satan. I am not suggesting that God simply played a game with the lives of hundreds of millions of people but I am suggesting that He intuitively knew that Israel was best suited as a people to accomplish his 'purposed' purpose. Satan could not see the pitch coming at him.

Notice that as a testament, the majority of the Old Testament has nothing to do (except as peripheral stories of fact) with the history of the Gentiles. Besides stories which must reflect historical context about figures like Caesar, or Goliath, or Pharaoh (etc.); there is no true instance where the direction of the storyline is specifically relevant to a Gentile.

Why is this true? I direct my evidence back to the book of Genesis once again and the story of Noah. In Genesis 6 there is wickedness on the earth that is unprecedented. This level of sin existing occurred before God established a **standard** with Abraham and his faithful righteousness; and Moses under the law. Satan had established his own standard. On the Earth at that time, satan was roaming about with the other fallen angels and chaos was consuming the world. As a result of satans activities, God is fully aware that satan is attempting to change the course of creation. God makes a statement that most may interpret as either an admission of being wrong or an attitude of giving up. Neither assertion is true. What is true is that even though God is fully aware of satan's schemes; it does not mean that He is not 'touched' or grieved to see the extent of the suffering and carnage that satan brings. Through it all, God prospers His unyielding love for man. In Genesis 6: 7- 8, the Lord said, "*I will wipe from the face of the earth the human race I have created—and with them the animals, the birds and the creatures that move along the ground—for I regret that I have made them.*" *But Noah found favor in the eyes of the Lord.*

An expression, which seems appropriate here is, 'power corrupts and it corrupts absolutely'. We are aware that satan is a principle power in the world system. He has so corrupted his mind that what has emerged is a blind assumption that he has become an ultimate power. He is so emboldened, that he even took the liberty to stand before Jesus to attempt the unattainable; to place God in the person of Jesus, under his worldly control.

1 Peter 5:8 states; '*Be alert and of sober mind. Your enemy the devil prowls around like a roaring lion looking for someone to devour*'.

In the book of Job 1:7; 'The LORD said to Satan, "*Where have you come from?*" Satan answered the LORD, "*From roaming throughout the earth, going back and forth on it.*" Then the Lord said to Satan, "*Have you considered My servant Job, that there is none like him on the earth, a blameless and upright man, one who fears God and shuns evil?*" This for me is one of the first insights into the secret why God used the Israelites. The fervour and unyielding faith that Job showed to God was a milestone testament to what zealous conviction the Israelites would show once they come to the conviction that Jesus is the Messiah.

I believe that God did not want satan to plunder the true treasure on Earth so God kept it a secret until after the resurrection of Christ. The time had not come. The level of chaos that satan unleashed throughout the Old Testament was primarily against the nation of Israel. I believe that if satan was fully aware that the Gentiles would also become redeemed sons of God; the level of chaos in this world after the flood and before Christ, would have been similar to the time before Noah. When nations such as the Philistines, Egypt and Rome (among others) prospered; I posit that satan was under the false opinion that these nations were completely under his control. His focus remained on Israel. Notice that God was wisely using other nations to accomplish great things in the development of man. Rome developed and proliferated the text of the Bible as well as Christianity far beyond any nation at that time but Rome began as a very pagan nation.

The birth and resurrection of Christ brought in a new dispensation of life for which death was no-longer a tool that satan could use as a hostage taker. I use 1Corinthians 2:7 - 8 as a marker to show how even the Sadducees and Pharisees, the men of learning, were even blinded by the influence of satan and could not see into the mysteries of Jesus according to Paul. It states; '*But we **speak the wisdom of God in a mystery**, even the hidden wisdom, which God ordained before the world unto our glory: Which none of the princes of this world knew: for had they known it, they would not have crucified the Lord of glory*'.

What I see in Israel is a nation that mirrored the life of Christ on Earth. Consider the reading of Hebrews 2: 10 from the Living Bible; '*And it was right and proper that God, who made everything for his own glory, should allow Jesus [Israel] to suffer, for in doing this he was bringing vast multitudes of God's people to heaven; for his suffering made Jesus a perfect Leader, one fit to bring them into their salvation.*'

I put forth, that Israel was the precedent of Christ and that we find the end result of this fact mirrored in the birth of Christ out of Israel.

Verses 14 – 15 of Hebrews 2 states; '*Since we, God's children, are human beings—made of flesh and blood—he became flesh and blood too by being born in human form; for only as a human being could he die and in dying break the power of the devil who had the power of death. Only in that way could he deliver those who through fear of death have been living all their lives as slaves to constant dread*'.

This is why the secret was kept; satan was under the assumption that Israel was the only 'prize' and that if he destroyed Israel he would end Gods proclamation of a kingdom on Earth. Satan has deceived himself. He assumed in his corrupt mind that because God is so very orderly, He would continue to allow the '**prince of the power of this air** (Ephesians 2:1-3)' to rule.

What God was able to achieve through these 'stiff-necked' people was a distraction before satan, such that this resilient people, through the greatest of adversities was able to produce a Messiah. This Messiah then **remarried Judah and Israel** and through His resurrection He redeemed Israel to God. His resurrection also revealed the mystery miracle; **Jews and Gentiles were made one flesh, united in our ability to be re-married to God through atonement of sins.**

3)   One Flesh – This is a very curious phrase. It has the complexity of a physics equation which has no solutions but this is the reason why it is a mystery. The immediate and perhaps most important implication of the phrase is its direct correlation to marriage.

It is generally agreed by Christian Apologist that the hermeneutics of Genesis 2: 18 – 24 denotes and is consistent with a marriage relationship. What has become controversial are the implications and interpretations of that relationship.

In an effort to streamline clarity to this conversation we will look at the points of interest that are based primarily on the words attributed to what God has said or conversely what Jesus has said; because, it is my view that the true authority on the matter is derived from the source or maker of the comment.

215

i. Genesis 2:18 - *The Lord God said, "It is not good for the man to be alone. I will make a helper suitable for him"*.

The understanding of this statement has to come from a rummage through all the preceding verses and those directly following which gives a fair understanding of where God was in His thoughts.

First of all; the statement is a declarative one. God is not unsure or using an interrogative to ascertain a truth. In verse 8 God has made a decision that He will place Adam in this beautiful natural habitat which He has created and make Adam the chief caretaker.

Even-though Adam was given dominion over all that was created back in verse 26 of chapter 1; God sets out rules for him to follow as he works in the garden. This is the very first precedent of law and obedience given to Adam. There was no doubt that God establishes this standard for Adam to adhere to. It is the principle of rules and punishment. If it were not so, Adam would not have received the punishment of being cast out of the Garden.

After making the statement in verse 18, God proceeds to give Adam the direct task of naming all the living creatures. What is curious is that God never goes back to his statement to justify or clarify why it is not good for man to be alone. I believe that no level of explanation is given because God had no need to justify what He ordained as 'good'. What is more interesting is that God has already established that Adam will be the caretaker of the garden but we are given a first-hand view of what he is to do in verses 19 to 20. Why? It is noticeable that in correlation to Adam naming all the animals, verse 21 begins with the conjunction 'but'. It is a conveyance of sorts. The placement of the word at the beginning of a new verse seeks to convey the occurrence of a sequence of situations which have influenced or will influence a new set of events to occur. There had to be some level of significance to the actions in verses 19 and 20 for God to produce an indicator of change.

What the conjunction signified was that God had given life to procreation synergies through creating male and female species of animals '**but**' Adam was without such a companion. This must follow as logically true because after previously saying that man should not be alone and then showing that Adam was responsible for naming all the species; God provides an **immediate** solution. What God did by creating a companion was, again, to stay with His 'ordered' nature and simply place Adam within the scope of what had already been mandated as a natural consequence; one male specie with one female specie.

He did not solve the problem by giving Adam a male friend that could share in all the 'manly' task at-hand. He did not direct him to the species of dogs or cats or any animal that has a compassionate quality of companionship. God unequivocally provided the only solution to His holy purpose which He prospered as a decree in Malachi 2:15; "…He seeks godly offspring".

This attaches true depth of meaning to Genesis 1:28 which God spoke with entrenched intention. It states, *"Be fruitful and multiply; fill the earth and subdue it; have dominion over the fish of the sea, over the birds of the air, and over every living thing that moves on the earth."*

God's solution is then an evolving confirmation of His other purposes because He then blesses the words of Adam after Eve is created. Immediately into the verses which follow God refers to a marriage situation whereby Eve is called 'wife'. In Genesis 3: 20 it states that *'Adam named his **wife** Eve, because she would become the mother of all the living'*.

This verse clarifies the sexual relationship between Adam and his wife because she is only made a 'mother' through the sexual union of both.

God's words in verse 18 were spoken with such authority that He allowed His actions to authenticate His thoughts. He did not say that Adam should not me alone. He said that 'man' should not be alone. Adam being the first 'representation of man' carried the blue-print of God's intention forward. Unyielding companionship (marriage) through being '**one flesh**', must have been the intended solution to being alone; because, in Malachi 2: 14 – 15 God states that any action of removal or separation from the wife is in fact treachery done to your companion who is a wife by covenant (thus we know that it is an unyielding relationship) and who He has made one with the man.

ii.   Matthew 19:3-6 – If ever there was doubt about the meaning of marriage through the reading of Genesis and Malachi, we find that Jesus gave such force and clarity to the intention of God that it becomes the standard of authority among the Pharisees.

Jesus was asked, *"Is it lawful for a man to divorce his wife for just any reason?"* Here is what Jesus told the Pharisees who were attempting to test the authority of Christ; *"Have you not read that He who made them at the beginning* **'made them male and female***, 'For this reason a man shall leave his father and mother and be* **joined to his wife, and the two shall become one flesh***'? So then, they are no longer two but one flesh.* **Therefore what God has joined together, let not man separate***."*

This pronouncement at the end of the verse 6 is a statement of authority. Jesus quotes words given by God the Father verbatim in Genesis 2 then adds, "Therefore what God has joined together, let not man separate".

Unless I am proven wrong at some later stage; I have never seen a quote of God used in the Bible which was repeated either out of context or added to. We know that God takes this very serious since He curses those who would do so in Revelations where it says', *"For I testify unto everyone who hears the words of the prophecy of this book,* **if anyone adds to these things, God will add to him the plagues** *that are written in this book; And* **if anyone takes away** *from the words of this book of this prophecy,* **God shall take away his part from the Book of Life***, and from the holy city, and from the things which are written in this book."*

Unequivocally, Jesus (as God on Earth) had full authority to do so as confirmed and pursuant to Matthew 28: 18; 'And Jesus came and said to them, *"All authority in heaven and on earth has been given to me"*.

The statement of Jesus places a heavenly decree by God on marriage. It indicates that it is not a mere union of two physical bodies but a marriage of two becoming one and overseen by the covenantal decree of God himself. 'One Flesh' is only achieved through the covenant of marriage.

iii. Copyright Blueprint – For lack of a better description, I have used the term copyright blueprint to connote a plan by God that can't be replaced, transformed or tampered with in any way. I believe that God's choice of wording was very deliberate in conveying His message. His words from Matthew 19:3-6 infer a physical imperative and a command. When a woman and man come together under marriage the one thing that is completely expected is that they will have sex. If we digest all the words used between Genesis 2 and Malachi 2 we would recognize that the sum total of the meaning derived has a heavy suggestion that copulation must occur after the couple becomes one to produce 'godly' offspring.

What is also certain is that two men (women) cannot become one flesh because they can't copulate to produce heirs. It is impossible. This is why the godly offspring is so significant. **God did not prescribe the marriage of man and woman to only sex** because as a physical act sex can be accomplished or replicated in many ways that does not involve a man and woman or more importantly, God's will.

God understands in full this disparity of depraved actions that satan creates in the consciousness of man; this is exhibited in Acts 13:10 which states emphatically, *"You are a child of the devil and an enemy of everything that is right! You are full of all kinds of deceit and trickery. Will you never stop perverting the right ways of the Lord?"*

God knew that satan had perverted the act of copulation so He differentiated the act by descriptive words which showed His abiding intention.

He calculatingly accomplished this when He made the outcome of **marriage, procreation;** a 'godly or holy' purpose. Not only can't two same gender humans accomplish the miracle of birth but they can't attain the holy purpose. This is a key reason why God drew a descriptive standard in relating to the act of sex. He was again fully aware that men and women would be tempted to have sex outside of marriage. He described this act as 'sexual immorality' in 1 Corinthians 7:2; but when it came to sex between two males he used the adjectives 'detestable[219]' and 'abomination[220]' because whiles sex outside of marriage is wrong and sinful, He did not leave room for doubt that satan would blur the lines between premarital sex and homosexual sex. They are both wrong but distinguished by description.

To be fair to this line of reasoning; there are other acts called abominations in the Bible[221] but the point still stands because God uses the same dynamics to convey the degree of His disdain for acts which create chaos towards the testimony of God and His created intentions.

4) The mystery of Melchizedek – Going through the reading of various chapters and verses in the Bible allowed me to understand much about the divine intention of God towards His created institution of marriage. When I wrote about the heritage of Jesus I felt that there was something missing in the equation.

I knew that Jesus unified the tribes of Israel through His kingly heritage in the line of David to establish a kingdom where 2 Samuel 7: 12 -16 is established. This line of heritage fulfilled the exultation of prophecy found in Revelations 19: 16 which states; 'On his robe and thigh was written this title: **"King of Kings and Lord of Lords."**

I also recognised that His earthly heritage from Mary to Adam was purposed as the '**Redeemer**' to His people as seen in Psalms 111:9; '*He sent redemption unto his people: he hath commanded his covenant for ever: holy and reverend is his name*'. This is then confirmed in 1 Corinthians 1:30 (NKJV) '*But of Him you are in Christ Jesus, who became for us wisdom from God—and righteousness and sanctification and*

---

[219] Leviticus 20:13
[220] Leviticus 18: 22
[221] Proverbs 6:16 - 19

redemption—'. For additional emphasis I will quote from the Living Bible so that the point on **redemption** is not misunderstood; "*For it is from God alone that you have your life through Christ Jesus. He showed us God's plan of salvation; he was the one who made us acceptable to God; he made us pure and holy and gave himself to purchase our salvation.*"

Where I remained somewhat perplexed was in understanding the lineage of the Levites because it seemed that in the orderly nature of God, there had to be provision made to account for heritage of the keepers of the Tabernacle.

Attention is brought to 2 Samuel 7 once again where God is speaking to the prophet Nathan. He dialogues on a deeply personal level as illustration of His relationship with the people of Israel; verses 5 – 7 state, "*Go and tell my servant David, 'Thus says the Lord:* **Would you build me a house to dwell in?** *I have not lived in a house since the day I brought up the people of Israel from Egypt to this day, but I have been moving about in a tent for my dwelling. In all places where* **I have moved with** *all the people of Israel, did I speak a word with any of the judges of Israel, whom I commanded to shepherd my people Israel, saying,* **Why have you not built me a house of cedar?**'"

I have already clarified that within the Tabernacle there was the Holy of Holies, or the Most Holy Place which was the inner chamber where God received the High Priest personally once a year. We understand from 2 Samuel 7: 5 - 6 that God in a conversation with great humble overtones, tells Nathan that it is time that David makes plans for his son Solomon to build a permanent Tabernacle. What really intrigued me most in the language is the image of our creator living in a simple tent environment to meet the judges (the Levite priest). We gain a sense of God's love towards His people as He subjects Himself to such a state of diaspora and instability imagined in a tent setting. In essence it was a 'make-shift' environment which moved when the people moved; it was not permanent. This is where God met the spiritual requirements of the people. At this time God was literally protecting the needs of Israel. **His dwelling place was less than perfect** but He fulfilled all their necessities. Although the tent enclave was not permanent, the instructions God gave to Moses in Exodus 25 on how to construct the Tabernacle and to keep the 'tent' environment were very specific and even elaborate.

The work of the Levite priest to maintain the Tabernacle and to receive instructions towards the people was not understated. If we closed our eyes for a moment and imagined the most powerful God, Yahweh, placing us into service to carry 'His person' in a box; we would then understand the indelible importance of the work that the Levite priest had to fulfil. Also; we should not forget the fact that the people needed the enforced imagery of God being physically with them as assurance.

This necessity and rigid instructions on the upkeep of the Tabernacle is understood through Deuteronomy 23:14 (ESV) where God gives a purpose of why the Tabernacle was needed; *'Because the Lord your God walks in the midst of your camp, to deliver you and to give up your enemies before you, therefore your camp must be holy, so that he may not see anything indecent among you and turn away from you'*.

Primarily then, God travelled with the people of Israel in His 'Holy environment' of the Tabernacle which the priest protected. Let's bring notice to the fact that it is stated by God that the judges (priest) of Israel were '**commanded**' to shepherd the people.

The very inquisitive nature of this is finding the answer to why God made such a 'fuss' about lineage and the ordered nature of His purpose for the Levites whiles also commanding them to carry-out this mandate.

On the surface, one would believe that all the Tabernacle work and order that was established in the Old Testament by God in relationship to the Levites, was then circumvented by the apparent removal of the 'shepherds of the Tabernacle' through the establishment of the perfect priesthood by Jesus.

We have already recognized the lineage shown in Revelation 5: 4 -10 which confirms the positioning of Jesus as *'the Lion of the tribe of Judah, the Root of David'*; this is the Kingly discretion. He is also acknowledged in verse 9 as *'the redeemer of the people';* but; and in verse 10 Jesus is attributed with carrying out the **appointed Levitical task**

of shepherding as the people are made 'holy seed' or priest so that His kingdom may reign on Earth.

That is a revelation because we know that Jesus was not a Levite. His lineage is not in line with the tribe of Levi. Did God break His orderly nature in restoring the Tabernacle through Christ? Certainly we can see again, that God took a determined route to verify the heritage of the priest by specifically naming their generations through 1 Chronicles 6:1-30; so we know that He had a great purpose for them through lineage.

I posit that God made provision for this transition from Genesis. Let's reason this out. Through all that I have presented on the priesthood it can easily be understood that there was a failure in their ministry as seen from the book of Malachi 2 which states that they 'profaned the Holy institution' of God's marriage to man. Drawing our attention forward to Malachi 3: 2-3; Jesus is characterized as the one who will 'refine', clean and 'purify', the sons of Levi so that (verse4) "the **offering** of Judah and Jerusalem, **Will be pleasant to the Lord, As in the days of old, As in former years**".

What did God mean when He alluded to the 'offering' so specifically and when was it so 'pleasant'. Even more, considering the tumultuous years of the priest; which 'days of old' is God referring to?

Special attention is paid to the fact that as a priest Jesus is called, in Hebrews 5:8-10, by God to be high priest. It states; "*though He was a Son, yet He learned obedience by the things which He suffered. And **having been perfected**, He became the author of eternal salvation to all who obey Him, called by God as High Priest "according to the order of Melchizedek*,"

In earnest then; Jesus received the authority through God to be 'High Priest' but the curiosity remains as to why the lineage was not accredited.

If we look at verse 9 it uses the past participle 'perfected' to describe the state of being for Jesus. Again I will parallel two translations to give effect to the point at hand. Hebrews 7:11 rhetorically places the question in the New King James which asks; '*Therefore, if **perfection were** through the Levitical priesthood (for under it the people received the law), what further need was there that another priest should rise according to the order of Melchizedek, and not be called according to the order of Aaron?* '.

In the Living Bible the verse reads; '*If the Jewish priests and their laws had been able to save us, **why then did God need to send Christ as a priest with the rank of Melchizedek**, instead of sending someone with the rank of Aaron—the same rank all other priests had?*'

As yet another rhetorical question, the answer is implied; the Levite priesthood was subject to imperfection and God needed the perfect priesthood to establish his new tabernacle so that He could perfect what happened in 2 Samuel 7; He would perfect how He was '**with**' us.

Before I jump the gun to pull this theory together; let me clarify who I have determined Melchizedek to be.

In Genesis 14: 18 – 20, a battle has taken place between a conglomerate of opposing kings which has resulted in Abrahams' nephew (Lot) being captured. The victories kings have successfully looted the spoils of Sodom and Gomorrah. After Abraham learns of this, he pursues the kings and is successful in defeating them and returning the riches which they confiscated.

A great mystery of the Bible then occurs. Abraham is approached by the 'King of Salem' who is called **Melchizedek**. There is no part of the Biblical introduction of Melchizedek that does not play into prophetic analogies.

1. He is called 'King of Salem'. It is generally accepted by scholars that Salem is equivalent to Jerusalem and that the word connotes

'peace[222]'. According to an official Israeli tourism site[223] the old city of Jerusalem was built in 1004 B.C.E by King David.

2. Abraham gave a tithe offering to Melchizedek. Hebrews 7: 4 -10 draws a conclusive statement of the authority that Melchizedek has. Abraham is without doubt the chosen leader in the plan of God. He is called the 'patriarch' to satisfy his standing as a progenitor of single authority among the people. The verses describe Abraham as the biological premise of the Levi priest who out of the 'loins' of Abraham inherit full authority to manage tithe offerings. Why then would Abraham offer a tenth tithe to an earthly King and not God?

The quick but most complex answer is because this man is not a man, but a physical aberration of the spiritual Jesus. This can be debated from now until the 'second coming' but again I will take an analytical and evidentiary angle to this paradoxical mystery.

- Verse 4 says', 'Just think how great he was'. I ask; how could an Earthly king of such distinction, who could command a tithe from Abraham (who God bestowed such favour that nations came from him), not be given a place of Earthly prominence in the developing tribes or kingdoms that came from Abraham? Melchizedek is mentioned in Genesis and Hebrews under the exact same account. It is not rational that a person so important would not be spoken of in a definitive way that testifies to his work on Earth. Every major figure in the Bible has been enshrined according to their purpose. Moses is the deliverer and prophet. King David, Solomon, Saul etc, have all had their kingdoms written about. Why not Melchizedek if he is only an earthly king?

222

223 http://www.goisrael.com/Tourism_Eng/Articles/Attractions/Pages/ OldCityJerusalem.aspx

- In verse 3 it says that Melchizedek resembled Jesus but had no father or mother and had no genealogy. We are aware that Jesus had a physical Earthly mother and adopted Earthly father. His genealogy is traced to the tribe of Judah. Here is the big question; did Jesus only come into existence when He was born to Mary? If that is so, then every prophetic verse in the Bible that speaks of Jesus would be the seed of who Jesus is. This means that Jesus only came into existence and was shaped by the conversations of Him through the Bible. I posit that this is false. In Genesis 1: 26 it says', 'Then God said, "Let **us** make mankind in **our** image, in **our** likeness,…" This is taken to mean that God's natural state already was (still is) the Holy Trinity. Jesus appears to Abraham in the 'likeness' of the physical person He would become.
- Consideration also has to be made to God's natural order on Earth. Even God made provision for His person of Earth to appear as man in the flesh with an adopted father and 'surrogate' mother. In this same natural order; it is impossible for an Earthly King of such importance to not have parents and no genealogy.
- There is an old adage which says', 'what is good for the goose is good for the gander'. How could Abram say to the king of Sodom, "*With raised hand I have sworn an oath to the Lord, God Most High, Creator of heaven and earth, that I will accept nothing belonging to you, not even a thread or the strap of a sandal, so that you will never be able to say, 'I made Abram rich.'*"; but offer a tenth tithe to the King of Salem from the very same spoils? Psalms 24: 1 says', 'The earth is the Lord's, and everything in it, the world, and all who live in it;' I state emphatically that Abraham was giving to God Himself.

3. From constructing this point, attention is then drawn to the reaction of the King of Sodom who in Genesis 14: 21 has asked Abraham to, "*Give me the people and keep the goods for yourself.*" Abraham's reply to this, establishes four Biblical standards (which

exalts the Trinitarian hypothesis) when he tells The King that he would refuse any such offer to avoid the possibility of an inference that this earthly King has provided the blessing of riches to sustain himself (Abraham).

- The **first** standard is that 'the father of nations' Abraham has shown that his **pledge** (any pledge or oath thereafter) **to the Lord must be kept**. Ecclesiastes 5:4-7 says', *'When you make a vow to God, do not delay to pay it; For He has no pleasure in fools. Pay what you have vowed- Better not to vow than to vow and not pay. Do not let your mouth cause your flesh to sin, nor say before the messenger of God that it was an error. Why should God be angry at your excuse[a] and destroy the work of your hands? For in the multitude of dreams and many words there is also vanity. **But fear God**.'* (emphasis added)

I contend that tithes are a vow we spiritually take as Christians in recognition of God's grace in our lives. Abraham would not have given a tithe to an earthly king as demonstrated.

- He **secondly** establishes the **purpose** for the tithe in the Old Testament. Notice that the account of Abraham and the King of Sodom takes place after Abraham has already given his tithe to Melchizedek. Abraham acknowledges the King of Salem before he acknowledges the King of Sodom. Furthermore, Abraham has distributed from the spoils a portion to his men, which means that he has acted with authority to remove from the spoils only after Melchizedek has received the tithe but before the King of Sodom makes an impotent gesture of offer. Deuteronomy 14:22-23 says', " *Be sure to set aside a tenth of all that your fields produce each year. Eat the tithe of your grain, new wine and olive oil, and the firstborn of your herds and flocks in the presence of the Lord your God at the place he will choose as a dwelling for his Name, so that you may **learn to revere*** *(fear) the Lord your God always."*(emphasis added). In my laymen's understanding, I would say that this precedent was established to 'keep man honest'. Men often revile in their own accomplishments as if they are the only source of their own goodwill and fortune. Deuteronomy 8:18, says, *"And you shall remember the LORD your God, for it is He who gives you power to get wealth, that He may establish His covenant which He swore to your fathers, as it is this day"*. The reaction of Abraham shows that he trusts only in the Lord as his source and shows the pre-eminence of respect to God as the owner and Creator of all when he gives to Melchizedek.

- **Thirdly;** even though Adam gave an offering to God in Gen. 4:3-5, the first true precedent on the 'tenth tithe' was through Abraham. I posit that the Priest to God, Melchizedek, had this ceremonial tithing done to establish the faith of Abraham by tithing which propelled him to success through (at that time the 'Law') the grace of God. In verse 19 of Genesis 14 it says' that Abraham was 'Blessed' by God and that blessing signified a return or reward byway of defeat of Abrahams enemies because of his faith to give back to God. I believe that the seed[224] for the beginning of the prophetic tribe of Levi (as quoted in Hebrews 7: 10), was blessed by Melchizedek through Abraham. I posit that this was the beginning of the prophetic covenant work of the Levite priest, which, under the law, brought forth the transition into the new dispensation of grace. Melchizedek, I believe, was the preeminent positioning of the 'perfect cure' that the Messiah would bring to the earthly priesthood as the one who would also establish the 'power of an endless life[225]'.

- **Finally; I contend that this is the perfection of the offering which God alluded to in Malachi 3:3 -4; which is given in the days of old.**

---

[224] Hebrew 7: 10
[225] Hebrew 7:16

My postulation towards this mystery is that Jesus and Melchizedek are one in the same. Genesis 1: 26 states; *'Then God said, "Let Us make man in Our image, according to Our likeness..."* In Genesis 3:21 it is further stated; *'Also for Adam and his wife the Lord God made tunics of skin, and clothed them'.*

These two verses are the truth of a certain fact; there had to be a slight physical change to Adam after he was in the image and more importantly the 'likeness' of *'Us'* (as stated in Genesis 1: 26). Adam was in the 'likeness of image' to God but he was transformed into a different image by having skin placed upon him.

We are aware from previous scripture quoted here that Jesus existed before creation; so the only deduction that I can draw is that Melchizedek, as the pre-existence of Jesus, appeared in His spiritual avatar similar to the form Adam existed in before his fall.

I draw my conclusion from that contention which is; the new Tabernacle which God perfected through Jesus in the order of Melchizedek is where the light now dwells in man. The golden lampstand which is spoken of in Exodus 25:31-40 is a magnification of Jesus in John 8: 12, *"I am the light of the world. He who follows Me shall not walk in darkness, but have the light of life.";* and John 9:5 which states *"As long as I am in the world, I am the light of the world".*

Let's transpose Malachi 2:15 with 2 Samuel 7: 10 – 16 and emerge the reasoning. I surmise that Malachi 2:15 is the prophetic procreation of God's intention throughout mankind. Before the resurrection of Christ, the Levitical priest carried the Tabernacle in their midst. God lived in a tented area. The people received instructions to move in His righteousness but their intimate relationship with God was only achieved through the intercession of the judges (priest). When God gave instructions in 2 Samuel 7 to establish a permanent home and He further tells them what that permanence would mean in verses 10 – 16; it is recognised that this is the precedent of how the New Covenant Tabernacle will exist. The 'Holy Seed' as a procreated reality is achieved through a permanent home for God. In verse 12 where God speaks of the seed of David being established; He confirms that His promise will be everlasting in verse 13.

Final thought to this process is that we have seen that Bible verses over a plethora of hidden treasure in meaning. My most profound contention is that the perfection of the ministry which Melchizedek offered, was the perfect ministry to usher in the marriage between God and man once again, which brings permanence. That perfection could not occur through the 'Ministry of Death' which the Levites where shepherds of. True confirmation of this is the parallel of meaning found between 1 Corinthians 3 and Malachi 3. In verses 5 – 6 of 1 Corinthians (TLB) Paul tells the Corinthians that, He and Apollos are, '…. *just God's servants, each of us with certain special abilities, and with our help you believed. <u>My work was to **plant the seed** in your hearts, and Apollos' work was to water it, but it was God, not we, who made the garden grow in your hearts.</u>*' In Malachi 3:3 attention is brought to the work of the Levite priest where it says', '*He will purify the Levites, the ministers of God, refining them like gold or silver, <u>so that they will do their work for God</u> with pure hearts.*' Both chapters set the foundation of providing the service of work. Malachi is in the Old Covenant where the work of the priest is 'procreational' in terms of impregnating the people with the laws and ways of God. Corinthians is a book under the New Covenant where the work of the priest is still procreational through preaching the acceptance of Jesus as the Messiah, which is the work of planting the seed.

The work of the priest has not changed but the orifice to the Tabernacle is no-longer a tent where the judge enters the Tabernacle to receive the blessings to and for the people. Its' opening is now directly through the faith of man receiving and believing in the message of the Gospel of Jesus Christ.

In a burst of revelation one can see that Malachi 3 is also a depiction of the judgement of man shown in the book of Revelations (this is important because from the Old Testament to the New Testament man has paid a price for rejecting God's Holy word).

Notice that the transition to judgement in verse 5 occurs after the perfection of the sacrament, which is the purifying of the sons of Levi who are then able to offer righteousness to God. Malachi 3: 4- 5 (TLB); '*4 Then once more the Lord will enjoy the offerings brought to him by the people of Judah and Jerusalem, as he did before. 5 At that time my punishments will be quick and certain;...*'

This is the exactness of salvation through Jesus found in the correlated chapter in Corinthians. Just as the metals are tested in Malachi for the result of purity through the heat of fire; the elements are tested in verses 12 -13 where it states, '*Now if anyone builds on this foundation with gold, silver, precious stones, wood, hay, straw, each one's work will become clear; for the Day will declare it, because it will be revealed by fire; and the fire will test each one's work, of what sort it is*'.

Why are they being tested? They are being tested because God now has the perfect foundation which He Himself is married to as a standard. That standard has a **resolve of judgement if rejected** as also seen in Malachi. In 1 Corinthians3: 16 – 17 we are given the outcome of any Tabernacle that has either rejected God or not utilized the 'proper materials. It states; so he will either not endure or "*endures, [and] he will receive a reward. If anyone's work is burned, he will suffer loss; but he himself will be saved, yet so as through fire* ". Verses 16 – 17 states; "*Do you not know that you are the temple of God and that the Spirit of God dwells in you?* **If anyone defiles the temple of God, God will destroy him.** *For the temple of God is holy, which* <u>*temple you are.*</u>"

God achieved perfection of the Tabernacle in the perfect priesthood of Jesus (in the line of Melchizedek) so that He (God) no-longer had to live in a tent or have a separate conversation through a priest. His convictions, instructions and glory are now all achieved through the anointing of the 'Spirit of God' residing in the perfect Tabernacle which is '**each person**' that accepts the gift of salvation.

As stated previously, **Jesus did not 'do-away' with the work of the Levite priest; He perfected their work.** Jesus did not do away with the chastisement upon the priest; he established the dispensation of 'Grace' that we would be convicted and forgiven of our sins and trespasses as each of us walk in His righteousness.

Jesus perfected the procreation of the 'Holy Seed' by the word dwelling in us.

Conclusion on the Importance of Covenants towards Spiritual Marriage

The evidence has shown the importance attached to the legality of covenants where marriage is concerned; but the most salient evidence uncovered was the marriage relationship between the covenants themselves.

There is progressive unity between the Abrahamic, Mosaic and Levitical covenants such that the latter two justify the promise and truth of the first. Here is the catch; it is through the marriage of those three covenants that we are able to receive the birth and promise of the New Covenant. All three aforementioned covenants are under the law. In the NKJV bible, it states in Galatians 3:19-25 that the purpose of the law was to keep mankind under instructions (from a tutor who would invariably be the Levites giving the law). This tutelage was to prepare us to accept faith in the promise of the New Covenant, which is Jesus Christ.

Further, marriage of the 'Kingly' inheritance; marriage of the inheritance of 'redemption through the promise; and marriage of the perfect priesthood; all three were personified and aligned to the importance of marriage as justified through the death and resurrection of Jesus Christ. There is no better proof than Galatians 3: 28-29 (NKJV), that the covenants are not divorced or abrogated from each other but all form a married bond to redeem humankind to the salvation of Christ Jesus. It states; *'There is neither Jew nor Greek, there is neither slave nor free, there is neither male nor female; for you are all one in Christ Jesus. **And if you are Christ's, then you are Abraham's seed, and heirs according to the promise.***

At the very heart of God's salvation to man is marriage.

Trivialising marriage to a civil formality does not sit as justified before God. If it were so; we would not find that in the very book where God defines the covenant relationship of marriage, He also defines the foolishness that follows as mankind reasons into his own justification.

Malachi 3: 13 – 17 (TLB) is the most appropriate conclusion to what God thinks of man's own attitude towards spiritual marriage;

> *"Your attitude toward me has been **proud** and **arrogant**,"* *says the Lord.*
>
> *"But you say, 'What do you mean? What have we said that we shouldn't?'*
>
> *"Listen; you have said, 'It is foolish to worship God and **obey** him. What good does it do to obey his laws, and to sorrow and mourn for our sins? From now on, as far as we're concerned, "Blessed are the arrogant." For those who do evil shall prosper, and those who dare God to punish them shall get off scot-free.'" Then those who feared and loved the Lord spoke often of him to each other. And he had a Book of Remembrance drawn up in which he recorded the names of those who feared him and loved to think about him.*
>
> *"They shall be mine," says the Lord Almighty, "in that day when I make up my jewels. And I will spare them as a man spares an obedient and dutiful son. Then you will see the difference between God's treatment of good men and bad, between those who serve him and those who don't.*

Conclusion

This is my conclusion to sum-up many of the matters that I have spoken on and to also address in a smaller framework some materials that were not specific to my topic but are relevantly needed to an overall conclusion. I'm sure that it will appear as a running commentary but I am passionate about lighting a fire under the LGBT and Humanist community as well as docile, if not atheist Christians[226] to rethink a rationality that has too many faulty premises to simply continue following. The way of a fool is right in his own eyes.....but open to wise counsel....

I say again; there is no denying the elements of complexity and emotionalism in the whole debate on homosexuality. Finding a balance of demonstrating God's love whiles standing on the truth of His word without offending individuals can teeter on the illustration of walking on a high wire.

From the start of writing this book, issues have remained relevant and continue to explode onto the headlines. The political landscape has been infused with the pungency of defeat especially where specific provisions in DOMA[227] have been ruled as unconstitutional; a key victory

---

[226] Revelations 3: 9

[227] In the DOMA case, U.S. v. Windsor, a divided court ruled 5-4 that by denying legally wed same-sex couples marital status under federal law, DOMA overreaches into states' legitimate authority to regulate marriage http://www.pewforum.org/2013/06/26/high-court-strikes-down-doma-but-leaves-fate-of-prop-8-uncertain/

for LBGT enthusiast. There seems to be a bold sense of self-actualization as professional US athletes are now making history and 'coming out' in celebration of their lifestyle. In the modern history of the fight for 'gay rights', there has not been a moment such as this in over 500 years where there is such a level of visibility and support. That backing has been registered from congressional members to celebrities; from priest to nationally recognized organizations. Without doubt, the preeminent support garnered has been from the President of the United States. Factually, there has never been a sitting President that has shown such liberalism towards unequivocal support. One can argue that his patronage has pushed the balance of acceptance towards a majority support of gay rights (marriage). Former President Jimmy Carter was quoted in a 'gay blog[228]' as supporting civil unions and the article went on to praise him for, 'reconciling his Biblical faith with the reality of the modern world'.

With this level of support, there could be little doubt that the LGBT has gained the mirage of 'moral' high-ground in the quest to legitimize the full scope of their philosophy; or have they?

Proverbs 29:18 which says, "Where there is no vision, the people perish" is aptly applied to the context of support for the Gay Rights agenda. On the principle that the people are void of understanding and belief in the 'vision' of God's Word; we recognize that our society is falling into moral decomposition.

Prof Jens Krause from Leeds University[229] performed a rather interesting experiment. What they did was to arbitrarily select persons as their test subjects to walk at random around a designated 'large' room. The volunteers were asked not to speak with each other. As the experiment proceeded, a specific selection of individuals received more in-depth instructions on where to walk. The results were amazing. The 'scientist' were able to determine (as quoted) *that people end up blindly following one or two people who appear to know where they're going. The*

---

[228] Full story here: http://www.queerty.com/jimmy-carter-supports-gay-marriage-jesus-never-said-gay-people-should-be-condemned-20120320/#ixzz2japOaWoz

[229] http://www.adsavvy.org/understanding-the-human-herd-mentality/

published results showed that it only takes 5% of what the scientists called "informed individuals" to influence the direction of a crowd of around 200 people. The remaining 95% follow without even realizing it.'

The results are not random. In fact, this is a scenario that has played out consistently by social scientist and is known as the 'herd mentality'. She submits in her findings that the results can be rather unfavourable when understanding that a small minority can in fact influence a vast majority. In her experiment it only took 5% to have 95% follow. Historically one can postulate that the Nazi regime operated along the same sociological extreme. What is certain of these results is that, whether 'right' or 'wrong' uninformed people can be influenced by an informed minority.

I would take that conclusion a step further and posit that an informed minority is even more influential when they can successfully transfer and <u>teach</u> their knowledge (whether the truth or not) to those who are uninformed. Here is an example.

> The 1970's for women was earmarked by incredible progress in the fight for women rights. The feminist movement, on the heels of rulings in the case of *Schultz* v. *Wheaton Glass Co[230] (a U.S. Court of Appeals rules that jobs held by men and women need to be "substantially equal" but not "identical" to fall under the protection of the Equal Pay Act);* the 1972 Equal Rights Amendment (Equality of rights under the law shall not be denied or abridged by the United States or by any State on account of sex."); and the very polemical passage of the US Supreme Court decision in Roe v Wade; was at the height of its political strength.
>
> Fuelled by fire and brimstone rallies such as the most effective 'Women's Strike for Equality[231]'which saw thousands of women

---

[230] Leagle, Inc; http://www.leagle.com/decision/1970548319FSupp229_1507
[231] Gourley, Catherine. Ms. and the Material Girl: Perceptions of Women from the 1970s to the 1990s. 1st. Minneapolis, MN: Twenty-First Century Books, 2008. 5-20 via http://en.wikipedia.org/wiki/Women%27s_Strike_for_Equality

fall under the guidance of such institutes as the Women's Right Movement and National Organization for Women (NOW); many national women issues, including abortion, were tabled and supported by a well-informed and agenda driven few. Prominent national leaders such as Betty Friedan and Gloria Steinem used these platforms astutely by galvanizing their base through the indoctrination of information and properly characterizing the nature of the debates. Although America was in the midst of a cultural sexual revolution in the 'disco' 1970's; it was still considered that most Americans had conservative values[232]. What NOW and other liberal feminist movements were able to achieve on a national level was to redirect and usurp the relevant argument of killing a human being[233] (fetus) to the new important and relevant topic of women rights. I doubt that many people in the 1970's would have accepted the thought of killing a baby so their tactic was clandestinely ingenious. They cleverly defused the emotional bomb of killing and gave new energy to the emotional bomb of a woman's right to manage her own body.

A small minority of persons (NOW) where able to inform and educate a vast majority of women to support their cause through deflection and in turn, that support was not prepared to acquiesce or give up ground on the many achievements for equality.

Primarily the 'natural right' under the constitution to 'not be killed' was adjudged as inferior rights (one can posit) to the right to privacy as ruled on by the Supreme Court[234].

---

[232] Jacobs, Meg; Zelizer, Julian E. (2008). "Comment: Swinging Too Far to the Left". *Journal of Contemporary History* **43** (4): 689–693. doi:10.1177/0022009408095423. JSTOR 40543230. via Wikipedia

[233] *Gerard Nadal, Ph.D. | Washington, DC, Scientist: Human Life Begins at Conception, Fertilization, LifeNews.com*

[234] Chase, H. et al. *Supplement to Edward S. Corwin's The constitution and what it means today: Supreme Court decisions of 1973, 1974, and 1975*, page 36 (Princeton

I would submit that the prevalence of information at the time of the ruling was very relevant to the outcome. The leading opinion was given by Justice Blackmun who claimed that a fetus isn't a person within the language and meaning of the Fourteenth Amendment. He noted that "the Constitution does not define 'person' in so many words." His contention was that the word 'person' "has application only postnatally." The Justice went on to say that, *"We need not resolve the difficult question of when life begins. When those trained in the respective disciplines of medicine, philosophy, and theology are unable to arrive at any consensus, the judiciary, at this point in the development of man's knowledge, is not in a position to speculate as to the answer."*

This dissection of the major opinion in Roe v Wade shows that the pro-abotion lobby presented information which was adequately ruled in favour of; but what would the result have been had the anti-abortion lobby presented indefeasible arguments on when life begins? This obviously calls for much conjecture but one can assume that the 7 -2 ruling may have been turned on its proverbial head had today's technology been available which shows indomitable proof that a foetus has life from conception and human attributes as early as 5 weeks.

> *"[At] five weeks old, [the embryo] is well past the stage when it looks like a formless clump of cells. The skin layers are still barely developed, and the tiny body is quite transparent. The head and tail can be distinguished, as well as the heart, the vertebrae of the spinal column, and the beginnings of a tiny hand."*[235]

University Press 1975): "The abortion cases afforded the Supreme Court another opportunity to caress the Ninth Amendment without embracing it. via Wikipedia
[235] Lennart Nilsson and Lars Hamberger, *A Child is Born, 4th edition*. New York: Bantum Dell, 2003. p. 98.

Many women will automatically be put off by my postulation which implies that they were led blindly into supporting abortion but this is not my complete submission. I am in fact suggesting beyond the conclusions of Prof Jens Krause. She concluded rather succinctly that, *'This is [an] excellent example of how the human brain is setup for social life. Even without a top-down organizer or any obvious rules, society just falls into place'. Unfortunately, that "follow the herd" mentality isn't always beneficial. If we're not fully versed on a subject, we tend to follow the guy who appears to know more than we do'.*

I believe that women (and men) in the aforementioned scenario started off very uninformed, jumped on the bandwagon, became very informed through stark indoctrination of misinformation and stood firm on their new knowledge. This premise is still not the completed litmus test in my opinion for the 'herd theory'. What is omitted from this theory is the fact that people don't simply follow for the singular reason of being uninformed. Other 'herd-like' social sensibilities also factor in.

- I will go out on a limb and postulate that humans are prone to the 'popular vote' culture where it becomes psychologically irrational to vote against what is popular. If we were to be honest, there are many people in society that hate being on a losing side.
- The 'clique' factor is another sensibility which differentiates because it is not simply about being an uninformed follower but also a follower based on 'close association'. I opinion that it was this very factor in the 'Sandusky[236]'affair which caused grave wrongs to be committed by the 'clique'- like atmosphere at Penn State.
- Emotionalism over rationalism or as some may say 'irrational exuberance' is a strong predictor of support. Former Vice

---

[236] http://www.forbes.com/sites/robertwood/2013/07/19/penn-states-60m-abuse-settlement-wont-erase-sandusky-name/

President Dick Cheney who is considered a poll bearer for the conservative movement in the US, supports gay marriage primarily because his daughter has declared herself as gay. Recently a Republican Senator, Rob Portman found out that his son is gay. He quickly switched sides in the argument declaring his support based on 'love[237]'.

- Communication overload in an age of technological sophistication is the progressive way of inundating a message. Everywhere that we look today, there is a message about the gay lifestyle. It is no longer a pariah. In fact, it is 'in vogue' to be associated with a gay person or lifestyle. There is a proliferation of celebrity women having a 'trophy GBF' (gay best friends) as if it is standard. Literature, pop culture, TV, politics; religion; sports; there is no avenue which this issue has not influenced and traversed. The easiest way to desensitize the public on an issue is to 'brow beat' them with it.

The fact is, with all the sensibilities added in, I believe that the herd theory is a simple but true theory on how the gay movement went from being 11% supported in 1988[238] to 46% in 2010. Unfortunately, it is still not enough to thoroughly explain such a dramatic change in philosophy. Here are my additional conclusions why the gay movement has gained such prominence.

1. **The 'moral majority' has minimized and lost its way.** There is nothing that threatens the existence of an organization faster than the death of its leader. Where there is no vision becomes an exact dilemma. In the early 1980's the Protestant fundamentalist, Jerry Falwell, formed and led a conservative organization that became very vocal on national issues. His aggressive style in confronting topics

---

[237] http://gawker.com/5990719/top-republican-switches-sides-on-gay-marriage-after-son-comes-out

[238] Americans Move Dramatically Toward Acceptance of Homosexuality; NORC at the University of Chicago.

galvanized many Christians to stand proudly on their fundamental beliefs. Like any 'controversial' group the fundamentalist came under scrutiny and pernicious damage was inflicted on the reputations of many persons who were affiliated with the group. Christians became reluctant to be associated with being called a fundamentalist where in some political and social quarters it was seen as a group of 'good 'ole southerners' with racial appetites.

This was most unfortunate. Even if that roamer may have festered a degree of truth; the Christian community and organization misunderstood the fundamental in fundamentalism.

What the pastor was fighting for was not the personal whims of a bunch of 'duck dynasty' southerners. He coined (or extended) the term fundamentalism to embrace the very core values inextricably linked to the Bible. I submit that the pastor wanted to assert that those values could never die because the Bible is the testament of the living God. Where the moral majority has gone wrong is that it has relied on the fallible leadership of men and lost sight of the infallibility of the risen Savior, Jesus Christ.

In today's world, it becomes increasingly difficult when setting up platforms behind avatars such as Jimmy Swaggart or Jim Bakker[239]. The true leader of the moral majority is Jesus Christ. Christians need not worry when so-called leaders fall or aspersions are cast because the testimony of Jesus is the only standard which we should live by.

Conservative Christians in America have lost the plot. They have fallen prey to the 'good guy' mantra of appeasement. The words moral and fundamental cannot act as an oxymoron. They must coexist as coercive synergise of infallible pragmatism.

Exactly what do I mean by that? I am asserting that there is and must always exist an unchangeable truth such that an accolade given to

---

[239] http://en.wikipedia.org/wiki/List_of_scandals_involving_American_evangelical_Christians

President Jimmy Carter as 'reconciling his Biblical faith with the reality of the modern world' becomes nonsense within the reality of indefeasible truth. Here are examples of propitiation and changing values:

> ➢ Men who assume that the moral compass changes direction based on 'love' are acting on the fallacy of love. I ask the question; is there any difference between two separate parents that stand, one against paedophilia and the other against homosexuality but both switch and support those behaviours out of 'love' for a child that is revealed to be involved?

Is there any difference between the actions of parents that abhor theft and fraud as both morally wrong but support children that are revealed to be involved? I say no. I have already clarified my position on truth and knowledge. It makes no sense that people are willing to stretch the truth to their own means and sensitivity of knowledge.

It is easy for the man who is away from the flood to talk about the necessity of rain. I understand that dilemma but the Bible never has an instance where Jesus compromised His standard.

In Matthew 4: 1 – 11 we are drawn to the scene of Jesus in the wilderness. One can imagine vividly how famished He was, having fasted for 'forty days and forty nights'. In real talk, it was the perfect time to bribe Jesus into supporting another agenda. It is recorded that the devil offered *all the kingdoms of the world and their splendor* if Jesus would compromise and bow to him.

What was the answer; did Jesus say that He would change His position? What Jesus did show was **love through moral fortitude**. He said to satan; "Away from me, Satan! For it is written: *'Worship the Lord your God, and serve him only."*

Real love does not compromise. I will never forget watching a program on drug addiction where a mother was adamant that her daughter's drug addiction was wrong; but out of 'love', she had become a cohort in supporting the daughters' addiction. That 'love' was only acquiescing and creating a new standard based on her sensitivity to the situation.

In John 14:15 & 23, Jesus states; *"If you love Me, keep My commandments."* and *"If anyone loves Me, he will keep My word; and My Father will love him...."* **Fundamental to love is the discipline of keeping standards**.

2. **Men are transfixed into reverse psychology and philosophy**. Reverse Psychology is now the sword of choice. When I first started to take up this conversation, I noticed that many homosexuals were speaking of the gross social atrocities being committed against them. Let me state out-front that I do not support any illegal act of physical harm against Homosexuals.

Without any research and understanding, I would have been immediately swayed into believing that a 'gay holocaust' was taking place. Now to be honest, I personally applaud the gay community for standing up against acts of blatant discrimination but they have cleverly gone beyond rhetoric of discrimination. Homophobia is now the sword of righteousness. We have evolved from a society of gay persons who were conscientiously contrite (if not morally convicted) and private in revealing their sexual perversion; to a society that is now afraid to speak out against this perversion lest you be labelled the socially unaccepted term of 'Homophobic'. Gays have used this perversion and reverse morality (actually very perverse) as a type of 'race' card into acceptance. It is reverse psychology.

I cringed the other day when I read an article that used the expression that being gay was the 'new black'[240]. If that is true, they certainly have the 'gay card' to play. In December of 2012 the last FBI[241] statistic on hate crimes was released in the US. Of the 6,222 crimes, 20.8%

---

[240] http://www.nytimes.com/roomfordebate/2013/06/26/is-the-civil-rights-era-over/ the-court-should-focus-on-justice-rather-than-rights

[241] http://www.fbi.gov/news/stories/2012/december/annual-hate-crimes-report-released/annual-hate-crimes-report-released

were due to sexual orientation bias. That does not mean that 20% of the crimes were attributable to crimes against gays. The 2004 report clarified that of the 15.6% of crimes committed that year on the bases of orientation, 'sixty-one percent of those attacks were against gay men, and 14% against lesbians'.[242] What the stats did reveal was the clear and present danger posed to the racial and ethnic community where 58.5% of hate crimes were committed as such.

This point has already been discussed at length on the exclusive new legal dynamic being created for gay persons; there are already existing laws that protect against discrimination of human beings of all race and ethnicity. What is abhorrent is that whiles blacks continue to struggle with racism (at least eight black people, three white people, three gay people, three Jewish people, and one Latino person become hate crime victims every day.)[243]gays are succeeding in usurping the position as if their proclivity is of an ethnic 'persuasion'. They plant the argument that they are superlatively entitled beyond the legal realm created for all people and minorities primarily because of the created stigmatization which the word 'homophobics' conveys. The scenario of stigmatization asserts that there is a concerted effort and movement of people against them. Well; blacks can attest to this based on a plethora of radical organizations such as the Klu Klux Klan and a number of Aryan[244] hate groups.

So well have the LGBT succeeded in this argument that the former Anglican Archbishop of South Africa was bold enough to challenge the very God he purports to follow. He proclaimed that he would not go to heaven but choose hell if he thought that God was 'Homophobic' and against gay rights.[245]

---

[242] http://en.wikipedia.org/wiki/History_of_violence_against_LGBT_people_in_the_United_States

[243] http://www.dosomething.org/tipsandtools/11-facts-about-hate-crimes

[244] http://en.wikipedia.org/wiki/White_Aryan_Resistance

[245] http://now.msn.com/archbishop-desmond-tutu-would-pick-hell-over-an-anti-gay-heaven/

People are systematically being singled out as homophobic for standing up for Biblical moral rights. Gays have successfully made the case that their 'created' moral standard is beyond the moral standard set out by God in the Bible. It is so amazing to see Christians accept moral definitions from a community who have formulated their own version of who Jesus as God is; but even more perplexing is when Christians acquiesce to Humanistic lexicon based on knowledge that does not recognize the existence of God in the first instance.

The Homophobic sword has cut through the meaning of Sodom and Gomorrah in Genesis chapter 18 and 19 and fulfilled the word in Romans 1:22, which says, "Professing themselves to be wise, they became fools."

Here are simple moral laws from the Old Testament to the New Testament which set a clear standard on Homosexuality.

> If *a man lies with a man* as one lies with a woman, both of them have done what is detestable. They must be put to death; their blood will be on their own heads. - **Leviticus 20:13 NKJ**

> For this reason God gave them up to degrading passions. Their women exchanged **natural intercourse for unnatural**, and in the same way also the men, giving up natural intercourse with women, were consumed with passion for one another. Men committed shameless acts with men and received in their own persons the due penalty for their error. **Romans 1:26-27 NRSV**

> Do you not know that wrongdoers will not inherit the kingdom of God? Do not be deceived! Fornicators, idolaters, adulterers, male prostitutes, sodomites, thieves, the greedy, drunkards, revilers, robbers--none of these will inherit the kingdom of God. **1 Corinthians 6:9-10 NRSV**

I would understand if a gay person complained that he (or she) was not allowed to enter a public cinema or walk into a department store; that would be gross discrimination and should not be allowed.

What about long held societal standards? I can remember a time when heterosexual couples would be asked to leave a public forum if they were being overtly sexual. We are at a place now were the rights of a family that wants to protect its' children or religious belief against certain sexual innuendo is socially boorish[246]. This is again a reversal. Years ago the key argument among homosexuals was that morality should not be legislated. In the most cleverly heinous way, gays are succeeding in legislating their penchant to perversion by hiding behind sexual discrimination laws. We are seeing it happen in the Boy Scouts and in other organizations across the world. Gays are actively fighting to legislate what they view as a moral right to impose their way of life.

This precedent is so dangerous that any private organization will have its mandate challenged.

It is time for Christians to stand up for the rights of heterosexuals. It's important that laws are adhered to. <u>Justice must be on a level playing field to stop blatant and harmful discrimination against gays and all individuals</u> but **Christians must stop giving up legal and moral ground to appease perversity**.

The precedent set already seems far too difficult to reverse. Legally, other groups such as paedophiles, marijuana smokers and the prostitution industry will use the same legal model successfully. Paedophiles will soon use the term 'Paedophobia'. Marijuana smokers will claim discrimination based on a need for the 'healing properties' of THC[247]. Prostitutes will claim discrimination based on a need to earn a living and the fact that their trade 'doesn't harm' anyone. These are all legal arguments which can be placed before the court based on the precedents being set by the LGBT movement.

Here is a quote from an article which appeared in the Northern Corlorado Gazette and previously qualified in this writing.

---

[246] http://www.dailymail.co.uk/news/article-1350764/Second-gay-couple-sue-B-amp-B-turned-away-owner-said-convictions-didnt-allow-men-share-bed.html

[247] http://www.health.harvard.edu/newsletters/Harvard_Mental_Health_Letter/2010/April/medical-marijuana-and-the-mind

Using the same tactics used by "gay" rights activists, pedophiles have
begun to seek similar status arguing their desire for children is a
sexual orientation no different than heterosexual or homosexuals.[248]

I say that fools speak loudest as wise men remain silent. The Christian community must **reverse** this trend of conceding moral ground because in fact the gay community is standing on their own created morals. Gays are actually **not** compromising their own morals whiles Christians are! The reversal of philosophy or reverse psychology must be recognized and stopped.

3. **Mental slavery is just as bad as physical slavery.** The African American community has turned its back on virtues of the past to be accepted into the irreverence culture of today. I can't stress how hard it is to make that statement considering the fallout that will result; but the fact that I am a Black person means that I ought to be sensitive to the continued moral health of this community. Unfortunately, I have had to speak as I see the truth even if it is contentious.

Open your eardrums for a moment and imagine listing to that 'old Negro spiritual' sang by our forefathers. What was the significance of it? Was it merely the frightened undulation of voices crying out for justice; or was it a song from the depths of the soul, believing that the God of Justice would deliver them from bondage? Songs like, 'A LITTLE TALK WITH JESUS'[249] and the many other spirituals; who were our forefathers singing about?

I'm sure some liberal deconstructionist will rebuild this spiritual timeline to reflect a mere symbolic affluence of a pseudo religious god that was only like a teddy bear set upon the minds of slaves to comfort them in brief moments.

---

[248] Northern Colorado Gazette, http://www.greeleygazette.com/press/?p=11517%20 %20%20paedophilias%20want%20same%20rights%20as%20gays

[249] http://www.negrospirituals.com/news-song/

I posit differently. I am in full belief that our enslaved forefathers were deeply converted into the faith of Christianity. They exhibited virtue and spiritual serenity based on principles learned from the Word of God.

How do I reach this conclusion? Let's select as our premises two charismatic and venerable Black leaders from the 1800's; Sojourner Truth and Frederick Douglass.

As a litmus test, I have chosen to build my case around two individuals that certainly would have represented the common and affluent thinking of the day, combined with the scholastically verifiable truths of their stance in life. Even more important for my premise, is the fact that the two individuals depict the dynamics of Black Christian leadership by a man and woman.

The first individual is a powerful instrument of inspiration who I had to take the opportunity to present and delve deep into.

> Sojourner Truth – Born in 1797 as Isabella Baumfree, this emancipated slave of no formal education, carved an impeccable history in the landscape of America. Her uncanny intelligence which must be attributed to 'mother's wit' made her a formidable figure among the leaders of the abolitionist and women's suffrage movements.

In 1843 After her conversion to Christianity, she is quoted as saying that she sensed God calling her to adopt a new name; Sojourner Truth: *"My name was Isabella, but when I left the house of bondage, I left everything behind. I wa'nt goin' to keep nothin' of Egypt on me, an' so I went to the Lord an' asked him to give me a new name. And the Lord gave me Sojourner, because I was to travel up an' down the land, showin' the people their sins, an' bein' a sign unto them. Afterwards I told the Lord I wanted another name, , 'cause everybody else had two names; and the Lord gave me Truth, because I was to declare the truth to the people."*[250]

---

[250] Sojourner Truth words, Harriet Beecher Stowe, author of the famous Uncle Tom's Cabin:

There could be little justice in paraphrasing the powerful words of Sojourner so I will not; but, in catalysing the point being made, it is very interesting to understand from the extensive quotes, the depth of wisdom that exuded from this uneducated landmark woman.

Here is a lady who has absolutely no formal education. Her words in verbatim, demonstrate her belief that God is her instrument of strength and knowledge yet she could not read the Bible.

> *At a gathering of prominent clergymen and abolitionists at the home of Harriet Beecher Stowe, author of* Uncle Tom's Cabin, *Stowe was informed that Sojourner Truth was downstairs and wanted to meet her[251].*
>
> *"You's heerd o' me, I reckon?" the former slave asked Stowe when she came downstairs.*
>
> *"Yes, I think I have. You go about lecturing, do you not?"*
>
> *"Yes, honey, that's what I do. The Lord has made me a sign unto this nation, an' I go round a'testifyin' an' showin' on 'em their sins agin my people."*
>
> *Fascinated by Truth's stories and demeanor, Stowe called down several of the more well-known ministers at the party. When asked if she preached from the Bible, Truth said no, because she couldn't read.*
>
> *"When I preaches," she said, "I has just one text to preach from, an' I always preaches from this one. My text is, 'When I found Jesus.'"*
>
> *"Well, you couldn't have found a better one," said one of the ministers.*

Consider the qualities of true moral leadership; the faithful words of a former slave who believed on Jesus when she could not even formally read His words. Her access to the truth which she professed, which would have been the Bible, was certainly limited at best yet she achieved

---

[251] http://www.christianitytoday.com/ch/131christians/activists/sojourner.html

more virtue and character of belief than leaders of today who have full literacy and access to the Word of God.

She did not move the 'land post'. She didn't reinvent a morality which did not exist. She did not adapt any heathen practice to suffice her situation and as we know it; she did not compromise her belief.

Imagine the boldness of a Black woman slave (emancipated) standing up among White men and making a statement which went against their sensibilities of what Christianity was; she said:

> *"But I believe in the next world. When we get up yonder, we shall have all them rights 'stored to us again."* (*Anti-Slavery Bugle,* Oct. 1856)

> *"Does not God love colored children as well as white children? And did not the same Savior die to save the one as well as the other?"* (Sabbath School Convention, Battle Creek, June 1863)

I place it before the consciousness of leadership that this hero of the first kind is what true moral character and leadership looks like. She did not appease the masses and she did not go for the popular vote.

What I love most about her as a leader is her fulfilment of the Word which says' in 1 Corinthians 1:27-31;

> [27] *But God hath chosen the foolish things of the world to confound the wise; and God hath chosen the weak things of the world to confound the things which are mighty;*

> [28] *And base things of the world, and things which are despised, hath God chosen, yea, and things which are not, to bring to nought things that are:*

> [29] *That no flesh should glory in his presence.*

> [30] *But of him are ye in Christ Jesus, who of God is made unto us wisdom, and righteousness, and sanctification, and redemption:*

³¹ That, according as it is written, He that glorieth, let him glory in the Lord.

A Black woman considered scholastically destitute was inspired by God to deliver words of truth and moral character where learned men were made to look foolish. Her weakness became her strength. Her words were not pointless elocutions from studied habits but from inspiration of the Holy Spirit where she boasted only (in her words), *"When I found Jesus."*

The second individual is no less impressive than the first and offers stark inspiration for his adherence to an uncompromising set of truths.

> ➤ Frederick Douglass – Education was never a luxury or prerequisite in the lives of slaves, especially considering that there was a ban throughout Southern States on educating them[252]. Mr Douglass received his initial training from his master's wife who felt it essential for him to read, so she thought him to read the Bible. In his book, <u>Narrative of the Life of Frederick Douglass, he says,</u> "Once you learn to read, you will be forever free."

His accomplishments as a statesman and leader for the abolition of slavery are far from simply historic. He is the poster child for moral leadership in the Black community. He can be contextualized as a course study in leadership perseverance.

Like Sojourner, his leadership qualities and moral aptitude were engrained in his words and are inescapable. He wrote:

"I have, in several instances, spoken in such a tone and manner, respecting religion, as may possibly lead those unacquainted with

---

[252] Bradley Skelcher Professor of History, Delaware State University http://www. brownvboard.info/popup/01_Early.htm

my religious views to suppose me an opponent of all religion. To remove the liability of such misapprehension, I deem it proper to append the following brief explanation. What I have said respecting and against religion, I mean strictly to apply to the _slaveholding religion_ of this land, and with no possible reference to Christianity proper; for, between the Christianity of this land, and the Christianity of Christ, I recognize the widest possible difference--so wide, that to receive the one as good, pure, and holy, is of necessity to reject the other as bad, corrupt, and wicked. To be the friend of the one, is of necessity to be the enemy of the other."

*"I love the pure, peaceable, and impartial Christianity of Christ: I therefore hate the corrupt, slaveholding, women-whipping, cradle-plundering, partial and hypocritical Christianity of the land. Indeed, I can see no reason, but the most deceitful one, for calling the religion of this land Christianity. I look upon it as the climax of all misnomers, the boldest of all frauds, and the grossest of all libels. Never was there a clearer case of 'stealing the livery of the court of heaven to serve the devil in.' I am filled with unutterable loathing when I contemplate the religious pomp and show, together with the horrible inconsistencies, which everywhere surround me. We have men-stealers for ministers, women-whippers for missionaries, and <u>cradle-plunderers</u> [**please note here that he was referring to the rape of young black children**] for church members. The man who wields the blood-clotted cowskin during the week fills the pulpit on Sunday, and claims to be a minister of the meek and lowly Jesus....... Here we have religion and robbery the allies of each other—devils dressed in angels' robes, and hell presenting the semblance of paradise."*[253]

---

[253] -Narrative of the Life of Frederick Douglass by Frederick Douglass;/Appendix

I read his words and found myself riveted to the substance and character of what he postulated. His intelligence towards Biblical exegesis was quite evident and impressive. He was not confounded by a misunderstanding or the prevailing interpretation of slavery in the Bible. Again; I would walk out on a 'plank of assumption' and posit that he was guided in his logic by the Holy Spirit. This is not to impute that Douglas was not an incredibly intuitive person. I believe he was but there is a certain component beyond mere intellect which can be detected when reading his words. He has a bravado and boldness that is exerted beyond the academic knowledge he would have attained.

How else does one explain his ability to differentiate Biblical connotations which are until this modern day still misinterpreted. I doubt very much that Mr. Douglas had access to Latin and Hebrew language or historical data on cultural norms during the age of Abraham, and Moses, or the time of the kings of Israel. He quarantined his thought process from the slaveholding religion of the day to find his true North. His faith in Jesus Christ was a compass of truth as he rejected the axioms of false religious beliefs.

Why is this important?

The prevalence of religious dogma, which would have surrounded Mr. Douglas, also would have validated slavery as an accepted practice in Christianity. Considering that he was converted into a religion[254] which was tolerating the practice of slavery as an acceptable truth speaks volumes. He was not swayed to accept as truth what he knew to be false. Mr. Douglas in my opinion, was not a mental slave to religion and religious practices but had freedom through his understanding of the Word of God.

That stands in clear contrast to leadership that we are seeing today. Leaders are acquiescing to the pressure of being 'politically correct' or

---

[254] Many scholars estimate that **15-30% of Africans imported as slaves were Muslim**. The majority of the remaining practiced indigenous forms of worship. All were converted to Christianity. Most became Baptist although slaves from Louisiana became Catholic because of the French settlers in that area. http:// blackdemographics.com/culture/religion/

socially relevant. Even where biblical[255]falsehoods are espoused, there are persons surprisingly still supporting heresy. There are numerous instances of 'so-called' Christians, gay activist and secular humanist supporting a theory that homosexuality is perfectly acceptable in the Bible. Apparently, Mr. Douglas was not only astute to understanding the Bible but he was also not a conformist.

Contrast the character of Mr Douglas with the prevailing 'moral' leadership in the Black community of present and a real deficit appears in the comparison. There are pastors and reverends and all make of civil leaders who support the most liberal agendas of homosexuality and other perversions that present. They continuously align themselves with the 'worldly' populist view.

Mr Douglas' understanding of slavery is further commendable because often in the conversation on gay rights an easy retort (defence mechanism) by supporters and advocates of the LGBT is to point out how disenfranchised people were in the Bible through slavery. This type of attack is suggestive of a bible (the Christian bible) that supports repression and is not egalitarian. There are a host of facts in the bible that would argue and refute this notion. I can reference this argument primarily to the book of Genesis, which has a brilliant revelation to elucidate this area of ecclesiastical debate.

Was the bible against the free and democratic way of thinking? Consider this illustrated rationalization.

- For the skeptic and believer, if we were to simply understand the story of Adam in the Bible it would clarify many arguments that men wrestle with. Whether you choose to treat this story as a fairy-tale or as literal; the moral of the story will remain the same.

---

[255] The Daily Beast; Were Christians Right About Gay Marriage All Along? Jay Michaelson. http://www.thedailybeast.com/articles/2014/05/27/did-christians-get-gay-marriage-right.html

In Genesis 1: 27 God has made the decision to create man after completing His work of creating a perfect living environment. He names the man Adam, who inherits complete serenity to live in Shangri-La; Paradise; Garden of Eden. His instructions to man are fairly simple. He tells man to have sex and procreate; place ownership over all that he surveys and have dominion over all other living things.[256] Adam receives one important further instruction. He is told in Genesis 2: 16-17; *"You are **free** to eat from any tree in the garden;[17] but you **must not** eat from the tree of the knowledge of good and evil, for when you eat from it you will certainly die."*

The key dynamic to the story is the illustration of death from consuming off the tree of knowledge. It is an allegory of moving from the perfect creation without sin to the fall from grace by eating from the tree and entering into the dispensation of sin.

By Genesis 3: 14 – 20, we learn that Adam has succumbed to the inquisitive nature of man; the penance of which is banishment from the perfection of creation into a world where he must suffer the toils and trials of life.

The jest is that God never intended for Adam to suffer the impracticalities of man's sin nature.

Shortly after his banishment we find out what type of fruit has been produced from the decision of Adam. There is jealousy and strife between two brothers; Cain and Able. There is deceit and covetousness. There is abandonment and lying, but far worse; there is murder. A good read of further passages in Genesis and the true story of man's battle with sin unfolds.

Genesis 6: 5 – 8. God must wrestle with His decision to destroy His very creation because he has looked at the heart of man and sees that man is wrought with wickedness.

The pressing question is now this; <u>why would an omnipotent, ever powerful God allow His perfect creation to fail</u>? **The rather sobering**

---

[256] Genesis 1: 28

answer is the fact that God did not create man to robotically worship Him out of compulsion. God gave man free will to democratically choose his way.

So, is the bible against the free and democratic way of thinking? No!

The greatness of God is found in the **free will** of man to choose Him by faith. God's glory is seen through man who is immersed in sin but can find his way to God's grace.

I submit that Mr. Douglass found God's Grace and that his moral leadership was to God's glory.

Douglass was a firm believer in the equality of all people, whether black, female, Native American, or recent immigrant. He is famously quoted as saying, *"I would unite with anybody to do right and with nobody to do wrong."*[257]

A skeptic to my narrow methodolatry can easily point out that I am painting a picture of an entire people based on the views of just two persons. I admit that this can be scrutinized as a blanket statement but consider this; over the past 40 years in America, the majority of what we know of the socio-political mind of the African American has been publically characterized and espoused by the reverend, Jesse Jackson.

I mean no disrespect to the legacy of Andrew Jackson; Congresswoman Maxine Waters; Colin Powell; Condoleezza Rice and the myriad of exceptional African Americans that have contributed to the advancement of blacks. There are thousands of influential African Americans in sports, entertainment, banking, law etc.

Whiles everyone knows of Oprah Winfrey and many also know of Rev. Al Sharpton; the vast rhetoric of representation, as the **major voice** in the Black _political_ community over the past **40 plus years**, has been from Rev. Jackson[258]. As a matter of fact, Rev. Jackson can say that he

---

[257] Frederick Douglass (1855). _The Anti-Slavery Movement, A Lecture by Frederick Douglass before the Rochester Ladies' Anti-Slavery Society_ via Wikipedia

[258] http://newsone.com/2001240/african-americans-are-sorely-disappointed-in-black-leadership-time-to-change-the-game/

was a member of the civil rights 4 X 4 team; including Andrew Young, Martin Luther King and John Lewis,

I used this analogy to illustrate that in consideration of someone who would have had a national voice over Black socio-politics; Rev. Jackson definitely was handed the baton. The reserve runner in the race and now leader of the team is President Barack Obama.

To the point, there have been diminutive and defined figureheads in the Black community over a 40 year period. If I were to gauge my opinion based on the political cogency of their life's work; I would unfortunately conclude that the trends I see in moral leadership leaves this community in a quandary.

I found only a small percentage of Black leaders, who hold political sway as identified on a national level, which did not support positions antithetical to values in the Bible. Even worse is that there are so many leaders (obviously this is happening in other ethnic persuasions) being caught with drugs; committing adultery; stealing and cheating on taxes.

I have heard so often the 'cop out' that no person is perfect. That is true but we have seen examples of great leaders illustrated here (let's include M.L. King) who have traversed extraordinary adversity to stand on moral ground; yet the modern Black community seems to lower its standard to accommodate frail leadership.

Hebrews 13:7 say's; *'Remember your leaders, those who spoke to you the word of God. Consider the outcome of their way of life, and imitate their faith'*.

Which leaders (not pastors) in the Black community can be emulated based on speaking the word of God? Considering the level of support for gay marriage and homosexuality by the Black caucus, I would have to say that the results show a real lack of moral integrity.

I very humbly submit that whether Democratic or Republican, the Black community needs to rediscover their moral compass and reject the populous influence. If they would stand on sound moral principles from both sides of the political divide; the black community would lead a revolutionary positive change in America. All other issues (welfare, taxes, crime etc) would fall into place.

> *"Blessed are those who are persecuted for righteousness' sake, for theirs is the kingdom of heaven. Blessed are you when they revile and persecute you, and say all kinds of evil against you falsely for My sake. Rejoice and be exceedingly glad, for great is your reward in heaven, for so they persecuted the prophets who were before you.* (Matthew 5:10-12)

4.   'Suffer the little children to be rebels'

When I was a younger person, I started to formulize where I saw my existence. I can always recall that I harnessed feelings of grandeur and the desire to live in the abundance of life. I was very driven by the theme of being rich.

Now that I am older and perhaps a little wiser, I've been able to reconsider and adjust those principles. What I have come to understand is that my grounding on basic biblical principles passed down from my parents has been the impetus that allowed me to see and reconcile the errors of my thinking.

There is a very serious position, which I believe has been virtually lost in understanding the implication of what the proliferation of gay marriage means. In the book of Malachi 2:15 when it was revealed that God *'seeks godly offspring'* it dawned on me that satan had to come against this intention by all possible means.

It's staggering to recognize the level of attacks that satan has mounted against the proposition of accomplishing godly offspring.

I have already touched base on the assured outcome expected due to the psychological indoctrination children will begin to have who are normalized under a homosexual relationship from birth.

Satan has not stopped there. We are aghast at the systematic exploitation of children around the world where they are being subjected to prostitution; slavery; various labour camps and even crime syndicates.

Although this mental scaring is occurring in America (and all around the world); I thought I would elucidate my conclusion here on another facet of child rearing which changes the scope of families and is having devastating results on the prospect of 'Godly seed'.

I posit that satan has deceived parents into becoming **caretakers** as opposed to parents. Parents are abdicating parenting skills of teaching and instilling values in concession to a new world ideology that children are smart enough to find their own moral being.

Has anyone watched TV lately to see the level of disrespect that emanates from the portrayal of children in families. I have seen programs where children freely smoke drugs with parents. I have watched parents apologizing to children when the kids are upset about not having their 'free way'. I have seen kids hitting parents and the parents become victims in their own homes. I have even viewed programs, which glorify and cast as celebrities teens who become underage parents; where they move their sexual partner into the house and engage in verbally abusive relationships with their parents.

I indicated previously in this writing also, how there is little support for any level of corporal punishment in America today and many organizations are quick to report parents (as well as kids doing the same) who attempt to physically discipline children.

For me; this is all an amazing game thrown onto the landscape of parenting to change the dynamics of any precedent towards holy offspring. I tend to believe that we are ill prepared to entertain a return to corporal punishment because of the level of real abuse that has occurred for so many years. What we don't recognize is the clear and present danger signs that God has mounted in the Bible and we certainly have misunderstood (as always) the role of deceit stretched out by satan.

Let me give a vivid example of the deceit before going into the Biblical argument. Once we are capable of digesting the insurmountable evidence that there really is an entity called satan who seeks to devour our lives, in direct opposition to God; we become aware of another immutable fact that his antithetical nature is set to place man in enmity to God. The very same way that God cursed satan in the Garden and brought man in enmity with him; satan has tried and is trying to reverse that operation.

The very fact that God has so fervently directed man on how to bring up a child means that satan has attempted to reverse those instructions.

Consider this; there are many marriages that are of the worst sort. Adults (man and woman) fighting against each other to the point of death, in some instances. Marriages have become so bad that a huge percentage of persons refuse to consider marriage and instead live lives of open promiscuity or simply live 'together' in defiance of God's will against premarital sex. Well; I guarantee that there is not a person who can identify an instance in the Bible that subscribes to either premarital sex or abuse by husbands or wives. As a matter of fact, the content in the Bible where marriage is involved gives instances of the most nurturing environment in which a relationship should be conducted.

Because we know there are so many instances of abuse in marriage; does that mean that people should stop getting married? Is God responsible for a man physically abusing a woman? Is God responsible for people having adulterous affairs?

In each instance God has spoken out vehemently against these behaviours but man continues to turn his back. Hollywood places a real emphasis on two persons getting married to only start counting the time at which they will divorce. It is all a worldly game and God is not subscribed to it, where marriage is concerned.

Through it all; marriage remains very serious to God. If one were to compare marriage to parenting and add all the ingredients of abuse; the question and the answer would remain the same. Is God subscribing to parents abusing children sexually, physically or mentally? No!

I completely agree with various border rules on abuse but the very ironic part of this is that God already established borders to instruct on how to rear children. We have allowed psychologist and sociologist, many of which are atheist, to draw up borders that reshape the scope of parenthood.

Let me just say that God is very aware of the plight of children. He warns us about turning our children over to Molech in Leviticus 18:21. I think I indicated earlier in this book that Molech is in fact satan but this cult (which there were several at the time such as Baal-peor) was specifically fixated on child sacrifice. In the context that it is used in Leviticus, the scope of it is encapsulating all the vices which result from neglecting the proper care of a child. Those vices are; children turning to crime and also being subjected to abuse and sexual debauchery.

So again the question; is the Bible or God accepting the abuse of children or is it in fact the prince of deceit who inflicts this level of sinful carnality once we are unfaithful to God's will?

Here is what the Bible has to say.

> The Bible says in Proverbs 22: 6 ' *Train up a child in the way he should go: and when he is old, he will not depart from it.*' In the same book at Proverbs 13:24 it is also states, '*Whoever spares the rod **hates** their children, but the one who loves their children is **careful to discipline** them*'. Very controversial of course is the implication of using a 'rod' to accomplish disciple. This I understand and will address. Further reading and we find that there is a common and repeated theme of disciple towards the child.
>
> > (1) Proverbs 22: 15 - **Foolishness** is bound up in the heart of a child; The rod of discipline will remove it far from him.
> > (2) Proverbs 19: 18, 19 - Discipline your son **while there is hope**, And do not desire his death. A man of great anger will bear the penalty, For if you rescue him, you will only have to do it again....

(3) Proverbs 23: 13, 14 - Withhold not correction from the child: for if thou beatest him with the rod, **he shall not die**. Thou shalt beat him with the rod, and shalt <u>deliver his soul from hell</u>.

(4) Proverbs 29: 15 – 17 - The rod and reproof give wisdom: but a child left to himself bringeth his mother to shame. **When the wicked are multiplied**, transgression increaseth: but the righteous shall see their fall. Correct thy son, and he shall give thee rest; yea, he shall give delight unto thy soul.

Combined with the concurrent theme of disciple, which is transparent throughout the book of Proverbs, is a prophecy of sort; it predicts that sparing disciple will result in the death of that individual. I posit that this is a figurative and literal expression.

Here's where I take another unorthodox route of explanation. I have never seen a person, whether a true dog lover or casual owner, not subject a dog to some degree of disciple. Before that statement causes indignation; I'm not suggesting that children are dogs **(far from it)** but I am attaching to the principle of why the dog is disciplined. If a person loves an animal to discipline it; how much more should he show love to discipline a child? It is easily seen that a dog that is not trained and shown the parameters of acceptable behaviour will grow and either be unable to stay in a house for lack of disciple/training or the dog can even be aggressive towards its owner.

Perhaps we assume that children are so supremely intelligent that we are foolish enough to dismiss the need to establish disciplinary perimeters as parents.

It's beyond my reasoning how we have come to believe that children need not be disciplined. **I completely understand the unacceptable consequences of abuse towards children but it is never suggested that a child should be abused.**

The result that the Bible is trying to obtain through disciple is not child abuse. Liberal (mostly Humanist) social scientist will have us believe that all physical discipline is abusive and stagnate learning.

The American Academy of Paediatrics states:

> **It is true that many adults who were spanked as children may be well-adjusted** and *caring people today. However, research has shown that, when compared with children who are not spanked, children who are spanked are more likely to become adults who are depressed, use alcohol, have more anger, hit their own children, hit their spouses, and engage in crime and violence.*

The data which they have used to acquire this position is specious to me, not because it is invalid in the conclusions but because the course of child discipline in America has been on a path of psycho-rationality for some 30 to 50 years now. I posit that there are second generation parents in America who have never experienced discipline beyond 'time-out' but if we gauge the level of disciplinary problems that exist today among children there would be a clear implication that the methodology over the past 30 years has produced results that do not reflect the aforementioned prognosis.

Children have become progressively worse over the past 30 years under mandated and uniformed methods prescribed by law and the paediatric association. With the amount of children fighting in schools where weapons are used and the amount of reported homicides by children on the rise[259] it's amazing that social psychologist can only attribute the behaviour to exposure to drugs or guns as a trend.

Call me crazy but I would guess that children who have exposure to guns only use them as a higher percentage towards crime based on not being disciplined. The whole system, where kids are concerned, is

---

[259] http://futureofchildren.org/futureofchildren/publications/docs/12_02_03.pdf

in a degenerative state. There are heightened incidences of bullying[260]. Across the US and UK there is a precipitous increase in students being expelled from schools[261]. It was reported in the Independent[262] that 'in the United States.... between 7 and 18 per cent of two-parent families and up to 29 per cent of single-parent families may suffer at the hands of their violent children'.

Despite the horrendous statistical data which is readily available to disseminate, every endeavour is being pursued to keep the status quo of the 'new-age'(as I would term it) discipline techniques which reject any type of corporal punishment.

I believe that the results quoted above by the American Academy of Pediatrics can actually be worse in terms of abusive children. Many parents attempt to discipline children when it is far too late. I believe that most forms of corporal punishment will not work when children have already formulated world views and have already been deeply exposed to a 'no-standard', low consequence disciplinary system.

A study by the American Psychological Association in 2002[263]interestingly concluded that corporal punishment was ineffective. In each analysis of various methods of discipline in comparison with corporal punishment (CP), the other methods used collaborative methods to reach a desired goal. CP was given negative results based on the singularity of the method. It did not demonstrate what happened in the event that a parent applied CP using the 'Authoritive[264]' method of control which incorporated (collaborated) love and affection. The

---

[260] http://www.bullyingstatistics.org/content/bullying-statistics.html

[261] http://www.telegraph.co.uk/education/educationnews/10201763/Huge-rise-in-number-of-expulsions-from-primary-schools.html

[262] http://www.independent.co.uk/news/uk/home-news/rise-in-parents-terrorised-by-their-children-7079798.html

[263] Is Corporal Punishment an Effective Means of Discipline? Elizabeth Thompson Gershoff, PhD, of the National Center for Children in Poverty at Columbia University, 2002

[264] Best method of discipline http://www.focusonthefamily.com/parenting/effective_biblical_discipline/effective-child-discipline.aspx

study showed no type of SWOT analysis on the effects of introducing CP at late stages of child development as opposed to introducing it in approved forms from infancy.

Given the certainty of so many esteemed, affluent and learned societies on paediatrics and psychology; we can assume that children in the US are adapting and exceling with so many freedoms; that's a joke!

Contrarily, there is current data, which shows that American teens have the highest rates of drug and alcohol abuse in the developed world along with violent deaths[265].

The Committee for Children (2004), delineate from this view somewhat. They state, *'the purpose of discipline is "to encourage moral, physical, and intellectual development and a sense of responsibility in children.* **Ultimately, older children _will_ do the right thing**, *not because they fear external reprisal, but because <u>they have internalized a standard initially presented by parents and other caretakers</u>[266].'* They went on to state in what I would term purely opinionated lunacy that corporal punishment stagnates the child's ability to learn. They state, *'Instead, it may halt the unwanted behavior only while the child is in the adult's presence, or it may scare a child into submission. <u>While it may teach a child what **not to do**</u>, it fails to teach a child what is expected of him or her and what is an alternate behavior.'*

It's appalling how many persons are functional literate adults and 'good for it' through being disciplined as children but are too timid to stand up for disciplining children today based on these 'learned' doctrines.

Let me make that stand if only by myself; I got a very good dose of 'spanking' when I was young. I would actually like to state that more emphatically but those words are better left on the streets.

What I can succeed in saying is that I stand as witness that I am neither minimized socially or intellectually.

---

[265] Read more: http://www.dailymail.co.uk/news/article-2135057/U-S-teens-worst-western-world-binge-drinking-drugs-violent-deaths.html#ixzz2am5pbDSs

[266] http://www.americanhumane.org/children/stop-child-abuse/fact-sheets/child-discipline.html

Dubious to the statement by The Committee for Children is the last part which basically says that children may learn what not to do but corporal punishment fails to 'teach a child what is expected'. What nonsense! It is like the cookie in the jar story. We have all heard it. These social scientist (don't forget the 'herd theory' here) would have you believe that parents are too dumb to correct a child using CP in correlation with love whiles also explaining to the child that they should not remove a cookie from the jar. It gives the picture as if all parents would inexplicably whip out a belt and beat a child with absolutely no explanation or justification. Perhaps they have watched too many 'B' movies which are all too happy to portray horrific scenes of back-wood incestuous hillbillies abusing children; or drunk 'getto' cursing single mums who become urban legions holding a spiked heeled shoe as the weapon of choice to abuse.

Well, I stand against that thinking. Clearly the wisdom of the Proverbs speaks beyond the perimeter of discipline and understands that 'the enemy' is plotting a humanistic intellectualised theory of discipline.

In Proverbs 13: 24, there is a diminutive statement. It says, '… *one who loves their children is **careful to discipline***'. Make note of the word 'careful'. It is a statement of responsibility on how the measure of discipline is given.

There are many who will use every method of interpretation to negate what these verses are saying but how does one account for the physicality of the following scriptures.

Proverbs 23: 13, 14 is very obvious in its guidance and offers the parent solace in understanding the practicality of being firm and following through with corporal punishment. It says', '*Withhold not correction from the child: for if thou beatest him with the rod, he shall not die. Thou shalt beat him with the rod, and shalt deliver his soul from hell*'.

For those who are not aware, Jesus said[267] that He came to fulfil the law and not to abolish it. I am sure that persons will feel that my next comment is too tangential but I am anticipating that rules and stories from the Old Testament will be viewed as antiquated.

---

[267] Matthew 5:17

In Deuteronomy 21:18-21 there is an alarming story of discipline that takes place under the laws of Moses. It is so crude and seemingly uncivilised that any person who is outside of Biblical exegetical understanding would simply promote this Bible story as barbaric.

The story tells of parents who have tried everything to discipline their son. The final resolution is being exhorted to physically place the son before the elders of the city. A picture is drawn which shows us that the son is obviously a 'good-time' person. In a modern day context, he is probably a womanizer who uses illicit drugs. We find out that the parents call him a 'glutton'. Besides the fact that he is eating excessively, the word further shows us that the son exhibits no sense of discipline and lives in excesses; he is unstable and has no standards. The son is a 'bum'! The ensuing result is very draconian. The son is to be taken out to the city gates as an outcast and stoned by 'all' the men of the city.

Why would such a benevolent God allow such an extreme remedy? As shown previously; God did not subject men before the flood to robotic dictatorial rule. After the flood man still ran wild in the lust of his flesh. The law was given to Moses to introduce standards. If anyone took the time to understand the extent of the law given to Moses by God and the laws God allowed Moses[268] himself to impose; the extent and physical count of laws implemented would be 613[269].

That is an incredible amount of laws to follow but it has a rationality; the men of the day were so wicked that God had to allow strict guidelines to prepare and discipline man in wait for the coming of Grace through Jesus Christ. Men were given up to all manner of lewd behaviour from bestiality to idolatry to incest[270]. What God is demonstrating in the Old Testament through such rigid and extensive laws is the 'reflective' nature of the laws needed to discipline the wide range of sin emanating

---

[268] Deuteronomy 31:9, "And Moses wrote this law."

[269] Understanding the Law by Keith Sharp

[270] Colossians 3:5 - Mortify therefore your members which are upon the earth; fornication, uncleanness, inordinate affection, evil concupiscence, and covetousness, which is idolatry:

from the human nature. This is confirmed in Romans 5: 12 – 19 where we understand that sin is engrained and inescapable.

Once the laws were implemented as a standard, there was a need to show the natural consequences that flowed from circumvention of the standards. In this story of the unruly son, the epidemic of his nature was a threat to his peers and to the orderly nature of parenting with discipline. It profited that society nothing to leave the problem unaddressed, so a staunch remedy to the law was applied. This action took place to assure that the behaviour did not subsist. I can guess that not allowing this problem to fester sent such a powerful message that the negative dimensions of the son's attitude and behaviour had no further influence on other children. It's almost as if God was 'cutting to the chase' in the conversation of discipline of kids. **Actions, which go unpunished spread like a virus; from one parenting situation to another.**

Any society that believes that it can allow children to grow up without strict guidelines and punishment risk spreading the apocalyptic disease I call 'death of the soul'. What a child sows as a child he will reap as an adult. We are continuously surprised by the amount of 'boy next door' characters that are hauled before the courts. From individuals who have been accepted as 'upstanding members' of society to individuals who are quiet and reclusive; we are seeing a proliferation of atrocities committed by persons who are missing the fundamental attributes of parenting which utilizes strict discipline.

Consider the following verse about the plight of salvation for a rich man. Matthew 19:23 – 24 'And Jesus said to His disciples, "*Truly I say to you, it is hard for a rich man to enter the kingdom of heaven*. *"Again I say to you, it is easier for a camel to go through the eye of a needle, than for a rich man to enter the kingdom of God*."

This level of undisciplined stupor in children is creating the moral dilemma of no standards and failing to produce the intention of holy offspring. Many adults today are drunk in the naivety of living rich with no borders because they had no provable standards as kids. They support philosophies with no true borders.

The next time homosexual rights are debated, ask a heterosexual person why they support gay rights. I almost guarantee the answer will sound like a narcissistic philosophy of self-invented belief; "**I** believe", "**I** think".

Maintaining self-belief is not wrong per se; but all beliefs are thought to be from verifiable standards. Unfortunately today, there are many beliefs contained within a vacuous space of self-invented standards.

I put forward then that the Bible standards are not contained in a vacuum but are proven from centuries ago. Think about that statement. Besides homosexuals fighting on the issue of gay rights; consider the many other standards that are adhered to which are all ecclesiastical in nature. I have already mentioned many; but here are a few standards from the Bible that people may not be aware about.

- Standard for money management - Proverbs 22:26-27 (TLB) Unless you have the extra cash on hand, don't countersign a note. Why risk everything you own? They'll even take your bed!

- Standard for Taxes – Romans 13: 6 – 7 (TLB) Pay your taxes too, for these same two reasons. For government workers need to be paid so that they can keep on doing God's work, serving you. Pay everyone whatever he ought to have: pay your taxes and import duties gladly, obey those over you, and give honor and respect to all those to whom it is due.

- Standard for obeying government – Romans 13: 1 – 5 (Living Bible) Obey the government, for God is the one who has put it there. There is no government anywhere that God has not placed in power. So those who refuse to obey the laws of the land are refusing to obey God, and punishment will follow. For the policeman does not frighten people who are doing right; but those doing evil will always fear him. So if you don't want to be afraid, keep the laws and you will get along well. The policeman is sent by God to help you. But if you are doing something wrong, of course you should be afraid, for he will have you punished. He is sent by God for that very purpose. Obey the laws, then, for two reasons: first, to keep from being punished, and second, just because you know you should.

I could quote all day from the Bible on standards but the point is; which standard listed is not applicable today.

The Bible is an accountable and proven standard which man finds himself antagonistic to because man seeks to create his own justification of standards which conflict with the Bible.

I believe in the mantra of the Bible, that children are better adjusted as adults when strict discipline guidelines are enforced from infancy. I posit that many adults who acquiesce to new standards such as gay marriage or rights are reflecting their psychological endowment of no true standards.

Voting in favour of Gay Rights is not only moving with the herd but also a safe vote for persons who are inebriated with their own standards and don't want to feel 'dictated' to.

Hear counsel, and receive instruction, that thou mayest be wise in thy latter end. Proverbs 19:20

5. Reality is stranger than fiction.

Isaiah 5:20

> Woe to those who call evil good
> and good evil,
> who put darkness for light
> and light for darkness,
> who put bitter for sweet
> and sweet for bitter.

We live in a world were fiction has more rationality than reality. It's rather absurd that man places more reality into fiction than recognizing the truth of his own existence.

It's impossible to find a blockbuster hero movie where there was not a villain attached to the plot. Year in and year out, we see the horror genre placed onto the movie screens with characters like, Jason, and Freddy Krueger. The themes of the movies get darker and depict sub-cultures of evil incarnate. Whether watching horror movies or a superhero flick, the prevalent theme of a villain or subculture of evil remains as the plot.

The world understands the relationship between good and bad in the fictitious world of movies, novels, and cartoons but completely rejects the notion of evil or the reflection of evil in the reality that is life.

Man conceptualizes the reality of evil in fiction as a **necessary** nemesis or balance to all that is good. In psychological terms, this is like reality projection. We project rationality into the fictional world that is rejected as irrational in reality; that is truly irrational thinking.

In reality, the themes of good versus bad; light versus darkness; righteousness as opposed to sin; are all seemingly accepted as having no merit because they presuppose an underlying theme of clandestine influence from a force that is rejected as non- existing.

Exactly what does make sense then? Are we in an existential existence where our thoughts are actually remotely related to our actions such that the result of what we do is only a pariah of what is true. In other words; aren't we really in an existence of non-accountability towards our behaviour because our behaviour has no base from existence? That would mean that having standards and accountability towards criminal behaviour is really a measure in futility because all behaviour can't be patterned or categorized as it is only attributable to the instincts and derived by that given individual.

The laboured point that I am driving to is that accounting for evil in our fictional subculture is the reflection of our subconscious that there has to be a given cause for our behaviour. It can't simply be held in a vacuum because that type of existence can't be held accountable. If evil does not exist, and I decide to kill a person; who are you to tell me that what I did is 'evil' or bad or immoral?

The book of First John 1: 8 states; *'If we say that we have no sin, we deceive ourselves, and the truth is not in us'*. This is the point; the world has become so very deceived by deceitful worldly philosophy.

The funny thing about that statement is that it sounds like a religious zealot but has anyone stopped for a minute to observe how very zealous the LGBT community is about espousing their philosophy?

1 John 2: 15 – 17 goes on to state:

> *Do not love the world or the things in the world. If anyone loves the world, the love of the Father is not in him. For all that is in the world—the lust of the flesh, the lust of the eyes, and the pride of life—is not of the Father but is of the world. And the world is passing away, and the lust of it; but he who does the will of God abides forever.*

What the world does not want to acknowledge is that there is sin and that sin is a composite of evil and that evil is incarnate to satan. One very shocking statement that I would make is that I do appreciate the candour of the group that calls themselves 'satanist'. I would say that in a 'can of pagan worms'; satanist[271] are the most honest. Unfortunately their honesty to the existence of a deity finds them on the side of defeat (my opinion). To their credit; they acknowledge who they follow. One has to appreciate the temerity; the sheer audaciousness of their position.

---

[271] Sean Murphy, The Associated Press via http://usnews.nbcnews.com/_news/ 2013/12/08/21820518-satanists-want-statue-beside-ten-commandments-monument-at-oklahoma-legislature?lite&

This point has already been made but the nail being driven in attempts to illuminate the state of deception that has placed man's knowledge into a stupor. Man does not believe or know or can conceptualize that he is being deceived because this is the greatest strength of the enemy. It was the tool of choice in the Garden of Eden. Satan did not resort to a feat of magic or physical force to induce man to betray God; he used something much more perverse. It is perverse because of how clandestinely it is introduced and accepted; something that we can't see coming at us. He used **deception**.

So great has his deception evolved today that those situations, which should seem perfectly logical and rational, are today, perceived as absurdities. The absurdity of two men or two women having sex has moved from being the unnatural and perverse sexual proclivity, which absolutely cannot produce the intended natural progression towards childbirth; to the naturally accepted standard of love for one another, which progresses towards adoption.

We have been deceived into believing that 'love' is the force majeure of verifying that a relationship is good and natural.

Even evolution can't really believe this. If it could, we would be sure that men would have naturally evolved to compensate for this 'natural' need of humankind to produce, give birth or procreate through love.

Man needs to return to reality and know that satan is a real entity. He is very serious about deceiving man and is at work with the reality of directing gay marriage.

6. **Sodom and Gomorrah are like the lost city of Atlantis**; they never existed except in mythology.

This is a topic that I considered placing into the main content of the book but it is not a direct argument used in relationship to gay marriage.

It is a topic that has general relativity to the topic of homosexuality so I have chosen to address it in my conclusion.

The denial of the existence of Sodom and Gomorrah is another patented defence mechanism by homosexuals. The story has such far reaching implications that every effort has to be made by the LGBT to discredit the account as either a sham, an ancient conspiracy by 'homophobic' church persons or a complete misinterpretation. For lack of an example which is more vivid; I will illustrate the absurdity of this thinking using the US President.

Whether interpreted as good or bad, President Obama has been a polarizing figure in American socio-political development. What is a fact is that every decision he makes will be recorded in history and saved into the vestiges of time. In 20 to 50 to 100 years' there will still be historical imprints of his presidency. Oddly enough, given the controversy of his birth record; many dissenters will argue in years to come that the President was not born an American. Whatever good is attributed to him, will be un-pragmatically flagged by them with the footnote which will indicate this 'proven lie'. His birth record will continue to be expunged from the minds of those persons who refuse to believe that he was/is a legitimate American sitting President. **For the record let me be clear that this whole argument is repugnant and a waste of time.**

People will believe what they want to believe to serve their own agenda.

I certainly don't want to go on a long anthropological expedition into verifying that the sister cities of Sodom and Gomorrah existed so I will settle for basic rationality to move beyond this one of many relevant points.

Rational:

- Sodom and Gomorrah is mentioned in Genesis 13: 10 where Abram and Lot agree to separate and Lot decided to settle his family among the cities of the plain.

Approximately more than **2000 years later** Jesus references Sodom in Luke 17:29 along with the exact story of the city being destroyed.

- City of Arad in Numbers 33:40, which says, "Now the Canaanite, the king of Arad who lived in the Negev in the land of Canaan, heard of the coming of the sons of Israel." "Arad was discovered 30 km NE of Beersheba, and excavated from 1962 to 1974 by Y. Aharoni and R. B. K. Amiran[272]." This city along with numerous cities (such as Bethel in Amos 7:12-13; Capernaum in Matthew 17:24; Gaza in Acts 8:26; Jericho in Numbers 22:1; to name a few) are all cities which have been either excavated or are still in existence. The rhetorical question is: with all the cities virtually verified as mentioned in the Bible along with the referenced characters; why would Sodom and Gomorrah be falsified.

The salient and pressing position with Sodom and Gomorrah (SG) is not really on whether or not the city was destroyed by God. That is only confirmation of the consequence which flows from the most important point. That point revolves around why God destroyed the city.

I have not seen any data from any gay friendly group or organization that acknowledges or supports the language used in Genesis 13 when describing SG and its' demise. Gay apologist have offered every interpretation; from SG being destroyed because the people of the city placed work above helping the poor to an interpretation that there was cannibalism which accounts for the terminology of 'strange flesh' in the account.

To all the liberal academics who would not find my suggestions insolent; let's place the most rudimentary context into focus and

---

[272] Achtemeier, Paul J., *Harper's Bible Dictionary*, San Francisco: Harper and Row, Publishers, 1985. http://carm.org/archaeological-evidence-verifying-biblical-cities

determine whether it is prudent to conclude anything beyond the obvious.

(1) Genesis 18:23-33 – In this account, we find that Abraham is so troubled by the plan of God to destroy Sodom that we find him pleading and bargaining with God. He differentiates what God sets as a standard for destruction. The standard is simple; God will not destroy the righteous. In fact, Abraham succeeds in negotiating the non-destruction of SG if only ten righteous persons are found in the whole city. According to 'The Ancient Hebrew research Centre'[273] the word righteous (tsadiyq) when used in relation to the word 'wicked' (rasha) usually means, 'the one who remains on the path'. It is in contrast to wicked, which means, 'to depart from the path and become lost.' All indications are, that the path is set out under the law in the Torah. Jesus says in Matthew 6: 31 – 33 by confirmation; *'Be not therefore anxious, saying, What shall we eat? or, What shall we drink? or, Wherewithal shall we be clothed? For after all these things do the Gentiles seek; for your heavenly Father knoweth that ye have need of all these things. But seek ye first **his** kingdom, and **his righteousness**; and all these things shall be added unto you".* Jesus was not speaking about the righteousness of man but the righteousness of God as found in the Bible. **This was the standard; to remain on God's authentic path of righteousness and not our invented paths.**

(2) What path did the law set out for righteousness according to Leviticus 18:20 – 23? - *"And you **shall not** lie sexually with your neighbor's wife and so make yourself unclean with her. You **shall not** give any of your children to offer them to Molech, and so profane the name of your God: I am the Lord. You **shall not** lie with a male as with a woman; it is an abomination. And you **shall not** lie with any animal and so make yourself unclean with*

---

[273] Jeff A. Benner, http://www.ancient-hebrew.org/27_righteous.html

*it, **neither shall** any woman give herself to an animal to lie with it: it is perversion.* There are five explicit commands which are stated as syllogistic imperatives. The first four use the obligatory exhortation 'shall not' to declare that there is no other path but what is being directed. The final instruction is also compulsory but as a declarative, it simply attaches itself to the unavoidable implication of the preceding sentence. It is interesting that this final verse is homogeneous in its command but leaves no room for speculation that a woman is not included in the 'you' of verse 23.

Now; the most interesting dynamic is that of the five directives only one is currently contested as abhorrent, irrelevant, or misinterpreted. How could that be? There is support by most (I assume most homosexuals and Christians do not supporting bestiality) to the language and actions of having no sex with animals; barring men and women alike. We reason here that this Biblical law is 'spot' on. We consider the law on adultery in general as 'spot on' (even though there are a good percentage of Homosexuals[274] who support the ideology of 'true tolerance' and a degree of heterosexuals who also support 'open marriages'[275]) There is also broad agreement (homosexuals and Christians) that infants/children should not be sacrificed or exposed to paedophilia (even though I believe this to be the case; homosexuals are on a slippery slop on this topic because the paedophiles are now organizing[276] to use the very same language that homosexuals used to justify their propensities).

The one imperative that is singled out and attacked by the LGBT is the verbiage in verse 22. All of a sudden; the LGBT are absolutely sure that Moses either got this law wrong or it is interpreted or transcribed

---

[274] http://www.patheos.com/blogs/getreligion/2013/08/npr-true-toleranceopen-marriages/

[275] http://www.huffingtonpost.com/rachel-a-sussman-lcsw/do-open-marriages-work_b_1222016.html

[276] http://togetherweheal.wordpress.com/2013/07/28/pedophiles-call-for-the-same-rights-as-homosexuals/

incorrectly. The mere fact that anyone could be so morally selective should send up smoke signals that something is wrong with this standard.

This is a key reason why there is animosity against the Bible. God sets a rigid and strict standard which is commanded to adhere to. Let's be honest; man in all of his carnality, the man who embraces the 'born to be wild theme', hates to be told that he 'must' hold to a standard. No person in the LGBT wants to assume that they are wrong much less be told that they cannot usurp the authority of that law.

Righteousness was not aligned with the actions of men sleeping sexually together nor with women sleeping sexually together. The standard was clearly against it.

(3) How do we know that the people of SG were unrighteous and off the path? Take a close look at the attitude of Abraham. Besides the fact that his family was in Sodom, he must have had a real understanding of how draconian Gods edict could be against the unrighteous.

We all know how families transfer generational history; there is no doubt in my mind that Abram was aware of the full circumstance of the flood story. Here is the genealogical proof. According to the scriptures, in Genesis 9:28; Noah lived 350 years after the flood and died at the age of 950. Genesis 5:32 states that Noah had three sons when he was five hundred years old. Genesis 11:10 records that Shem was one hundred years old when his son Arphaxad was born; this would mean that Noah was then approximately 600 years old by the birth of Arphaxad. In the account of Genesis 11: 10- 32 the generations of Shem to Abram is approximately 400 years. Abraham, by all accounts, was born 50 years after his grandfather Noah died.

I see a vivid picture of understanding from Abraham. He knew that God was burdened by man's unrighteous actions and he knew that God's plan to destroy SG, as a consequence of man straying from the path; was a burden that his grandfather experienced.

I posit that Noah did not have a vision of the coming Grace through Jesus and the 'law' (which was given to Moses) was not sufficiently in place; but he was a man of great faith (haven't built a 'super tanker' on faith).

I believe that it must have been surreally stressing psychologically to live through the phenomena of the destruction of mankind; to only realize that man was again becoming, in a relatively short period, hedonistic and antagonistic to God again. So great was that burden on Noah that I believe it attributed to his drinking in Genesis 9: 20.

I believe that Abraham pled with God not simply to save his family but because he knew that man's unrighteousness would cause far ranging devastation physically, financially, psychologically and spiritually.

One has to understand that Abrahams' situation was no different than communal tribal living today. Abraham was a leader and knew these people. If he had family living in SG, imagine how many other persons in the camp of Abraham also had relatives there. How do you, as leader deal psychologically with the horrific destruction which is about to happen to the relatives of all the people you are leader to?

In Genesis 13: 10 it is apparent that Lot chose to live on the plain because it was very fertile. Abraham knew that another repercussion of the destruction was that God was going to kill the land itself, such that it would be barren for years. Abraham was familiar with the fertility of the land. In verse 14 of chapter 13 one can posit that God made plans years before to destroy SG and allowed Abraham to grow in fulfilment of the covenant[277] and moved his vast amount of livestock across the land[278] of the plains until he was safely miles away from what would become 'damned earth' because of the sulphur that fell into it. Abraham and his camp had settled comfortably into the land years after separating from Lot who dwelled in Sodom and would have to uproot his vast holding of livestock to move away before the destruction took place.

---

[277] Genesis 18: 18 as fulfilled in Acts 3:25
[278] Genesis 13; 1 -10

The move was an economic inevitability that no fair person would wish on anyone. The house of Lot paid a huge financial and moral price because of the unrighteousness of the people he dwelled amongst.

Confirmation that the people in SG (who, by-the-way, were all descended from Noah), had lost their path and were blindly living in their own unrighteousness is found in Matthew 11: 23 – 24.

> Jesus says', "*And you, Capernaum, will you be exalted to heaven? You will be brought down to Hades. For if the mighty works done in you had been done in* **Sodom**, *it would have remained until this day. But I tell you that it will be more tolerable on the day of judgment for the land of Sodom than for you.*"

Jesus had travelled vastly in the area of Capernaum[279] and it was commonly known that great miracles[280] had been performed by him. In John 12: 9 we see the fascination among many who followed Jesus as he sat to have dinner in Bethany, which is in the area of Capernaum. The people gathered to see Lazarus, who after being raised from the dead, was now sitting and having dinner with Jesus. There is no doubt left that this miracle alone was vastly heralded throughout the land. News of the miracles had even reached the ear of King Herod[281], so we are aware how vast information travelled. For anyone to reject the implications of what Jesus was doing, showed a high level of unbelief and unrighteousness.

Jesus had selected some of His disciples from Capernaum as we see in Mathew 4:13 & 18:22. There is little doubt that culturally this fact would have been known to the people in Capernaum. Unfortunately, the people had hardened hearts and did not repent. As prophesied, those cities[282] were destroyed. God uses Sodom as a precedent to justify under

---

[279] The area is located at the north corner of the Sea of Galilee, http://www.biblewalks.com/Sites/capernaum.html

[280] Matthew 11:20

[281] Mark 6: 10 - 14

[282] Matthew 11:21

the Grace of Jesus, the destruction of unrighteous people in Capernaum who once again rejected God.

(4) What was the unrighteous sin that caused the destruction of SG?

First of all; we already know that the Bible defines the word righteousness in this context according to a contrast with wicked and in accord with those who are walking on the path.

We know that the path is the law but exceptionally there is recognition that the law has not been established in the time of Abram. For this reason, God looks upon the heart of men who show the innate characteristic of faith such as Noah but he begins to establish the path of righteousness through Abram. In Genesis 17: 1 God tells Abram, *"And when Abram was ninety years old and nine, the Lord appeared to Abram, and said unto him, I am the Almighty God; walk before me, and be thou **perfect**."* In the sense that perfect is use, it is a connotation of Abram walking 'blameless[283]'. As a measuring stick, SG was judged to that standard.

In speaking to Abraham in Genesis 18:20 God tells him that the sin of SG 'is very grave'. Immediately Abraham starts to negotiate with God and uses the word righteous as a justification for God to change His intentions. Abraham was hoping that God as a 'just' God would change his mind. In 18: 25 Abraham says', *"Far be it from You to do such a thing, to slay the righteous with the wicked, so that the righteous and the wicked are treated alike. Far be it from You! **Shall not the Judge of all the earth deal justly**?"*

In law, connotatively, Abraham has set a legal precedent in first acknowledging God as the 'Supreme Judge' and then he further establishes that this judge must rule with justice (the rule of law). It is superb thesis of jurisprudence.

---

[283] Deuteronomy 18: 13

This verse is referenced to Deuteronomy 1:16-17 and 32:4. To put the verses in context first; we understand that Moses is explaining the law to the people of Israel. He says to them (with great significance);

*16 And I charged your judges at that time, saying, Hear the causes between your brethren, and judge **righteously** between every man and his brother, and the stranger that is with him.*

*17 **Ye shall not respect persons in judgment**; but ye shall hear the small as well as the great; <u>ye shall not be afraid of the face of man; for the judgment is God's</u>: and the cause that is too hard for you, bring it unto me, and I will hear it. Deuteronomy 1:16-17*

*4 He is the Rock, his work is perfect: <u>for all his ways are judgment</u>: a God of **truth** and without iniquity**, just** and **right** is he. Deuteronomy 32:4 (KJV)*

Judging was to be done justly and righteously and by the standard of God who stands as truth.

The important side of this legal equation is to understand that even though Abraham was negotiating with God; God already knew that the people of SG had fallen into unrighteousness so his judgement was not only justified but truthful to its' nature. Considering the fact that God entertains Abrahams negotiation; the consequences of the sin in SG and the outcome was immutable once verified because man (Abraham) was now witness to the irrefutable truth of the established standard. From verse 17 of Genesis 18, God indicates that He already knows what He will do but it is based on the standard of "righteousness and justice" already foreseen in Abraham in contrast to the sin of SG. Genesis 18:19 -20 says; *'For I know him, that he will command his children and his household after him, and they shall keep the way of the Lord, to **do justice and judgment**; that the Lord may bring upon Abraham that which he hath spoken of him. And the Lord said, Because the cry of Sodom and Gomorrah is great, and because their **sin is very grievous**'.*

Let me draw attention to the book of Romans 2 which states:

> [11] *For there is no respect of persons with God.*
>
> [12] *For as many as have sinned without law shall also perish without law: and as many as have sinned in the law shall be judged by the law;*
>
> [13] *(For not the hearers of the law are just before God, but the doers of the law shall be justified.*
>
> [14] *For when the Gentiles, <u>which have not the law</u>, **do by nature the things contained in the law**, these, having not the law, are **a law unto themselves**:*
>
> [15] ***Which shew the work of the law written in their hearts, their <u>conscience</u> also bearing witness**, and their thoughts the mean while accusing or else excusing one another;)*
>
> [16] *In the day when God shall judge the secrets of men by Jesus Christ according to my gospel*

The Apostle Paul, who wrote this, more than two thousand years after Genesis, is able to supernaturally frame the complete justification of judgement on the people whether there is law or no law. He points out that even those who have not received the law but act in accordance with '**the nature of things**' shall be a law unto themselves.

The curious wording of 'nature of things' gives us insight to what was unrighteous.

If we were to establish a linear perspective of natural and unnatural acts spoken of in the Bible; it becomes very clear what acts are unnatural and unrighteous.

Firstly; Let's look at sin placed in the context of being unnatural. In Genesis 19: 8 -9 the story of SG is at the stage where the Angels of God are in the house of Lot. Word of their encampment spreads like wildfire throughout the city. For all practicality, the scene becomes reminiscent to that of a mob. The men are implicitly desirous of knowing the pleasure of these strangers to their city in a sexual way.

Here is the key indication to all arguments which suggest that this was not a homosexual act and that it was not wrong; Lot tries to protect his guest by saying to the men on the outside that their act is 'wicked' (which we know is unrighteous) and he tries to balance the wickedness by offering his daughters.

There is no level of interpretation that can vitiate the impairment of this moment. Lot not only knows that the men are wrong for wanting to have sex with the 'Angelic men' but he actually offers his very own daughters as reparation for their lust in the hope that they would not persist. Why; because sex with his daughters would have been the '**natural use**' of sexual intention.

I believe the final judgement or the nail in the coffin for the men and people of SG, comes when Lot tells them in verse 8, that the reason the men are in his house is for protection. This society was so terminally ill in unrighteousness that no house was safe from the scourge of their actions.

The men were wroth with indignation and uttered xenophobic threats at Lot in verse 9. By their very own mouths they ushered in their destruction. They said (using the AMP version) *'This fellow came in to live here temporarily, and now he presumes to be [our] judge! Now we will deal worse with you than with them.'*

They basically were saying that no stranger had the right to judge them (this is very similar to today's culture with the LGBT) because in their community they saw themselves as justified.

To fully visualize the 'unnaturalness' of homosexuality; I am using the Amplified Bible which shares a translation from the King James Bible of Romans 1: 24 – 27, that has common language which epitomizes the unnatural behaviour of the people. It says:

> [24] *Therefore God gave them up in the lusts of their [own] hearts to sexual impurity, to the dishonoring of their bodies among themselves [abandoning them to the degrading power of sin],*

*25 Because they exchanged the truth of God for a lie and worshiped and served the **creature** rather than the **Creator**, Who is blessed forever! Amen (so be it).*

26 For this reason God gave them over and abandoned them to vile affections and degrading passions. For their women exchanged their <u>natural</u> function for an <u>unnatural</u> and abnormal one,

*27 And the men also turned from **natural relations with women** and were set ablaze (burning out, consumed) with lust for one another—<u>**men committing shameful acts with men**</u> and suffering in their own bodies and personalities the inevitable consequences and penalty of their wrong-doing and going astray, which was [their] fitting retribution.*

Secondly; let's examine the word abomination which describes this unrighteousness. The first contention a gay rights apologist will point to is that the word in the original Hebrew is in fact a different word and meaning. In Hebrew the word is *to'evah* which is a connotation of abomination. The basic meaning is 'not fit for use according to Jewish law'.

Now considering that the English translation of abomination which is 'a thing that causes disgust or hatred[284]', is far more unpleasant; many homosexuals see a type of victory in pointing out the small discrepancy between the Hebrew and the English.

I fail to see the moral victory here because when placed into full context using the Hebrew, one can't fail in deciphering a very negative attribute.

Leviticus 18:22 & Leviticus 20:13 both speak of abomination; *'You shall not lie with a male as with a woman. It is an **abomination**'.* (NKJ,)

*'If a man lies with a male as he lies with a woman, both of them have committed an **abomination**. They shall surely be put to death. Their blood shall be upon them'.* (NKJ,)

---

[284] Merriam-Webster

Let's cut through the conjecture and accept that the ramifications of Leviticus 18:22 is analogous Leviticus 20:13.

It would mean that whether we accept the Hebrew interpretation that the men committed an act that was not fit for use according to Jewish law or we accept the English interpretation which views the act as something abhorrent and detestable; both interpretations lead to death. The imminent nature of the conclusion is inescapable. The homosexual act was determined to be so egregious that death was the penalty.

Again before the apologist find some crevice to undermine this argument let me anticipate the elusion premise which may say that this is why the Old Testament's (OT) draconian laws are outdated and that abomination was about the illegal act of rape between men.

There is truth to the view that the Mosaic law was applied with morbid harshness but as alluded to earlier, by the time that Moses received the law, man was living in virtual spiritual anarchy. Moses, as led by God, had to impose strict standards because the pagan culture inside and outside of the nation of Israel was formidable. We know that even as Moses received the law from God in Exodus 32, the people were already rebelling and turning to a pagan ritual of worship.

The proviso to the whole thought of justifying words or an action in the OT is that when we take a look at the New Testament, the standard can be verified as the same and reinforced.

The beauty of the New Testament is that it is a fulfilment of prophecy in many instances and brings finality through the resurrection of Jesus in establishing the legal standard in grace.

In 1 Timothy 1: 9 we learn that the standards of unrighteous behaviour found in the Leviticus 18:20 – 23 is being mirrored and restated as ungodly in this New Testament chapter. It lays out various depravities, which are unacceptable and scrutinized by the standard of the law. For those who would believe that whoremongerers or ungodly cannot include homosexuals; the verse ends with the most inclusive language to behaviours outside of biblical standard doctrine.

It states:

> *"Knowing this, that the law is **not made for a righteous man**, but for the lawless and disobedient, for the ungodly and for sinners, for unholy and profane, for murderers of fathers and murderers of mothers, for manslayers, for whoremongers, for them that defile themselves with mankind, for menstealers, for liars, for perjured persons, and if there be any other thing that is contrary to sound doctrine"* (1 Timothy 1:9-10 KJV).

We are sure that homosexuality is in the litany of vices because we find in Corinthians a direct acknowledgement of it. It is an inescapable condemnation of the act.

> **Do you not know that the unrighteous will not inherit the kingdom of God? Do not be deceived.** *Neither fornicators, nor idolaters, nor adulterers, nor homosexuals, nor sodomites, nor thieves, nor covetous, nor drunkards, nor revilers, nor extortioners will inherit the kingdom of God. And such were some of you. But you were washed, but you were sanctified, but you were justified in the name of the Lord Jesus and by the Spirit of our God.* (1 Corinthians 6:9-11).

The final coup d'état in overthrowing any argument to justify the act of homosexuality is through understanding the exegetical emphasis of the resurrection of Jesus Christ. Consider Luke 17: 27 – 30 *"They ate, they drank, they married wives, they were given in marriage, until the day that Noah entered the ark, and the flood came and destroyed them all. Likewise as it was also in the days of Lot: They ate, they drank, they bought, they sold, they planted, they built; but on the day that Lot went out of Sodom it rained fire and brimstone from heaven and destroyed them all. Even so will it be in the day when the Son of Man is revealed"*. This is a reality check of where our society is presently. We have been deceitfully lulled to a spiritual slumber and we are content to remain drunk in our iniquities. Our societies have brazenly rejecting the righteousness of salvation in Jesus Christ; but God has shown from His word and like in the days of old that He will not tarry in the destruction of this evil.

For the wages of sin is death, but the gift of God is eternal life in Christ Jesus our Lord. Romans 6: 23

7. **Separation of paganism (church) and state** – Here is a very uncanny scenario; imagine if twenty years from now after homosexuality is completely legitimized, we find that the LGBT community is fighting to have the government refuse rights to the Paedophilia organization. This incongruity is in fact a real possibility in my mind. I would have said 30 years ago that there was no way possible for gay marriage to be legitimized but based on the legal precedent they have presented I realize that all other possibilities are legally cogent arguments which only need presenting in the courts.

The statistic has already been stated. America professes to be a Christian Nation. The Pledge of Allegiance of the United States reads; *I pledge allegiance to the Flag of the United States of America, and to the Republic for which it stands, one Nation under God, indivisible, with liberty and justice for all.* What is the point of this pledge? According to the American Legion[285] each refrain signifies a specific oath in creating allegiance.

What I would be concerned about if I were an American are the refrains, 'under God', and 'with liberty and justice'.

The refrain, 'under God' is not ambivalent in the acknowledgement of a deity. It is a clear connotation that the pledge as said, creates a suggestion of belief in a 'supreme' God. With the level of religious diversity in the US (Christianity being dominant) one can postulate that all persons who are under a hierarchy religion will have representation

---

[285] http://www.legion.org/flag/pledge

within their understanding. That means that there is room for plurality where different denominations can 'interpret' God into the deity of their worshiping denomination.

What creates more discourse for me is the refrain, with liberty and justice. If read in context with the three preceding and the last refrains in succession it becomes syntactically complimentary; so it reads, 'one nation, under God, indivisible, with liberty and justice, for all'.

If I were a Christian living in a country that is predominantly 'Christian', I would have to ask myself how it is that my views under a dominant Christian God culture are not being justified.

We already examined the support of other major religions supporting homosexuality and demonstrated that there was a very miniscule representation of support. Since the LGBT can't claim that Christianity predominantly supports homosexuality, it remains quite dubious that they have made the level of legal inroads as they have.

But what happens when they decide that the pledge is contrary to their shared believe (for a high percentage of humanist and LGBT that are atheist)?

Would it be in their best interest to either not pledge allegiance (which may or may not be politically treacherous), or should they petition, similar to a recent case in Massachusetts Supreme Court[286], to have the pledge changed to represent that they are not under God? Once again and for those who may think that my thinking is not practical; read this article about the proliferation of 'atheist super churches[287]'

The point that I am making is that the pagan religion or LGBT, along with the Humanist are obviously not in line with the Christian God of the Bible. In fact, they are not relative to any of the other major religious deities. It means to me that they can be classified as even

---

[286] http://usnews.nbcnews.com/_news/2013/09/04/20327848-pledge-of-allegiance-challenged-in-massachusetts-supreme-court

[287] Gillian Flaccus of Associated Press; MSN News; Atheist 'mega-churches' take root across US, world http://news.msn.com/us/atheist-mega-churches-take-root-across-us-world?ocid=ansnews11

'more' pagan in their culture; having to create their own standard of a god to meet their criteria. They will very soon petition for the rights to have Christmas, and Easter banned and holidays' realigned to reflect sensitivity to their way of thinking. Persons who are reading my words can easily reflect and know that what I am saying is a demonstrated fact every year. Nativity scenes are disappearing from the landscape of festive celebration.

So if individuals, who are acting independent of major religious doctrine, and are able to form a majority contingent to change what America represents (as in under God); then the 'One Nation under God' will be fully paganized and should then read 'One Nation under Pagan Self Actualization' (for lack of better terminology).

Where is God in this great movement of paganism and is it His intention to have His law separated from the law of the land? The full answer to the true question of 'separation of church and state' would again spur another fanatical debate.

Since this is really my conclusion; I won't take up the jurisprudence but I will continue to reflect on what I see as the indefeasible truth found in the Bible.

With all the political mileage and prevalence of legal victories, the LGBT may well assert (by their belief) that God is on their side. Quite frankly, with ambivalent statements by the Pope[288]and the aforementioned Bishop Tutu; one would understand their elation.

Perhaps the voices of gay right aficionados who herald the belief that gays have been in the desert for far too long are correct. Perhaps it is their time in history to assert and establish the truths of their beliefs!

Let me say; 'this is false!'

There is no period of entitlement for unrighteousness in the continual timeline of righteousness. God has not changed his opposition

---

[288] http://www.huffingtonpost.com/2013/07/29/pope-francis-gays_n_3669635.html

to unrighteousness. He is always interested in building righteousness. In Acts 10: 34-35 (AMP) Peter says:

> [34] *And Peter opened his mouth and said: Most certainly and thoroughly I now perceive and understand that God shows no partiality and is no respecter of persons,*

> [35] *But in every nation he who venerates and has a reverential fear for God, treating Him with worshipful obedience and living uprightly, is acceptable to Him and sure of being received and welcomed [by Him].*

No matter how emotional or seemingly convincing the arguments are by the LGBT, the standard which they adhere to is unacceptable by the standard of God. Let me act like a radio 'shock jock' and level the playing field; God is also unhappy and unsupportive of stances by Christians who allow for unrighteousness to fester in the land. Christians are not 'safe' from having a standard.

Take a quick rationale of what I have said. It is difficult for many Christians who live in this 'don't offend' culture to stand up for their beliefs. I recognise that standing for biblical principles garnishes criticisms that 'Christians' are hatemongers but it is inescapable that God has a standard and expects us to hold to it. If what I am saying is false examine the very moments leading up to the Resurrection of Christ.

The disciples were so afraid of being criticized as participants with Christ that some denied[289] Him when pointed out by the crowd. The Pharisees and Sadducees who considered themselves the religious standard amoung men found Jesus contemptible. Jesus knew this but never backed down.

In Matthew 15: 11-12 we have proof that Jesus was aware when he said; "*Not that which entereth into the mouth defileth the man; but that which proceedeth out of the mouth, this defileth the man.*

---

[289] Mathew 26:34,74-75

*Then came the disciples, and said unto him, Knowest thou that the Pharisees were **offended**, when they heard this saying?"* He was persecuted and crucified but never relinquished the truth.

Christians today are so very scared and afraid; they reason and believe that they are acting 'in love' by acquiescing and giving in to the world. This is the furthest from the truth. The truth of Christ is supposed to exist in the mouths of Christians. What emits from the mouth should increase truth on Earth. Christians, by shrinking from the truth create a spiritual void where false doctrine becomes the law of the land.

Every day in America (the world leader?) the cry among 'good' people is a question as to why there are so many crimes committed by children. We hear the cry concerning all manner of crime being committed but yet Christians continue to allow depravity to fill the void by replacing the law of the Bible. This is the very reason that God's feelings are indicated as being '***wearied***' in Malachi 2. The people continue to rely on their own understanding and standard of justice which fails them; yet they turn to God and say, *"Everyone who does evil is good in the sight of the Lord, And He delights in them,"* or, *"Where is the God of justice?"* God is saying to the people that the folly and repercussions of asking and agreeing to take prayer out of schools, and remove any indication of Him from our public are not His responsibility. We reap what we sow; we can't therefore choose to blame Him for the results.

In every part of the battle field we find Christians retreating; no prayer in schools, abortions, removal of Biblical references from public domain etc, etc. Romans 1: 28 says'; *Furthermore, just as they did not think it worthwhile to retain the knowledge of God, so God gave them over to a depraved mind, so that they do what ought not to be done'.* That is not harsh; it is a standard. Standard is standard!

As shown above; men are not simply given up to their reprobate minds without penalty. The Amplified Bible says in Proverbs 22: 28; '***Remove not the ancient landmark which your fathers have set up'***. The ancient fathers such as Abraham and Moses set out ecclesiastical law which nations have codified and followed as a standard for centuries. If this is doubted, look at the laws set down by God in the commandments and compare them with common law in almost any country; the similarity is indisputable. Look at the framers of the American constitution and read in-depth what their intentions were with regards to Christianity. Christians in America[290]must become indignant against wickedness.

Psalm 119:51-54:

> *The arrogant mock me unmercifully*, but ***I do not turn from your law. I remember, Lord, your ancient laws***, *and I find comfort in them.* ***Indignation grips me because of the wicked, who have forsaken your law****. Your decrees are the theme of my song wherever I lodge.*

What we find in the Bible is that God was establishing His laws not only into the hearts of the people but was giving the nation of Israel the fundamental rule by which it should govern.

Colossians 2: 8 (amp) epitomizes the movement of humanist and the LGBT into the contextualizing of political rhetoric as 'sound' and justifiable standards; '***See to it that no one carries you off as spoil or makes you yourselves captive by his so-called philosophy and intellectualism and vain deceit (idle fancies and plain nonsense), following human tradition (men's ideas of the material rather than the spiritual world), just crude notions following the rudimentary and elemental teachings of the universe and disregarding [the teachings of] Christ (the Messiah)'***.

Clearly I will be perceived as a broken record for stressing various points but it is overwhelming to understand what is happening in America. Statistical[291] analysis is contradicting facts which should

---

[290] I am speaking to all Christians in the World but using America as a precident.

[291] http://abcnews.go.com/US/story?id=90356&page=1

logically flow from those results. A staggering 83% of America considers themselves Christian. Without doubt this is the great hypocrisy of the 21st century. Unless Christians have become demi-gods who are now defining their own creed and theocracy or they have abdicated having a voice for righteousness; the statistics cannot be correct. For the amount of support being shown to antithetical positions to the Bible, the real conclusion must be that America is no-longer a majority supported Christian nation. It must now be pagan (just to be politically correct; The Bahamas seems to be moving in the very same direction).

There is a consequence to people and nations harbouring and implementing doctrine which stagnates the doctrine of the Bible. Reading 2 Chronicles 7:13 -15 (NIV), I recognized a peculiar attachment of words.

> 13 **"When** I shut up the heavens so that there is no rain or command locusts to devour the land or send a plague among my people, 14 **if** my people, who are called by my name, will humble themselves and pray and seek my face and turn from their wicked ways, **then** I will hear from heaven, and I will forgive their sin and **will** heal their land. 15 Now my eyes will be open and my ears attentive to the prayers offered in this place.

The very same logical syllogisms used in structured conversational paradigms which seek to reach truth conclusions, has been used in these verses. It starts with the imperative of 'when' to illustrate that there is a result, which absolutely will take place or is existing. Everything flows from the truth of that premise. 'If' is the logical collaborator which links the truth of actions taking place only predicated on the truth of the action called for. The conclusion of the logical syllogism is the revelation of an exact action taking place which flows from the truth expressed and derived from 'if'.

God tells Solomon that there will no doubt be spiritual drought which will cause plagues (in today's vernacular; crime) over the people. God did not tell His people (Christian) to hold hands with unrighteousness. He did not tell them to give in to faulty doctrine. He specifically said that the key to healing the people and the land was for the people to humble themselves (observe that he is God) and to pray.

Instead, we have replaced prayer with a moment of silence. I posit that God does not hear silence.

God always has a plan but He does not intervene in man's will. Here is what God says' about His plan; Jeremiah 29:11 (NIV)

> For I know the plan I have for you," declares the Lord, "plans
> to prosper you and not to harm you, plans to give you hope and
> a future."

He allows man to see and experience the glory of who He is and man is able to make a decision to follow.

Let me illustrate and explain. The **first** explanation deals with the 'heart of man and conversion'.

It will sound like religious garble to many but if a person had faith enough to recognize that the heart of man is deceitful[292]'we' would also recognize that it is not a simple task to have men follow God. This is the quintessential reason why God allows men to live in their circumstance. When men turn to God it is an extraordinary event. It is actually more extraordinary than a miracle. Never in the Bible does it reference any level of celebration or awe when a miracle is performed by God, God as Jesus Christ or any of the Apostles; but in Luke 15:10 it says "***In the same way, I tell you, there is joy in the presence of the angels of God over one sinner who repents.***" Just one! Man is so obstinate and singular in thinking that the job to have 'just one' person converted brings a celebration among Angels.

My **second** explanation takes into account, the necessity for God to reveal Himself to man.

---

[292] Jeremiah 17:9

Look at the story of Jonah. He knew[293] that God had directed a specific purpose or assignment into his life. One would think that if God spoke from above and revealed Himself to a mortal man, that man would do all of Gods bidding immediately. Not the case. Jonah rebelled as many characters in the Bible did.

I personally believe that God uses these stories of intrinsic revelation to demonstrate and show humans how fallible we are and that our impulsive nature for self-reliance is destructive. God is looking for humankind to have faith in Him; the Creator of all things. Everyone does not follow; so we find situations like Judas; and Samson (repenting[294]); Ananias and Sapphira to name a few.

Specific to my premise; in the Old Testament God used miraculous events to inspire humans to follow but satan's plan was to counter through pagan worship which increased and mankind became emboldened by demonic power and witchcraft. Moses and the incident with Pharaoh is a prime example. God had to use Moses to render the magic of the demonic priest as powerless against His divine will.

This will be difficult to explain from a modest journeyman perspective but the way that God goes about revealing Himself to the prophets and people of Israel in the Old Testament, I believe, is a foundation of the 'order' of God. Proverbs 29:18 says', '*Without guidance from God, law and order disappear, but God blesses everyone who obeys his Law.*' When Paul sets out to bring order to the church he establishes the precedent by telling the people, who are the church, '*For God is not the author of confusion, but of peace, as in all churches of the saints*[295]. God revealed Himself through miracles to humans because there was all manner of pagan worship with soothsayers spreading false doctrine and worshiping false deities (satan). God had to continually bring authority to His name because the enemy, satan, was misguiding and clandestinely attempting to undermine the plan of God. This had

---

[293] Jonah 1:1

[294]

[295] 1 Corinthians 14:33; KJV

been the case from Genesis (in the Garden of Eden) and will subsist until Revelations.

Consider Deuteronomy 13: 1 - 5

> *"If there arises among you a prophet or a dreamer of dreams, and he gives you a sign or a wonder,* [2] *and the sign or the wonder comes to pass, of which he spoke to you, saying, 'Let us go after other gods'—which you have not known—'and let us serve them,'* [3] *you shall not listen to the words of that prophet or that dreamer of dreams, for the Lord your God is testing you to know whether you love the Lord your God with all your heart and with all your soul.* [4] *You shall walk after the Lord your God and fear Him, and keep His commandments and obey His voice; you shall serve Him and hold fast to Him.* [5] *But that prophet or that dreamer of dreams shall be put to death, because he has spoken in order to turn you away from the Lord your God, who brought you out of the land of Egypt and redeemed you from the house of bondage, to entice you from the way in which the Lord your God commanded you to walk. So you shall put away the evil from your midst.*

America must decide whether it is a pagan nation with a mirage of evolving beliefs or whether it will make a stand for God's justice.

I very much doubt that 'separation of church and state' is anything more than a ploy to silence Christians from the affairs of their own country. How would it make sense to a Christian to sit back and remain silent as men decide to subject your home (America for Americans is home) to laws which reflect a culture supposedly alien to your core Biblical beliefs? How could it make sense for a man who professes no belief in God to put forth a law (in the guise of 'his' own beliefs) that subjects Christians to contradict God whiles also stating that religion has no place in politics? That is nonsensical! Wake up 'oh ye sluggard'. See with eyes beyond the world and recognize what you are being subjected to. Take back control over your children and what they are learning. Take back control of discipline and stop allowing your children and the state to tell you how to manage family crises. Stop being deceived by doctors and humanist agenda driven activists who convince expecting mothers that life conceived within is but a foetus, which is not human. Stand up for freedom of choice. Stop separating yourself from God, before God is fully separated from you.

My final word is to further my appeal to Christians around the world but specific to America. I began this book by indicating that America exudes critical influence on what happens in other countries. When America sneezes other countries catch a cold.

Christians in America can start a new spiritual revolution. The level of spiritual responsibility that America has built through powerful international Christian ministries, should never be misunderstood. This does not mean that God can't use a tiny nation like The Bahamas to change the world in positive ways; but it does indicate that the spiritual ground already gained in America, if surrendered, would leave an unprecedented void. I believe that there is a spiritual price to pay for such defiance. This is not a threat but a spiritual fact that has been demonstrated through the precedent nation of Israel in the bible and the many nations that sought to persecute and come against the will of God.

The special Tabernacle that God wanted built was actually in each person that commits in truth and believes in Jesus Christ as Lord. He established a special lampstand in us by which the oil will never run out and the light may shine forever. We are the lights of the world; therefore, love should shine in us such that all men would see the way, which is through Jesus Christ. Love should be exhibited along with truth and if we stand on truth they will see the light of the truth. Men have never found their way in the darkness of untruths. They are subject to failure. Hitler found this out. There is darkness in untruths but light prevails from the truth. We are to love our fellow men including Homosexuals but we are to vehemently speak the truth against sin. As inheritors of the promise and priest in accordance with Isaiah 61:6, Christians are responsible to put forth the truth of God. Thereafter, it is up to men to receive the truth because God is the final judge of any rejection.

Psalm 1:3, "And he shall be like a tree planted by the rivers of water, that bringeth forth his fruit in his season; his leaf also shall not wither; and whatsoever he doeth shall prosper."

About the Author

G. Deon Thompson is a qualified attorney-at-law in The Bahamas who has also been called to the Bar of England and Wales and is a member of The Honourable Society of *Lincoln's Inn*.

This book represents his first foray into non-fiction.

Born in the small island nation of The Bahamas in 1967 to devote Christian parents Mr. Thompson matriculated through the private school system and eventually enrolled in Liberty University (USA), where he pursued pre-law and psychology.

Mr Thompson pursued his entrepreneurial spirit after leaving university and worked as President of a family operated business until he finally settled on owning and operating his own business in the entertainment and tourism sector.

After some years Mr Thompson decided on a change in career paths to study law in the UK where upon completion he then found interest to work in the field of Wealth Management.

Mr Thompson was happy to meet his future wife whiles working in Brazil. They dated for 2 ½ years and married in the spring of 2014.

Mr Thompson is actively involved as partner in the development of a wealth management consulting firm.

As a loving husband Mr Thompson lives an active life indoors and out. He is a faithful member of Bahamas Faith Ministries and endeavours to support homeless shelters in Sao Paulo Brazil.

---

[1] This indication is inserted to bring clarity to the relationship with the heritage of Mary
[2] This indication is inserted to bring clarity to the Father-ship of God
[3] Capitalized for emphasis